THE
MAIDEN
KING

THE
MAIDEN
KING

*The Reunion
of Masculine
and Feminine*

ROBERT BLY
MARION WOODMAN

HENRY HOLT AND COMPANY · NEW YORK

Henry Holt and Company, Inc.
Publishers since 1866
115 West 18th Street
New York, New York 10011

Henry Holt® is a registered
trademark of Henry Holt and Company, Inc.

Published in Canada by Fitzhenry & Whiteside Ltd.,
195 Allstate Parkway, Markham, Ontario L3R 4T8.

Library of Congress Cataloging-in-Publication Data
Bly, Robert.
The maiden king : the reunion of masculine and feminine /
Robert Bly and Marion Woodman. — 1st Holt Ed.
p.   cm.
Includes index.
ISBN 0-8050-5777-3 (hb : alk. paper)
1. Maiden Tsar (Tale)   2. Tales—Russia (Federation—History
and criticism).   3. Psychoanalysis and folklore.   4. Femininity.
5. Masculinity.   6. Jung, C. G. (Carl Gustav), 1875–1961.
I. Woodman, Marion, date.   II. Title.
GR203.17.B59   1998
398.2'094702—dc21   98-21706
                                                          CIP

Henry Holt books are available for special promotions
and premiums. For details contact: Director, Special Markets.

First Edition 1998

Designed by Victoria Hartman

Printed in the United States of America
All first editions are printed on acid-free paper. ∞

10 9 8 7 6 5 4 3 2 1

This book is dedicated to
Marie-Louise von Franz,
great teacher and strong, stark soul

Contents

Interpretation by Marion Woodman

Acknowledgments

We wish to thank:

Applewood Centre, out of which the original idea for the video series *Bly and Woodman on Men and Women* came;

the forty-seven Limited Partners, whose faith in this work funded the film project;

the thirty participants in the original workshop and the many who have participated in workshops since;

William Patrick, our editor, who kept this book moving;

the men and women who believe a reconciliation of masculinity and femininity is possible.

Marion adds: I give special thanks to Ross, with whom I have learned so much about reunion, to Joy Parker for her generous help, and to Michael Mendez, my vigilant secretary.

Robert adds: I am grateful to Francis Quinn, who first pointed out the Maiden Tsar story to me; and to Gioia Timpanelli, whose subtle storytelling has alerted me to so many meanings. Thomas Smith has given thoughtful advice throughout the writing, and John Lee has helped in dozens of ways. I want to thank Martín Prechtel for the use of his story. Joy Parker has been a superb guide toward clarity in prose. Many conversations with Ruth Bly have helped me understand that the Love is not dead, only hidden.

Introduction

About seven years ago a friend recommended to us a story called "The Maiden Tsar," one of 178 stories collected by Aleksandr Afanas'ev in Russia and later translated into English by Norbert Guterman. The two of us had earlier begun working together because we each admired the other's thought and because it seemed right to have both a female voice and a male voice when interpreting these old stories. Two voices felt essential if the two roads taken by the genders were to be brought back in touch with each other. Our way was to announce a workshop and then throw ourselves and the audience into the ocean of the story; once in the ocean, we would all have to swim for our lives. The two of us and the audience would work together in making what Antonio Machado called "a road over the sea":

> *All things die and all things live forever;*
> *but our task is to die,*
> *to die making roads,*
> *roads over the sea.*[1]

As "The Maiden Tsar" demonstrates, this task is not an easy one; the building of a road over the tempestuous sea is a huge undertaking that requires more human resources than we have; particularly it requires leaps of imagination beyond the limits of our rationality or common sense.

In 1991, we recklessly allowed a filmmaker to film, before an invited audience, our first encounter with "The Maiden Tsar." Six hours of video were produced and shown on the CBC in Canada. We found the story magnificent but difficult. After working over the story three or four more times with audiences in various cities in the United States and Canada, we decided to collaborate on a book about it. The book would have to have new material, because we weren't satisfied with what we had found so far. We had swum for our lives, but we hadn't quite made it to shore.

In the book itself we decided that we'd each work on our own material alone. We had thought at first to merge our words, alternating our material section by section, but that just didn't work. The best approach seemed to be to present each one's material in its entirety, side by side, and then, in an epilogue drawn from telephone conversations, talk about what we had both left out, and how we felt about what the other had said.

Robert focused, as a storyteller, upon the story itself and, as a poet, upon the metaphors provided by the story. He worked to make sure all details of the story were brought forth, and that comparisons were made with stories from other traditions. He set himself the task of unpacking the main mythological images in the tale, in order to make them clearer—images such as the thirty ships, the pin, the sword, the Firebird, the casket, the hare, and the egg. Marion, as an analyst, focused on the griefs she had, over the years, explored with her analysands, both male and female. She compared the world of this fairy story with the realm of the unconscious, recognizing in Ivan's adventures a process of individual psychological maturing, which often appears in myths as a kind of collective dream.

While contemporary journalism tends to interpret every story literally, our task, both separately and together, was to interpret the events of the tale metaphorically. In doing this, we found ourselves in a metaphorical world that stretched us beyond our individual limits. The old patriarchal notion of the active male and the passive female was not adequate, nor was the idea that the role of the feminine is to help the male to ascend. In the fairy tale, the swan maidens, captured by the eternal, long for release into the fleshly human. Similarly, if Ivan's goal is to ascend, the Maiden Tsar's is to descend. Their "marriage," when it finally takes place, is a place of intersection where matter and divine intensity find a place to meet, and the radiance of the spirit shines through.

Readers will, at the end of this complicated story, find themselves in the position of the Maiden Tsar sitting at the breakfast table, eating the egg that Ivan has, after a series of difficult encounters, succeeded in bringing back to the birthday party. Whoever ingests that egg is partaking of what we would call the new paradigm, a realignment of the masculine and the feminine, that contemporary men and women are endeavoring to achieve as we move toward the new millennium.

Some of us received our first introduction to old mythological themes from Joseph Campbell's *Hero with a Thousand Faces.* We became acquainted with the heroic young man who leaves his village, dropping out of conventional life. After battling dragons or lions, he rescues a young woman, receives a reward of some sort, and returns to his village, bearing his gifts, there to be recognized as a genuine hero. In Campbell's brilliant summation, these ancient stories become vivid and invigorating reminders of the ever-present theme of the indomitable hero. In our fairy tale, however, we have a hero with no face at all, an ordinary human being with a thousand forgetfulnesses. Ironically, the young woman he sets out to rescue in our tale actually ends up rescuing him. The modest face he finally achieves is the result of his persistence and the persistence of the feminine in holding the tension of the opposites. It is a face that unites ecstasy and the Underworld. Together, our hero and his beloved tap into the power that can unite all opposites, a union that is seen in the fairy tale's title, "The Maiden Tsar."

Our story is not about heroism, but about failure and repair; it is not so much about bravado as about learning courtesy; it is less about doing and more about listening; it is not as much about ascents as about descents. It is about the forging of a new relationship within both men and women.

The young man in our story takes one look at the Ecstatic Feminine and falls asleep. He forgets—like so many of us. We have a remarkable ability for forgetfulness, ingenious methods for not being present, a delicious capacity for oblivion. It's not difficult for us to forget the shocks of childhood, our nature, our destiny, the divine, and all those tasks for which our soul actually came into this world. As Antonio Machado once asked:

> *"What have you done*
> *With the Garden that was entrusted to you?"*[2]

The tale is a story about Ivan's initiation into the feminine, into what we might call the ancient feminine, which through long years of patriarchal culture we have forgotten. In the tale, and in the experience of contemporary men and women as well, the young feminine is becoming conscious of herself in a new way.

This book differs from Robert's *Iron John* in that that book was intended for young men who for one reason or another are unable to move into a responsive form of masculinity, and consequently are obliged to accept the ready-made masculinity the corporate or military culture dumps on them. This book differs from Marion's *Leaving My Father's House,* which was intended for women who for one reason or another are unable to move into a responsive form of femininity, and have consequently been forced to adopt the ready-made femininity the patriarchal culture has imposed on them.

The story we have chosen to write about raises issues not addressed in *Iron John* or *Leaving My Father's House*. One of these issues is this noisy literalism that now characterizes the struggle between the ready-made masculine and the ready-made feminine. In the great world of metaphor, both masculine and feminine take on rigor and dimension. The feminine in our story is abundant, gorgeously articulated, dangerous, and related to spiritual worlds. The masculine is persistent, capable of tremendous courage when facing the Queen of Death, beautifully allied to the Firebird, and possessed of an energy that works with the feminine in finding the egg.

Thus, the concepts of "masculine" and "feminine" as used in this book are not to be associated with biological gender. In the metaphorical world, there is no "battle of the sexes." The feminine side of the young woman may find herself deeply at home with the feminine, or she may not. She may be a stranger to her own masculine energy, which in turn may know very little about the feminine. Certain fathers' daughters—Marion writes about them in *The Owl Was a Baker's Daughter* and *Leaving My Father's House*—through long association with the patriarchal world find themselves more strongly linked to abstract thinking, corporate planning, and to Platonic ascension than to flexibility, paradox, receptivity, and resonance. The masculine side of young men may find itself deeply at home with the masculine, or it may not. Probably not. And with its overemphasis on sports and financial success, our culture gives very little help to the feminine side of men. Thus, the masculine in young men may know almost nothing about the feminine, particularly its depth and fierceness.

When "masculine" and "feminine" are taken metaphorically, a sort of multiplication takes place. Antonio Machado said:

> *How strange! Both of us with our instincts—*
> *suddenly we are four.*[3]

When a man and woman are together, four are present. Four are present when two women are standing together, or when two men are standing together.

Furthermore there is an upper and lower level for both masculine and feminine. Each swan maiden is divine, but she is also that part of Robert who likes to be in vibrating space inside a poem. Ivan is an Eternal Energy, but he is also that part of Marion who drills into the ground, finding its way down into psychological depths that most people would prefer to leave alone.

So we leave you, the reader, with the story, which will be interesting to you whether you like our commentary or not. We leave you with our impressions of material that is too big for either of us to handle, in the hope that it will serve as a starting point for your own exploration. As Walt Whitman said, we take a few steps, leaving the rest to you.

—*Marion Woodman and Robert Bly*

A Note on the Storytelling

Norbert Guterman's translation of Afanas'ev's Russian story is set down word for word at the end of this book. Storytellers always retell; they are not allowed to omit a single image, or even significantly alter it, but they can add humor and contemporary or "village" references when they wish. So the rephrasings we use in telling this story have developed over the seven years we have worked together on this story.

THE
MAIDEN
KING

Interpretation by

ROBERT BLY

✦ PART I ✦

"Once upon a time" is the way a storyteller often begins a tale in English. By contrast, an old Persian storyteller might say, "At one time there was a story and there was no one to tell it," or "At one time there was a story, but there was no one to hear it but God." In other words, stories were in existence before human beings. That's a strange idea, but lays a lot of responsibility on the good storyteller. "The Maiden Tsar" is one of the most magnificent of all stories.

It has been preserved in the Russian language, but the storyteller does not say exactly where the story takes place: it is occurring "in a certain land, in a certain kingdom." That seems right, because the narrative is happening, one could say, simultaneously in the other world and in this one. A storyteller might say, "Our earth has four continents, and we are going now to the fifth," or "In our planet there are seven oceans; we are going now to the eighth." If you, as a reader, adore literalism, you may as well close the book now—you'll argue with our sallies so often that it will be bad for your health. Storytellers will mention that in "this kingdom" time is not linear, but persistently circular. When some event takes place in our world—a group of people walk into the desert—it never really happens exactly the same way again; new incidents replace the earlier incident. But in this "certain kingdom," the same events happen over and over; and that is what is so beautiful about that realm. People who live there love the way stories happen over and over again. They get a good look at the characters that way, because they know the old miser will come back, the dog with three legs will reappear, utterly unchanged, the prince will be just as foolish next time, the obstinate old woman just as determined, the father just as absent.

The Opening Situation

In a certain land, in a certain kingdom, there was a merchant whose wife died, leaving him with an only son, Ivan.

The father is a merchant, and so we know he will travel a lot. We are told then that his first wife, who is Ivan's mother, has died; so we could say both mother and father are absent in differing ways.

The merchant father marries a second time, and as usual in fairy tales, he picks the wrong second wife. We've learned to expect that. The blessings the motherless child will receive will come, as we know from dozens of other tales, from the mother who has died, who sometimes leaves a doll for her child, which the daughter or son can speak to in difficult situations. The departed mother generally protects the abandoned child from evil.

The trouble comes from the stepmother. It has to come from somewhere. If we omit literalism from our discussion of mother and stepmother, we can say that we are looking at two code words. "The mother who died" is a code word for the positive side of your own mother, which you probably felt deeply and unforgettably in the womb, and in very early childhood; and the "stepmother" is a code word for the dark side of that very same mother, who has, one might say, other invisible children besides you, and sometimes she prefers them to you. If you don't like this extravagant way of understanding a story, you can always remain with the more literal way; that is, Ivan's true mother did die, and a stepmother entered the family, and that's the way it was. Either way will work fine in this story.

> **In a certain land, in a certain kingdom, there was a merchant whose wife died, leaving him with an only son, Ivan. He put this son in charge of a tutor, and after some time took another wife; and since Ivan, the merchant's son, was now of age and very handsome, his stepmother fell in love with him.**

By the time we reach the word "handsome" in the second sentence we know that more than a little trouble is approaching. The father has hired a tutor to be a sort of mentor for the son, and that sounds fine, but it turns out that Ivan is handsome and the stepmother has fallen in love with him.

Stuff like that happens sometimes when a father is absent. Our storyteller casually drops the tutor and the stepmother into the same sentence, but from this cool juxtaposition we don't have any way of knowing what a team these two will shortly become. This team will undo the boy.

The Fishing Trip

Things move fast in a story like this.

One day Ivan went with his tutor to fish in the sea on a small raft.

The father apparently has wisely asked the tutor to teach the boy how to fish. We each need to know how to "fish." Psychologically, fishing amounts to an inquisitiveness about the "treasures of the deep." We float in broad daylight, on our well-constructed, rationally engineered raft or boat, looking down into the cloudy waters—inhabited by God knows what—the same waters each dreamer fishes in at night. Teaching people to fish is a just aim in education. We are fishing right now.

Fishing is a kind of dreaming in daylight, a longing for what is below. There are many mysteries down there in those waters over which these two dwarfed, half-abandoned people drift. I suppose we could say that as we brood over the story, we are fishing in the eighth ocean mentioned earlier, the ocean that amounts to a legacy left by our ancestors to living women and men. Novelists are fisherpeople; so are poets and psychologists. Many superb psychologists have been fishing in the last hundred years, among them Freud, Jung, Karen Horney, Marie-Louise von Franz, Marion Woodman, Heinz Kohut, Melanie Klein, Georg Groddeck, and Alice Miller.

A lot of our joy and happiness has come from these investigators of our legacy. Just as the fish "accidentally" bites on the worm, so a life passion may rise from below our consciousness during "fishing," evoked by an accidental reference noticed in a book that simply fell open. I know one man who found a book by James Hillman in a Goodwill dumpster, and it moved his whole life into psychology and mythology. Marie-Louise von Franz, at sixteen, the night before she was to have a brief meeting with Jung, dreamt such a powerful dream about "Virgin's milk" that when she told him the dream, he invited her to translate into German the medieval Latin of some ancient alchemical texts he had just purchased, and a sixty-year-long friendship began.[1]

A casual reference to a spider interests a young boy, and soon he is ransacking encyclopedias, studying webs, learning the ninety species of arachnids. When you visit his parents' house, he places a living tarantula in your hand. He has discovered his passion, or one of them, and in some way he is an individual.

Painters are always going on fishing expeditions. Chagall was amazed at what he saw in the waters beneath his little Russian village, and he spent his life bringing those violinists and horses and brides up to the surface.

Sometimes what we discover when fishing is a Presence. An event like that is about to happen to Ivan in our story. The boy and the tutor are looking down into the sea, one might say, for the Presence that swims about in the murky world below the surface of things; and all at once the Presence arrives on the surface of the ocean, coming in from the horizon, seemingly belonging to the sea itself.

One day Ivan went with his tutor to fish in the sea on a small raft; suddenly they saw thirty ships making toward them. On these ships sailed the Maiden Tsar with thirty other maidens, all her foster sisters. When the ships came close to the raft, all thirty of them dropped anchor. Ivan and his tutor were invited aboard the best ship, where the Maiden Tsar and her thirty foster sisters received them; she told Ivan that she loved him passionately and had come from afar to see him. So they were betrothed.

This is an amazing event. A fleet of thirty ships arrive. The thirty women, who as we later find out are both swans and women, arrive, one on each boat, and there is a thirty-first Being as well, who is the "Maiden Tsar," or the Maiden King. The phrase is meant to carry a contradiction: she is not a woman Queen, but a woman King. We know from other stories that this is a divine being, sometimes called the "Woman with Golden Hair." She isn't a Queen, for that term would imply a King of her same rank. She *is* the King. She doesn't participate in opposites: the Queen vs. the King, or night vs. day. She does not belong to this world of opposites; the world we live in is a place of opposites, moon and sun, right and wrong, left and right, joy and sorrow, Democrats and Republicans, masculine and feminine. She is the unity of opposites.

How could Ivan not be entranced? He is. She tells Ivan that she loves him and that they are betrothed. "Do you know my name?" "Oh, of course; we've known each other for a long time." He and this Golden-Haired Woman are already betrothed. That's the way it is in life.

The moment the flotilla arrived must have been that instant the Greeks called *kairos* or "the right instant." There is a certain particle of time in which the stars are lined up—then the shaman can actually heal the sick person, then silver will turn with the right tincture into gold, then the Holy One can be born. A fifteen-year-old can wake up one morning and for ten minutes understand all of mathematics in the world, or the principles of great art, or grasp ahead of time everything that will happen to her in her life. The *kairos* moment seems to be the moment when one world interpenetrates the other. It is hard to explain this in Freudian psychology, but it is very easy in Islamic psychology. Avicenna, also known as Ibn Sina, said there was a world Aristotle didn't know of, in which Spiritual Presences live. One world is mud and stone; one world is divine; and there is a third world, an in-between world. The name given to it so far in English is the Imaginal

World. St. Francis and St. Teresa can meet a human being there.
The thirty boats are arriving from that world.

The Moment When the Worlds Meet

The second when thirty silver and golden boats touch the boy's
raft is an astonishing moment; on the other hand, it is a playful
magnification of certain heated moments we have all experienced.
What are those moments like in human terms? Sometimes when
one reads diaries written in one's twenties, one finds written there
accounts of sudden illumination, perhaps a moment or an entire
morning when the spiritual goal of one's life is utterly clear: the
clarity is so amazing that we know we will never forget it. We feel
a bit of inflation that morning, but inflation is merely a drawing
in of breath, of air, of oxygen, which was always *out there*. It was
actually an *illumination;* some sort of light came in from the
other world, or from the stars. We were confused, but the visit
amounted to a *visitation*. A spiritual woman—some sort of messenger, or *angelos,* as the Greeks called her—entered our house,
interrupting those anxious hours when we brooded over our in-
adequacy, or schemed how to make some money. The angel said,
"I am a spiritual being visiting you." Some angel with wings
whose tips are violet at the edges descends to the young man or
woman. We understood our life had changed; we knew nothing
would ever be the same. We knew now that we were a person
with a calling—as St. John of the Cross was, or the author of *The
Cloud of Unknowing*. We carried inside a new dignity; we felt related to Buddhist saints or to monks who stayed in the desert hut
for thirty years. In that mood, I set down these lines, which I in-
cluded in my first book of poems:

We know the road; as the moonlight
Lights everything, so on a night like this,
The road goes on ahead, it is all clear.[1]

It *was* all clear, but two months later I wasn't sure. A renewed need to pick up dry cleaning, or perhaps a return of our old habit of self-absorption, turns our eyes away from the clear road. The superficial, greedy part of the soul that retired for a few days returns with the fury of all pushed-away beings.

Sometimes in early adolescence a love feeling will flood the brain with radiance again; a beauty glimpsed in another's face will bring all the radiance forward, and once again we have a sense of a Presence. A child of ten sees an unusual light flooding the fields. Blake saw angels sitting in a tree when he was ten; Thomas Traherne recorded a moment when he looked on the street and saw "boys and girls like moving jewels."[2]

Robert Johnson, in his new autobiography *Balancing Heaven and Earth,* describes a half hour when he stood looking down over the city of Portland, Oregon. A few weeks before he had lost part of one leg when a runaway car pinned him against a wall; he had come close to death, and he knew that. Standing on a hill, he saw that something had replaced ordinary sunlight, so that a heavenly light seemed to glow from behind every house and tree and person in Portland. The experience lasted only five minutes or so, but it determined the rest of his life.[3]

The New Life

The arrival of the thirty golden boats and the meeting with the "divine woman," who remarks that she and Ivan are already betrothed, reminds one of certainties associated with romantic love. Each person in love feels that he or she has known the other before, in some other life. This is the lightning bolt called *amor* celebrated so deeply by the Provençal poets of the thirteenth century, by Dante in *La Vita Nuova,* and by the Norman and Irish love sagas. The two lovers may feel so close that death together is—compared to parting—the lesser of two evils. Coleman Barks, in his translation of Rumi, depicts the mood well:

> *Come to the Garden in spring.*
> *There is wine, and sweethearts in the pomegranate blossoms.*
> *If you do not come, these do not matter.*
> *If you do come, these do not matter.*[1]

This intense awareness of destined love, of a unity bypassing all class and gender lines, the ecstatic sense that something divine is hidden in the meeting of these two, that "you" may be God, that each separate and foolish human being is actually participating in a holy meeting, occurs. Wallace Stevens says of Aphrodite in adolescence:

> *She causes boys to pile new plums and pears*
> *On disregarded plates. The maidens taste*
> *And stray impassioned in the littering leaves.*[2]

Romeo says:

> *But soft! What light through yonder window breaks?*
> *It is the east and Juliet is the sun! . . .*
> *The brightness of her cheek would shame those stars,*
> *As daylight doth a lamp; her eyes in heaven*
> *Would through to any region stream so bright*
> *That birds would sing, and think it were the night.*

Juliet later replies:

> *Good pilgrim, you do wrong your hand too much,*
> *Which mannerly devotion shows in this,*
> *For saints have hands that pilgrims' hands do touch,*
> *And palm to palm is holy palmer's kiss.*[3]

There is an ancient Egyptian saying that suggests that the divine power in woman is so strong that boys in some sense die simply from having experienced that power. "We must die because we have known them." Rainer Maria Rilke imagines the boy as a mountain valley, earthbound, rather inert. The feminine wind makes "his body leaves rustle."

> *The adolescent boy praises the death-givers,*
> *when they float magnificently through his*
> *heart-halls. From his blossoming body*
> *he cries out to them:*
> *Impossible to reach! Oh, how strange they are:*
> *They go swiftly over*
> *the peaks of his emotions and pour down*
> *the marvelously altered night into his deserted*
> *arm valley. The wind that rises*
> *in their dawn makes his body leaves rustle. His brooks*
> *glisten away in the sun.*[4]
>
> (Translated by R.B.)

At a certain age, then, a boy's emotional receptors become attuned to the wind of the feminine. And hers become attuned to the mountain valleys of the masculine, perhaps. How large is this attunement? Enormous. When two people are together, there are really four, so the attraction can happen many ways, between men and men, or women and women.

The arrival of the boats is a good development for Ivan. The "betrothal" has begun. The feminine has shown herself, bravely, vulnerably, ready for serious life. The Goddess has arrived from the In-between World.

The question is: What will happen to Ivan? When he got back on shore, he went to his room and thought about it. What did the stepmother do? She undoubtedly noticed a new expression on Ivan's face when he came ashore. As we know, she called the tutor into her room, gave him some brandy, and asked, "What happened today?" "Oh, nothing much." "Don't be foolish. Something happened, man. Tell me what it was!" "Well, about two o'clock or so some boats did approach, twenty-five or thirty of them, and there was one beautiful woman on each boat. That was about it." "Go on, have some more brandy." "One of the women was especially beautiful, I must say. Not as beautiful as you, of course." "Come to the point. What happened?" "The woman on the golden boat seemed to know Ivan, and it was quite a scene." "What happened next?" "She told Ivan she was coming back to the same spot tomorrow, and he should come. That's what she said. We pulled up anchor and came home."

How did the stepmother respond?

The Maiden Tsar told the merchant's son to return to the same place the following day, said farewell to him, and sailed away. Ivan returned home and went to sleep. The stepmother led the tutor into her room, made him drunk, and began to question him as to what had happened to him and Ivan at sea. The tutor told her everything. Upon hearing his story, she gave him a pin and said, "Tomorrow, when the ships begin to sail toward you, stick this pin into Ivan's tunic." The tutor promised to carry out her order.

"Tomorrow when the ships come into sight, I want you to slip this pin into the collar of Ivan's tunic." "Will it hurt him?" "How could a pin in his collar hurt him? Don't be absurd." The tutor promised to do what she wished.

The pin is an old shamanic tool. We know that Siberian shamans still will prick the finger with a pin, and if it is done rightly, the person will fall asleep. This is an old magical trick, and it seems to be flowing out of the stepmother's dark side, the power side. We notice the pin theme in many Central European stories as well, such as in "Sleeping Beauty." In that story, a King and Queen plan to invite all the goddesses or wise women of the neighborhood to the christening of their new daughter, but something goes wrong—perhaps they have only twelve golden plates. The thirteenth goddess or "wise woman" is not invited. She appears anyway, but she feels insulted. During the christening ceremony, while others are blessing the daughter, she cries out, "This girl will prick herself with a spindle on her fifteenth birthday and die!" The goddess who speaks next does what she can; she cannot cancel the curse, but she softens it so that the fifteen-year-old girl will merely fall asleep, though the sleep will be a hundred years long. The parents from that day on keep all needles and pins away from the girl. But one day, when the girl is fifteen, she wanders into a room high in the castle. An old woman sits there spinning, and when the daughter tries out the spinning wheel, she pricks her finger, and the whole castle goes to sleep. Even the slow kitchen boy, plucking a chicken, stops with his fist full of feathers; the cook falls asleep with his hand halfway to the boy, about to hit him.

The stepmother in our story comes forward as a practitioner of the magical arts. What is the insult or hurt the stepmother has received? Given the passion the stepmother feels for Ivan, perhaps the hurt lay in Ivan's failure to reciprocate it. If a human being or a goddess reaches for love and doesn't achieve it, he or she usually reaches next for power.

The Maiden Tsar's Second Visit

Next morning Ivan arose and went fishing. As soon as his tutor beheld the ships sailing in the distance, he stuck the pin into Ivan's tunic. "Ah, I feel so sleepy," said the merchant's son. "Listen, tutor, I will take a nap now, and when the ships come close, please rouse me." "Very well, of course I will rouse you," said the tutor. The ships sailed close to the raft and cast anchor; the Maiden Tsar sent for Ivan, asking him to hasten to her, but he was sound asleep. The servants began to shake him, pinch him, and nudge him. All in vain—they could not awaken him, so they left him.

That's the way it goes. Does the human being have the stamina to meet the Divine on the human plane? Can a young man truly stay in touch with the ecstatic force of the feminine? One boy in our high school dropped his prom date off at her house for a few minutes to change clothes; he himself went home to change, lay down on his bed for a few minutes, and woke up at eight o'clock in the morning. Other boys let the whole love affair lapse in order to spend a little more time with the guys. "I'll take a little nap now: When the ships come close, be sure to wake me." "Oh, certainly I will!" Perhaps this nap would take place even without the tutor.

But the stepmother and the tutor make sure it happens. The image of the pin placed by the "tutor" leads us to speculate about the part the American educational system plays in the deep sleep that seems to be falling on high school students today. Perhaps the falling SAT scores are a part of a large sleep.

The stepmother has contributed to that sleep. We know that her aim is to keep Ivan separated from any close connection with the young feminine. But, looked at more widely, is it the influence of the Divine Feminine that she wants to block? Is it possible that our educational system, so sociological and commercial in its orientation, finds it okay for girls and boys to meet, but doesn't want anything divine brought into the picture? Teachers are not supposed to pray anymore. Capitalism wants the schools to reflect its values.

The *New York Times* reported on January 11, 1998, that college freshmen are aiming not at high marks but income:

> A survey of college freshmen confirms what professors and administrators said they have been sensing, that students are increasingly disengaged and view higher education less as an opportunity to expand their minds and more as a means to increase their incomes.[1]

The Maiden Tsar told the tutor to bring Ivan to the same place on the following day, then ordered her crews to lift anchor and set sail. As soon as the ships sailed away, the tutor pulled out the pin, and Ivan awoke, jumped up, and began to call to the Maiden Tsar to return. But she was far away then and could not hear him. He went home sad and aggrieved.

Oh yes, of course he calls for Her to return. As the thirty boats disappear over the horizon, the tutor pulls the pin out of Ivan's collar. He leaps to his feet and he cries out pitifully to the departing boats, "Come back!" What good does that do? *They are too far away to hear.* So Ivan and the tutor drag the raft on shore.

On Top of Old Smoky

How does the young feminine feel about this sleep? Sometimes a girl gives her heart to a boy in true faith, feels herself at last to be a part of some genuine emotional exchange that she perhaps saw lacking altogether in her parents' house. Sometimes a girl's first love is the first great act of her soul. What happens? The boy may say: "I have to be leaving now." "On Top of Old Smoky" catches the story:

> *For courting is pleasure*
> *And parting is grief*
> *And a false-hearted lover*
> *Is worse than a thief.*
>
> *For a thief will just rob you*
> *And take what you have*
> *But a false-hearted lover*
> *Will lead you to the grave.*
>
> *And the grave will decay you*
> *And turn you to dust*
> *Not one boy in a hundred*
> *That a poor girl can trust.*
>
> *Come all you young maidens*
> *And listen to me*
> *Don't place your affections*
> *On a green willow tree.*
>
> *For the leaves they will wither*
> *The roots they will die*

You'll all be forsaken
And never know why.

Perhaps the young male has receptors more available for adventure, or warriorhood, or lion-fighting than he does for love. The young man's ability to stand in the truth of love is limited. However it happens, Ivan has fallen asleep. He is asleep right now to what thrilled him so deeply twenty-four hours ago.

Young women are not always up to the truth of love, either. Both genders fall in love and sometimes neither can sustain it. The intensity of romantic love falters. Only later can two adults, of different genders or the same gender, do the work necessary to create what Robert Johnson calls a "sustainable" relationship.

The Great Disappointment

We have the sense that both boys and girls fall asleep in slightly different ways. Joseph Chilton Pearce, in *Evolution's End,* remarks that in his childhood he felt a promise always that "something marvelous is going to happen."

Sometimes the Presence does come. But this sense of Presence doesn't last long. Wordsworth speaks so clearly of the luminosity he felt as a boy walking the hills. But "shadows of the prison house" begin to close in. As time goes on, the youth, as Joseph Chilton Pearce expressed in his own life, is hit with the awareness that something marvelous is *not* going to happen. The marvelous thing promised never does take place. The adolescent boy or girl then feels the Disappointment even more deeply in comparison with those earlier times when the brain felt full of light. One could say that he or she in late adolescence senses that the neurons no longer fire; now all the oceanic fluid has withdrawn; now the adolescent feels ordinary and empty.[1]

What has happened? Joseph Chilton Pearce concludes that a spiritual "opening" took place, but the world outside did not support it. "Openings" toward amazing abilities arrive on schedule, like molars. Each of these openings needs a response from family or culture in order to remain open, to become a part of the life. When the longing to draw arrives, most parents do provide crayons and paper. The gift of clairvoyance may arrive around the age of seven. When the Balinese child at seven suddenly knows who is standing outside the door, most Balinese families celebrate and praise the seven-year-old, recognizing the opening and providing support for it. But when a child in our culture remarks, "That's Aunt Mary on the phone," very few parents celebrate that moment. The genius for mathematical thinking may open around twelve or thirteen; sometimes the parents or the teacher respond to that, sometimes not. The conclusion is that if the outer world responds, the inner opening will remain open for life, and that corresponding power becomes an integrated part of the psyche.

There is evidence from many cultures that an opening toward spirituality arrives around fifteen or sixteen. What happens? In India the outer world "responds," so to speak. A child in an Indian village or city sees on the street constant religious processions. Everyday Ganesha receives showers of flowers. The religious impulse is everywhere. Religious festivals occur constantly. Holy men walk along with a begging bowl, representing renunciation. One hears on the streets ecstatic singers, in Pakistan, the Bauls. A kind of madness of religious feeling helps the adolescent whose spiritual chakra has just opened feel at home.

But in our culture, the adolescent does not see ecstatic religious singers on the street. What he or she does see is posters advertising sexual energy.

The sexual chakra in the adolescent opens a few months after the opening of the spiritual chakra. The adolescent in our culture sees sexual images on all sides—enormous billboards where half-naked women are lying on air, Victoria's Secret ads; he or she hears his sexual urges constantly alerted by sitcoms, talk shows, movies, hears the strong beat of the sexual chakra in rock music; he or she rolls around in the sexual vibrations as in a swimming pool. Average twelve-year-olds know more about human sexuality than the average sixty-year-old knew in 1890.

We could say, then, that the opening of the sexual chakra receives enormous support from the outer world, but the spiritual opening, having received almost no response, closes again. "Something marvelous is about to happen." But it doesn't. The result is that the American adolescent tries to receive from sexuality the marvelous ecstasy that his or her cells have been promised by the spiritual opening. "It must surely come." But the ecstasy doesn't come. What arrives is disappointment. The adolescent feels horrific despair when the sexual chakra does not deliver the ecstasy that he or she believes will come. Sex is brief and flat. No one can overestimate how huge this Disappointment is. Gerard Manley Hopkins said:

> *So be beginning, be beginning to despair.*
> *O there's none; no no no there's none:*
> *Be beginning to despair, to despair,*
> *Despair, despair, despair, despair.*[2]

The spiritual chakra closes; and sex has betrayed them. Some teenagers never pull out of that depression.

Adolescents in all societies, we suspect, feel the disappointed emptiness; but in our culture, it's as if adolescents are *sold* this emptiness. Consumer pirates and advertising agencies find the emptiness helpful to them, and a young American is urged to fill the emptiness with alcohol, sexual conquests, clothes, designer drugs, rudeness, flights from home, breakings of the law, self-pity, spiky hair, pregnancy, agreeing to be no one.

When we hear a genuinely spiritual poem or song, we feel different, but we don't know why. We feel we're being fed. But instead of receiving the honey from the spiritual chakra's opening, contemporary Western youth receive the stale, confusing substitute out of the sexual chakra, never intended to replace spiritual food.

So there we are. We can say that these images of the spirit, as an abundant, generous, lively, honey-loving energy, are really what appeared to Ivan when he was on the raft. That honey-loving, life-giving spirit, feminine in its love of dance, is what came to visit Ivan in the first place. That spirit visits almost all young people, but most young people like Ivan don't know what sort of courtly response they might make in return, so that the spirit or the Divine Feminine can stay close.

The current president supports the multinational capitalism that makes precisely the television programs that sell adolescents cheap solutions. Encouraged by business interests and the driving force of the pragmatic American consciousness, we insult the feminine at every turn.

Perhaps these assertions about our national life are too sweeping; perhaps we are learning, as the Cold War ends, some ways of living and letting live; perhaps certain forms of tenderness are appearing in our cultural and religious life. One can feel something tender in the wholesale apology the Southern Baptist Church offered recently to all black people. Perhaps the new attention our political culture pays to the women's vote will have a valuable effect in the long range. But the major drive is toward brutality in a way unheard of since the days of the Roman coliseums.

The invasion of intense feeling that Rilke describes as "the marvelously altered night" that is poured down into the other person's "deserted arm-valley" has a transcendent aspect. The young man has fallen in love with the Divine; as the young woman has. Falling in love, as our story suggests, is one of the adventures promised to the soul in return for its agreeing to be born on this planet.

The Tutor as Destroyer of Imagination

I once heard Marion Woodman tell an audience a story about an experience she had with a teacher when she was seven or so. A woman teacher gave each child in the class watercolors and told them to paint a house and a lawn. Marion liked the look of blue, so she painted the lawn blue. Her teacher was furious, and said, "You will stay after school until you learn to paint grass the right color—green!" This time Marion did paint the grass green, but also the house, the roofs, and the sky. The teacher wanted what was literally green to be green and what was literally blue to be blue, so her response was a redoubled fury. Marion said, "I put my head down on my desk, and didn't raise it again for six years."

This is the tutor as destroyer of imagination. In the opening paragraph of *Hard Times,* Dickens has Mr. Gradgrind, the teacher, say:

> Now, what I want, is Facts. Teach these boys and girls nothing but Facts. Facts alone are wanted in life. Plant nothing else, and root out everything else. You can only form the minds of reasoning animals upon Facts: nothing else will ever be of any service to them. This is the principle on which I bring up my own children, and

this is the principle on which I bring up these children. Stick to Facts, sir![1]

Mr. Gradgrind is the tutor, all right, in his negative mode, in his job as the destroyer of imagination. Blake refers to him in several proverbs: "Expect poison from standing water." "The tigers of wrath are wiser than the horses of instruction." "The eagle never lost so much time as when he submitted to learn from the crow."[2]

The tutor as the destroyer of imagination has always been a part of American public education, but he has seemed to receive even more leeway in recent years. Some grade and high school teachers today are marvelous encouragers of images, metaphors, and fancies, but others—among them, regretfully, many persons with education degrees—have become monsters of literalism who make class life hateful and contemptible. A few teachers have personalities flat as the abandoned parts of the Sudan. If we are looking for the force that puts the pin into millions of North American students, the American public school system, so tied to the sociological, the rational, the calculated, to computer information, is a likely suspect. Both teachers and students end up in despair. Great poetry and great fiction can come toward the young mind with the same excitement as the thirty brilliant boats approaching the raft. Great literature seems to "know" the very girl or boy who in fact hardly "know" themselves. "Do you know my name?" But the national drift toward eliminating music and art classes means that increasingly computer firms and right-wing "market forces" will dictate classroom structure and content. In one university in Minnesota, literature is now a part of the sociology department.[3]

Leftists don't like to talk about it much, but it seems clear that Marxists through the thirties and forties put the pin into their own children's collars, by mocking all religion and all talk of spirit. Despite Marx's acute grasp of economics, his jargon and his obsessions were for decades the pin that did the most damage. When deconstructionists use the phrase "hegemonic structures," we know there is a stepmother somewhere who is jealous. D. H. Lawrence, speaking of the mechanical metaphors, Marxist and behaviorist, that are adopted to explain human unhappiness, said:

> *I am not a mechanism, an assembly of various sections.*
> *And it is not because the mechanism is working wrongly, that*
> *I am ill.*
> *I am ill because of wounds to the soul, to the deep emotional self*
> *and the wounds to the soul take a long, long time, only time*
> *can help*
> *and patience, and a certain difficult repentance,*
> *long, difficult repentance, realization of life's mistake, and the*
> *freeing oneself*
> *from the endless repetition of the mistake*
> *which mankind at large has chosen to sanctify.*[4]

Mankind has chosen for centuries, for example, to sanctify the beating of students by teachers and parents, to sanctify shaming, war, and genocide. Mankind has begun now to sanctify pop culture. The pop culture pin, especially as transmitted by television, has caused a great sleep, so deep that many college students can no longer deal with Shakespeare's intensity. The *Christian Science Monitor* reported in January 1997 that fewer and fewer U.S. colleges now ask students to take a Shakespeare course, because their attention span has become too shortened. Interestingly, teachers who are allowed to teach Shakespeare in those colleges that still require such a course sometimes ask to be relieved of the task, because the resistance the students feel to any complicated language produces so much sadness in the teachers.[5]

Deconstruction is an attempt to right wrongs. But the obsessive hatred of canonical literature, the suspicion of almost all novels and poems written by our ancestors, whose sins of commission or omission can be so easily pointed out, and a generalized hatred of excellence separate the students from their own human past, and act as a pins in thousands of classrooms, with consequent wounds to the soul.

> **He went home sad and aggrieved. His stepmother took the tutor into her room, made him drunk, questioned him about everything that had happened, and told him to stick the pin through Ivan's tunic again the next day.**

Once more Ivan goes to his room to be depressed. Once more the tutor visits the stepmother's apartment; once more she brings out the alcohol; once more he tells everything that happened; once more the opponent of closeness is delighted to hear that the silver and gold boats have sailed away.

Marion Woodman has been saying for years that our culture has been steadily producing what this story calls the stepmother; that is, unconscious men and women, in this case mothers who have become so concretized that they block symbolic energy. Feminists have been rightly critical of the immense numbers of corporate, unconscious fathers, but women are not immune. Marion Woodman believes that one cannot be silent about the unconsciousness of many women, who have become concretized by materialism. In the malls we find materialized motherness. The concretized mother is hostile to symbolic food. An "unconscious father" is a force for tyranny, capitalist domination, and gender warfare. The "unconscious mother" is a force for psychic heaviness and literal-minded consumerism.

Woodman puts it this way:

> The old petrifying mother is like a great lizard lounging in the depths of the unconscious. She wants nothing to change. If the feisty ego attempts to accomplish

anything, one flash of her tongue disposes of the childish rebel. Her consort, the rigid authoritarian father,
passes the laws that maintain her inertia. Together they
rule us with an iron fist in a velvet glove. Mother becomes Mother Church, Mother Welfare State, Mother
University, the beloved Alma Mater, defended by Father, who becomes Father Hierarchy, Father Law, Father Status Quo. . . .

The effort of centuries to kill the dragon has ended
in the worship of mother in concrete materialism. The
sons and daughters of patriarchy are, in fact, mother-
bound.[6]

If you truly take in what she is saying, you will feel your hair
stand on end. The pin has long ago gone into millions of women,
and concretized mothers play a strong part in the tutor's work as
destroyer of imagination. Millions of people of both genders, addictive in different ways, participate in these nightly conversations
we have overheard, whose aim is to keep the Divine away, in this
case the Divine Feminine.

A Parallel Mayan Story

Let's go over the story again in a telling that doesn't blame either
the stepmother or the tutor. Let's say that Ivan's nap amounts to
a simple story of forgetting. Forgetting is what human beings do
best. It's their specialty. Even without the stepmother or tutor, a
human being will go to sleep, man or woman. It's as if we have
genes for forgetting.

A parallel story to this one is a Mayan tale, a story from Santiago de Atitlan, the Guatemalan village where Martín Prechtel lived for so many years. With his permission, I'll sum up the opening events of that story.[1] In a certain time which was no time at all, in a year which had thirteen months and no yesterday, a young boy with no father or mother went out hunting. He was so incompetent in making his bow that the arrows he shot always curved over and fell behind him. It was hard to hit anything. He met a young women one day while out hunting—unsuccessfully. Their affections grew rapidly, but when she took him home, her parents had a shock! Her whole family belonged to the race of gods and goddesses, and this boy was a ratty, seedy, smelly, insignificant human being. The father, under the guise of initiation, tries to kill the boy twice, once by placing him at the center of a forest fire, once by letting a landslide come down on him. Each time the daughter, with magical tricks, saves her lover. Finally, the daughter runs out of tricks, and the two of them flee, pursued by the murderous Divine parents.

The daughter, now pregnant, realizes that when the birth-time comes, she will not be able to protect herself, *and* the child, *and* the husband. So she settles on a good place in the forest, gives birth, and sends the young man with the two twin boys back to his human community. She will wait in that lonely spot for her husband to return. But the major thing about human beings is their forgetfulness.

The young man goes back to his village, is treated as a hero, and immediately disremembers his betrothed. We could say that he meets his old high school pals, has a pizza, and joins their life again. It's amnesia.

Months later, the young man suddenly remembers he is married, that he has a dear wife. He hurries out of the village, up the mountain, scrabbling, pulling himself up big boulders to go faster, and at last finds the meadow where he said good-bye to her. She is gone. There are only one or two bones lying in the grass. She died waiting. How could he have forgotten? He pounds the grass, he howls, he cries for hours, he feels horror when he looks at his own hands. He doesn't understand how he could have forgotten! How is it possible? The months with her were the most magnificent of his whole life; he was at last living a larger life. He had met the Divine and had two children.

So, that's the way it is with us. We forget our teachers, the authors we learned from, our sacred visitations, our meetings with the Divine. But the Divine will not wait forever for us. By the time our memory gets better, considerable damage has taken place.

We can see that the Mayan story throws a lot of light on the story of Ivan. The Young Man Who Hunts with a Crooked Bow is finally feeling the grief that Ivan is about to feel.

> **The next day Ivan again went fishing, again slept all the time, and did not see the Maiden Tsar; she left word that he should come again.**

The Maiden Tsar's Third Visit

The next morning Ivan gets up once more. Once more he and the tutor take the raft out onto the bay. Once more the thirty-one Presences appear, coming over the horizon.

> **On the third day he again went fishing with his tutor. They came to the same old place, and beheld the ships sailing at a distance, and the tutor straightaway stuck in his pin, and Ivan fell sound asleep. The ships sailed close and dropped anchor; the Maiden Tsar sent for her betrothed to come aboard her ship. The servants tried in every possi-**

ble way to rouse him, but no matter what they did, they could not waken him.

We don't know how many times these unsuccessful visits happen in our own lives. But eventually we come to the last visit, whether the visit has happened two times or six hundred times. Eventually a moment comes when all that is over.

The Energy that belongs to the Universe says, "I can't wait any longer. This is it." The Universe writes a letter to you and leaves it with your tutor. The Woman with the Golden Hair and the thirty swan women sail away, and they will never come back. Something final has happened. The mood reminds one of that summer of 1914—some joy disappeared in England and never came again. Eliot noticed it:

> *And when we were children, staying at the arch-duke's,*
> *My cousin's, he took me out on a sled,*
> *And I was frightened. He said, Marie,*
> *Marie, hold on tight. And down we went.*[1]

It's as if this instant—the moment when something marvelous is over—happened collectively in Europe at the time of the First World War. Eliot's poetry is the best report of all that. The one who abandoned the Feminine is now himself abandoned. The men and women who abandoned the Divine by brutalizing Africa are now themselves abandoned. Fitzgerald and Hemingway and Gertrude Stein happen after the Abandonment.

In our own lives, after too much sleepiness, so many insults to the Divine, so much materialism or TV, a moment arrives. It's all over. The crying out to the departing ships is even more pitiful this time—*they are too far away to hear you.*

The ships had no sooner set sail and put out to sea than the tutor pulled the pin from Ivan's garment;

he awoke and began to bemoan his loss of the
Maiden Tsar; but she was far away and could not
hear him.

Using the Sword

It turns out that when the Maiden Tsar, the Divine Lover, realized for the third time that Ivan could not be awakened, she
wrote a letter and left it for him.

> The Maiden Tsar learned of the stepmother's ruse
> and the tutor's treason, and wrote to Ivan telling
> him to cut off the tutor's head, and, if he loved his
> betrothed, to come and find her beyond thrice nine
> lands in the thrice tenth kingdom.

Ivan takes up his sword—which sword? Never mind, *his* sword,
and he cuts off the tutor's head.

> Ivan read it, drew out his sharp saber, and cut off
> the wicked tutor's head. Then he sailed hurriedly to
> the shore, went home, said farewell to his father,
> and set out to find the thrice tenth kingdom.

The matter of cutting off the tutor's head is disturbing
to some people. Isn't that violence? On the other hand, if
the tutor is inside you, no one will be harmed but you. Ivan's
brusque motion with the sword is a kind of healthy animal
act. The animal in us knows how to survive; the animal in us
will, when hungry in the desert, catch and eat a rabbit and it
is the right thing to do. Ivan would never have been taught

to cut off the tutor's head *at school.* It's a question of survival. The animal does the sincere things to save its life, it draws on its instincts. Hamlet, when he finds that Rosencrantz and Gildenstern have enlisted in the King's plot against his own life, sends them quickly off to their death—and thinks no more of it.

So if you take all events in a story literally, I suppose you would now say that Ivan has become a killer. But that doesn't describe it quite rightly. He offered the old animal in him—secretly set in his soul through a million years of life before this—a chance to act. The act was not sneaky, but clear.

If you prefer to imagine all the persons in the story as parts of one person, then you remember that some people achieve their proper work by cutting off their academic head. Albert Schweitzer would be an example; he abandoned his career as a concert organist in Europe and moved to Africa to run a hospital for black people. Beheading is not an unusual act for artists. Great art is associated with the same sort of renunication, often brutal to those watching.

The Hindu poet Kabir talks of the Great Sleep, and how weak our efforts against that Sleep are:

> *If you are about to fall into heavy sleep anyway,*
> *why waste time smoothing the bed*
> *and arranging the pillows?*
>
> *Kabir will tell you the truth: This is what love is like:*
> *suppose you had to cut your head off*
> *and give it to someone else,*
> *what difference would it make?*[1]

The beheading has taken place now, and the tutor is out of the story; and that is good. But before we leave it, we need to notice our own resistance to the swinging of the sword. Many of us don't want Shiva to cut off his son's head; we don't want Hamlet to stab Polonius or send Rosenkrantz and Gildenstern off to death; we don't want Arjuna to join the battle. We would rather smooth the bed and arrange the pillows, live naively, and hope for the best. Some people want to live their whole lives without taking a decisive action with their animal bodies. Through the whole play of Shakespeare's we feel it is a kind of miracle when Hamlet finally takes a decisive action.

Some women need to develop their masculine side deeply enough so that they can cut off the head of their interior tutor, who may be either masculine or feminine. The masculine is helpful to both men and women for this tutor-beheading business.

The story says nothing about Ivan punishing his stepmother. She acted out of some sort of love, but the tutor out of weakness. The story says merely that Ivan sailed to shore, said farewell to his father, and set out to find the Kingdom Difficult to Find.

PART II

Ivan is looking for the Kingdom Three Times Ten, which lies just beyond the Kingdom Three Times Nine.

Baba Yaga's Hut on a Chicken Leg

He journeyed onward, straight ahead, a long time or a short time—for speedily a tale is spun, but with less speed a deed is done—and finally came to a little hut; it stood in the open field, turning on chicken legs. He entered and found Baba Yaga the Bony-Legged.

We have arrived at something wholly different now. The story—in its print form—says amazing things in one sentence, but we know that if the storyteller were present, she or he would slow the speed down—way down—by "talking in voices" or through jokes and asides. So we'll do that as well here.

An enormous event has happened. How long has Ivan been searching—perhaps five years, perhaps ten? Ask a person who has left home, after cutting off a head, and is looking for a place he or she knows nothing of, and which other people don't know anything about either. We remember Bob Dylan's lines:

> *How does it feel*
> *To be on your own,*
> *With no direction home,*
> *Like a complete unknown,*
> *Like a rolling stone?*[1]

Ivan found himself unable to meet the Feminine Divine appropriately, when the Divine Energy came toward him. The Divine has, we might say, now withdrawn, and perhaps, in the time-worn tradition of withdrawing armies, has left roadblocks behind, blown-up bridges, burned barns, poisoned wells, gas tanks made useless by sugar, and so on. In other words, this young man will be passing, as he grows up, through a landscape of female anger. He wasn't warned about this, but each of us experiences landscapes that we weren't warned about.

So the three-times-ten kingdom is a sort of triple women's sphere, a *very* impressive place, gathering together powers of fertility, of magic, of the Underworld, of the sea and the moon. We are not told that the Kingdom Three Times Ten is a secret name for the realm of the magical feminine. It is possible, given the entirely female population of the boats, that the world of the boats was the Kingdom Three Times Nine. Now the Goddess has retreated, so to speak, to a still more distant place, to the Kingdom Three Times Ten.

It's even possible that this kingdom includes some trace of the union of masculine and feminine. We recall that Noah belonged to the tenth generation. In the Hebrew alphabet, the tenth letter, yod, is the Tree of Life; and Yahweh is said to have used ten words to create the universe. In many traditions the number ten represents the Fall; that is, the decisive descent of the soul into the

world of matter. We could say that the Ecstatic Feminine is returning now to a kingdom in which the soul has been joined to matter.
That will be a difficult place for an utterly uninitiated boy to reach.

Our whole story so far represents a parable of our Fall as human beings. If we as human beings had accepted the Divine when
it was first offered, our individual lives and our collective history
would be simpler. But we did not accept it. Now it takes endless
labor and trouble for human beings to get back to the divine. We
don't need poets to tell us that. We have each experienced it.

But García Lorca takes a stab at it:

To take the wrong road
is to arrive at the snow,
and to arrive at the snow
is to get down on all fours for twenty centuries and eat the
*   grasses of the cemeteries.*

To take the wrong road
is to arrive at woman,
woman who isn't afraid of light,
woman who murders two roosters in one second,
light which isn't afraid of roosters,
and roosters who don't know how to sing on top of the snow.

But if the snow truly takes the wrong road,
then it might meet the southern wind,
and since the air cares nothing for groans,
we will have to get down on all fours again and eat the grasses
*   of the cemeteries. . . .*

light shudders when it has to face the roosters,
and since all roosters know is how to fly over the snow
we will have to get down on all fours and eat the grasses of the
*   cemeteries forever.*[2]

Lorca wrote that poem in New York in 1929; and probably New York was a kind of underworld to him.

Who is Baba Yaga? Nothing is sure, even the era associated with Baba Yaga. We simply guess that the admiration for Kali or Baba Yaga belongs naturally to the time *before* cattle patriarchy, before the conquest of Greece by the cattle breeders from the Caucasus, before agricultural religions were paved over by the more abstract gods. We suspect that in the Baba Yaga's scenes we've revisited a time when women owned the center of the village, and men lived somewhere outside and had to be careful when they entered. We think that; we suspect it; but we don't know anything. No one knows. The fact that modern priests wear robes which are symbolically female may be a telling detail. The fact that judges in England still wear wigs implies that women once decided matters of law; just as the robes imply that women were once the priests. But we don't know. There are good arguments on both sides of this question. I'm perfectly satisfied to rest for a little in the concept that men's domination of things is fairly recent, and that women's earlier power had to do with food gathering, food preparation, their elaborate gifts of language, and higher socialization. Perhaps I'll change my mind later, but, for now, that's what I think.

There is a real need in our culture to have a wider mythology, one not so restricted by the typical patriarchal obessions. We are being invited to investigate the old mythologies, rather than simply accepting the mythology that has fallen on us. Of course, we are smart enough to know that no myth can actually be invented—it takes roughly 10,000 years to invent a new myth, and none of us are likely to live that long. But we can bring forward from the vast treasures of mythology the stories that more nearly answer this call, besides or beyond the heroic, and when we find those stories, we can relate them as we should to our houses, our food, our clothes, our psychology, etc.

Robert Johnson remarked recently:

> It is conceivable that what is required to round out a modern person, to help make us whole, is to incorporate the downward, earthly movement of things. This will require an entirely new ethos and mythology. New symbols may be stirring in the collective unconscious to reverse the movement that has been predominant for thousands of years.[3]

We are about—in our story—to meet the Goddess Who Eats People. She has an honored place at the center of much ancient mythology, but her greatness has been lost in the landscape of most Western stories. This being is not a witch, but a magnificent imaginative creation.

The greatest error that could be made around this story would be to declare the vision of Baba Yaga to be patriarchal propaganda, another attempt over generations to demonize women, a clever move in the war for power between the genders. The images in this Russian story reverberate to pain in both men and women. The story has the soberness of an Emily Dickinson poem:

> *There is a pain—so utter—*
> *It swallows substance up—*
> *Then covers the Abyss with Trance—*
> *So memory can step*
> *Around—across—upon it—*
> *As one within a Swoon—*
> *Goes safely—where an open eye—*
> *Would drop Him—Bone by Bone.*[4]

Marion Woodman and I have been engaged in the task of recovering old mythology for our whole adult lives. Marion, recognizing the amount of unconscious mother that we have all inherited from the nineteenth century, has asked mothers to become conscious. She has worked hard in fighting against the literalization of certain old myths, which results in what she calls a "concretized Great Mother," almost inseparable from materialism. I have urged men to take a conscious part in their own growth by stealing the key from under their mother's pillow, by respecting the wild part of themselves, by descending consciously into the underground and shame and failure rather than by letting nineteenth-century masculinity, as defined by bishops and businessmen, simply happen to them.

Some readers will refuse to put the mythological telescope to their eyes; they will insist on retreating inside the old interpretations, so that the intricate movements of heavenly bodies are reduced to a few mechanical theories of gender. With the help of Freud, Western culture has moved from a literal to a psychological understanding of the world in only a hundred years. But now we are receiving a request to move on still further, from the psychological to the mythological stage. This is more difficult. We are, at the moment, almost incapable of a mythological understanding of the world. That understanding is not behind us, but ahead of us. It does not involve adversarial thinking, but the sort of double vision that develops in the Underworld.

Who Is Baba Yaga?

From the mythological point of view, She out there is not exactly in the human world. She is a part of the inhuman Universe, not a mammal inside the menagerie of the human soul. She is a Force, a Being, probably older than the earliest human being, not made of projections, not evoked by denial, but an amazingly joyful Being. She is Existent; perhaps she is Existence. In any case, it would be wise to watch your step. She owes you nothing, and it is Her universe.

The young man cannot quite face the ecstatic energy of the feminine; the human being cannot quite take on the energy of the Divine when it arrives. The cure for that is the experience we will witness in our story: going down to play some bocce ball with the Lady of Death. In the Underworld we have to learn new rules of behavior; there courtesy is a matter of life or death; there the adversarial thinking that Fundamentalists and Marxists and all of us love has to go; there things our parents never taught us have to be learned, including the shift from seeing to hearing.

Baba Yaga, then, is a worthy adversary, a magnificent Empress of the Dead, and men or women who gamble with her usually lose. One would say *invariably* lose. The gamble is introduced by her question; the dice roll, and the human being dies.

It's fair to say that Baba Yaga is almost identical with the Indian goddess Kali and the Balinese goddess Rangda.

The word *kali* is the feminine form of *kala,* meaning "time." So Kali is Time. Painters show her wearing around her neck a necklace of skulls, which can change in a second to chrysanthemum blossoms and back again. So it is with Time.

Alain Daniélou, in *Shiva and Dionysus,* says:

> Death is a return to the mother's womb, to the earth from which we came. Kali alone is invoked by her faithful as "Mother," the protectress. From whom else can mercy be implored, if not from the all-powerfulness of Time?[1]

We're embarking here on a study of one of the greatest stories in world literature. It answers the question: Who is the Queen of the World? Who is this mysterious figure that people refer to in a mood of nostalgia as the Great Mother? Our minds go blank as soon as we hear that phrase, because the word "mother" picks up, for both men and women, images of nurturing, coziness, infantile delight, cribs, playpens, perhaps diapers, rebukes, table manners, someone who prefers your brother or your sister to yourself, a person perhaps too yielding, almost too self-sacrificing, perhaps a little codependent. How can this set of emotional reactions be correlated with the word "great?" By "great" do we mean a big mother? Do we mean a cosmic mother? Do we mean a mother so immense that she occupies all the space between your personal mother and the universe itself? Some of the confusion around the New Age comes from bewilderment at repeating this phrase "the Great Mother," over and over. In this story, that phrase isn't used. ("The Great Father" is no better, but it is not a part of our deliberations here.)

We are getting closer now to that Being whom the ancients sensed when they were walking in an oak forest, or the Being they saw in a hurricane, or the Energy who burned up their houses when the volcano erupted. In a culture as flattened as ours, I think we all have to stretch to imagine the height of such a being. This being is present in a thousand small details of our lives, but her power also reaches out to the very edges of the universe—I suppose we would say to the outer edges of our galaxy.

Many people feel a curious resistance at the prospect of discussing this large one.

Baba Yaga's Question to Ivan

Let's return to the story.

> **He entered and found Baba Yaga the Bony-legged. "Fie, fie," she said, "the Russian smell was never**

heard of nor caught sight of here, but now it has come by itself. Are you here of your own free will or by compulsion, my good youth?"

When Baba Yaga glimpses Ivan in her section of the forest, she is delighted. She sings her little song:

> *Oh it's more years than I could tell*
> *Since I've picked up the smell*
> *Of a Russian boy—*
> *Oh joy, joy, joy!*
> *And now his little bones*
> *Come on their own!*

The Queen of the Dead in the Russian style turns out to be quite high-spirited. In other stories we learn that she sometimes comes gaily riding into the compound, firmly sitting in a mortar, and rowing it with a pestle. The mortar and the pestle probably do not refer to alchemy, but rather to the thorough way Nature grinds up and reuses her children. Nothing is lost, it is all recycled, and one is not to take this grinding down personally.

In most stories, the hut of the Queen of the Dead stands on a single chicken's leg. This detail is strangely piquant and satisfying, so much so that the image appears over and over in other Russian stories of Baba Yaga. If you closely examine a chicken leg, you'll notice that its strong scales, often yellowish or grayish, remind you of the scales on fish, and on certain large snakes such as boa constrictors. The scales speak powerfully of some previous era, a reptilian era, one not known for mercy, an era that the crocodile and the alligator survived. As we look, the fundamental reptile-like foundation of earthly life becomes clear; we catch a glimpse of the scaly ancestors of all the present floppy-eared mammals with their charming faces.

Some stories add the detail that her hut is continually turning; "even though the hut is always turning, its door is always open to the darkest part of the forest." How that can be you'll have to figure out. But that irrational detail becomes clear when we understand that we are now in the Underworld, and everything in the Underworld is the mirror opposite of things in our world. In our world, doors face the light, but doors in the Underworld face the darkest part of the forest. Houses on earth stand still; but here the houses turn, for we are dizzy now; we are not in "our right mind," we are spinning as certain shamans spin in trance when they visit the other world, or certain dervishes whirl when they want to see what can't be seen.

We might mention that in some stories the traveler sees twelve stakes set around Baba Yaga's hut. Men's heads are stuck on eleven of the stakes, and the twelfth stake is conspicuously empty. Oftentimes a fence made of human bones encloses this clearing—the garden gate hinges are probably human bones: a thigh bone may act as a door bar, and the lock on the door is a jawbone with teeth. Everything points to an imminent loss of life; and we sense that Baba Yaga will not shed too many tears if that should happen.

> *Oh it's more years than I could tell*
> *Since I've picked up the smell*
> *Of a Russian boy—*
> *Oh joy, joy, joy!*
> *And now his little bones*
> *Come on their own!*

We know from other stories that Baba Yaga doesn't like to be spied on; most versions mention that when she arrives in a mortar, rowing with a pestle, she brushes away all traces of her path with a broom. Her possession of the broom doesn't mean she is a witch.

She simply likes things clean; sometimes Baba Yaga keeps a young girl (such as the girl called Vasilisa in another Russian story) for several weeks just to make sure everything in her house is clean.

The idea that goddesses dislike being spied on by human beings survives in many mythologies. Artemis, for example, was bathing, and Acteon, out hunting with his dogs, had the bad taste to watch her bathing. Artemis then turned Acteon into a deer, whereupon his own dogs killed him, in an economical move: Gioia Timpanelli tells a famous Sicilian story in which Mama Draga (the female dragon) asks a certain young girl who has wandered down into her area to comb her hair. This girl must have received some instruction or is naturally wise. She avoids expressing shock at the incredible animal life in the hair, even when Mama Draga asks what she sees there ("Oh, just some little nits, such as anyone might have!"). Mama Draga gives the girl many gifts. Another girl, seeing the gifts, rushes down, but, when combing Mama Draga's hair, she cries out, "Oh lice! Awful! Awful! Awful!" Her story doesn't end so well. In the Russian tale, Vasilisa survives because when she is cleaning Baba Yaga's hut, she decides not to ask questions about the skeleton hands that come up through the table and pour wine for Baba Yaga.

Baba Yaga carries strong remembrances of the old Mediterranean corn goddesses. In corn cultures, people recognize that every kernel of corn can experience one of two possible deaths. The kernel can be planted and so die, but will then be reborn. Or the kernel can be ground up, and become food for the village. Baba Yaga's mortar suggests that Ivan is about to experience the second sort of death. During the Eleusinian mysteries, the kernels of corn fall into the mortar the way the Greek dead fell into the lap of Demeter. The Greek dead in fact were called the *demetreioi*, those who belong to Demeter. At this moment, our traveler really belongs to the Queen of Death. He has arrived in Her world a little early, but it's too late now.

Ivan has arrived while alive to that place of which we are all most deeply afraid, the place under the ground where the dead "lean backward with a lipless grin." His arrival there is a restatement of the old theme of *katabasis*—the necessity to go down; he who wants to heal a wound will have to descend.

Ivan's descent will not be easy, either; it's not a weekend descent. His descent is more like Mandela's years in prison, or Lazarus's three days in the family tomb, or Holderlin's insanity, from which he did not come back. Ivan's descent resembles the Eskimo shaman's dive to visit Sedna at the sea bottom.

The Swedish poet Tomas Tranströmer gives the mood of the Underworld:

> A drink that bubbles in empty glasses. An amplifier that magnifies silence. A path that grows over after every step. A book that can only be read in the dark.[1]

The Saturn Who Eats People

Why did Goya do his great painting of Saturn eating his own son? We can see the anguished look on Saturn's face, but he can't stop eating. Saturn in Greek is Kronos; *kronos* is time, who can't stop. Another point of reminding people about Saturn's action is not to deepen our fear of fathers but to help wean each person from the illusion that it is the sole job of the father to provide food and encouragement always. Saturn's cannibalistic nature is the exact opposite of the Good Father nature that each of us carries inside us in our fantasy.

The Baba Yaga Who Eats People

Baba Yaga's vivid presence at the center of this story is meant to help wean the childish human being from the illusion that it is the job of the mother to provide food and encouragement always. Baba Yaga's raucousness and cannibalism is the exact opposite of the Good Mother image that each of us carries in our fantasy life.

People from earliest times have called nature Mother Nature. But whether we visit the Amazon or Hudson Bay, it's clear that Mother Nature gives life with gusto and takes it back with gusto. She hints at immortality, then kills you; she produces children and then eats the children with no more emotional distress than a boa constrictor. This is uncomfortable to contemplate.

If we imagine that the Mother's purpose in the universe is to bring us food, we will never grow up. Most cultures have their Baba Yaga creature; we've mentioned Kali in India and Rangda in Bali. In Greek culture, Persephone was the goddess of the underworld; Lilith is the dangerous one in the Bible; Ereshkigal was the Sumerian Queen of the Netherworld.

Kali suggests time and blackness; all things rise from time and return to it. Kali is usually shown with four hands. One right hand says, "Don't be afraid," and one left hand lifts a sword. The other right hand offers you a bowl of rice; the other left hand holds a head that has been cut off. So we are in her area, all right.

Erich Neumann in his book *The Great Mother* points out that the Goddess Who Eats People is the womb of the earth:

> Thus the womb of the earth becomes the deadly devouring maw of the underworld, and beside the fecundated womb and the protecting cave of earth and mountain gapes the abyss of hell, the dark hole of the

depths, the devouring womb of the grave and of death, of darkness without light, of nothingness.[1]

His prose is typically Germanic, without much humor. The Indians imagine Kali as the initiating, instigating, active, forceful divine energy in the universe. She starts things. We notice it was the Maiden Tsar who approached Ivan, not the other way around. Kali's male consort, Shiva, is imagined as quiet, quiescent, brooding, lying flat on the earth, asleep. Kali is shown pulling up and eating Shiva's intestines, but he doesn't take it personally.

Why Is Baba Yaga Female?

Before we go on with the story, we will stop a moment and ask this question: Why are Baba Yaga and Kali female?

We know several acceptable answers: Because Earth is female, and these beings represent the Underworld, the Womb of the Earth.

But we can add one other reason: She is huge and female because that's the way our early mother felt to us. Whether a boy or a girl, we stood in the crib, and the mother coming toward us was enormous. We are not talking here of Bad Mother—not at all. We are talking of the difference in size. Things go the way this large person wants them to go, and that is proper. If the mother did not make decisions on her own, so to speak, none of us would have survived.

When this story brings Baba Yaga in her confident, powerful form, riding in from the woods in a mortar, and rowing with the pestle, holding a kitchen broom, fantastically energetic in her demands, we enter—as Ivan does—into childish helplessness. We are contemplating Female Largeness, which our mother—whether she willed it or not—represented. The mother moreover has to take on Authority, or the child will choke, or crawl out a window, or eat the wrong thing, or stay up all night, or suck on the breast until it hurts unbearably, or kill a younger sibling, or crap on the floor for fun, and so on. Just as romantic love (for man and woman) is "shot through with the flavor of the original blissful mother-infant union," so this early infant nonromantic state, the helpless time, is shot through with the flavor of Female Largeness, which we each knew very well in the first months after birth.

It is Simone de Beauvoir (in *The Second Sex*) and her American student Dorothy Dinnerstein (in *The Mermaid and the Minotaur*) who have best brought forward this material around the largeness of the mother. It is largeness more than power. The de Beauvoir–Dinnerstein insights are disturbing, but it would be wrong to characterize them as misogynous. This is not material about the Bad Mother, simply the—to the child—large mother. Power is put into the hands of the mother simply because the human infant cannot—unlike the fish infant—get along in the world by itself.

Dinnerstein quotes the anthropologist Sherwood Washburn, who sums up the research:

> In humans adaptation to bipedal locomotion decreased the size of the bony birth canal at the same time the eugenics of tool use selected for larger brains. This obstetrical dilemma was solved by delivery of the fetus at a much earlier stage of development.[1]

But if the fetus is delivered before it can survive, then the mother has no choice but to exercise a lot of power, simply in order to keep the baby from getting killed. Dinnerstein believes that until men take a vastly increased part in early child-raising, the baby's experiences of authority will continue to be the will of the female.

We could say then that the reason the headstrong quality of Baba Yaga is so disturbing to the stomachs of both men and women is that it carries us back to the time when we were standing in the crib. We stood looking at someone whose will was stronger than ours. The whole mood of the exchange was life and death. Dinnerstein remarks that by the time we—boy or girl—are two years old, our "I" is just beginning to form, but our mother is not felt as a correlative "I" but as an "It." When a boy or girl is in the womb, the nurture-giving surrounding surely feels like an "It." That perception of an "It" is probably lessened in certain African cultures, when the mother stays alone in her hut until she hears the "song" of her approaching child; she communicates to the child by singing her own song to the pre-baby. But here in the West, pregnancy is imagined as less mysterious. In our culture the perception is that the mother is a kind of impersonal nourishing machine, exactly the sort of institution we can imagine as "It." The girl standing in the crib feels the danger to her individuality, her "I," just as deeply as the boy standing in the next crib.

Even beyond that, Melanie Klein has written convincingly about the child's fear of herself being eaten. Some children suffer from fantasies that she or he will, perhaps out of revenge for nursing so long, be devoured. Again, the child feels a threat to his or her "I." This is how it *seems* to the child, not how it *is*.[2]

The advantage of a story like ours is that we, as adults, are able, through the scene, to revisit the wounds we felt when we sensed how little our will counted in the crib situation. Dinnerstein writes of female *intentionality*:

> What makes female intentionality so formidable—so terrifying and at the same time so alluring—is the mother's life and death control over helpless infancy, an entirely

carnal control exerted at a time when mind and body . . . are still subjectively inseparable. . . . Through woman's jurisdiction over child's passionate body, through her control over what goes into it and what comes out of it, through her right to restrict its movements and invade its orifices, to withhold pleasure or inflict pain until it obeys her wishes, each human being first discovers the peculiarly angry, bittersweet experience of conscious surrender to conscious, determined outside rule. It is against this background that child's occasional victories over woman are experienced, and its future attitude toward contact with her are formed. . . . The defeat is always ultimately carnal; and the victor is always female.

The crucial psychological fact is that all of us, female as well as male, fear the will of woman. . . . Female will is embedded in female power, which is under present conditions the earliest and profoundest prototype of absolute power.[3]

Her startling statement is that when the boys or girls are small, perhaps two to four, the victor is always female. The awareness that a female was always the victor when we were small will remain part of the brain's equipment for years after.

We recognize then that our Baba Yaga story, with amazing swiftness and economy, has carried us—both men and women—back to that time, perhaps two to four years old, when we became shocked and frightened as we realized that the all-supportive, cooing mother sometimes became a Thwarter of Impulse, a dangerous figure with reckless will who would as soon eat you as look at you.

> *Oh it's more years than I could tell*
> *Since I've picked up the smell*
> *Of a Russian boy—*

Oh joy, joy, joy!
And now his little bones
Come on their own!

We can surmise that grown men, or some of them, will try to erase memories of their helplessness by strutting in front of women, ordering them around, denigrating them, working to erase all forms of female authority.

Understanding the fear that tiny children feel is not condoning male hostility to female authority. It merely points out the difficulty we face in getting rid of the fear. Fear of female authority is felt at all levels of culture, even in universities supposedly staffed by rational people. We've learned that both male and female professors in universities and colleges tend to be less sympathetic to the women candidates for a job than to male candidates. My daughter, who teaches at a university, notices that in hiring interns, different standards seem to be in place for women than for men. The roots of the hostility to female authority are often not very conscious. The hiring committee will aim to add women teachers to its department, but when the interview session is over, the men may remark, "Well, the women candidates were not so good this year."

Baba Yaga is female, then, in order to call us back to the reason that Ivan rejected the thirty-one boat women in the first place: because he was afraid. Thirty-one women arriving on thirty boats are too much. On the surface of his mind, Ivan has "forgotten" the early situation. But he is afraid. Women are not to blame for his fear. This is what happens on a planet in which people are born not from eggs, but from inside a woman. If we had been born from eggs, we would fall asleep whenever we saw an egg, and eggs would never get tenure. Dinnerstein repeats that this fear of female authority can only be alleviated if men learn to participate deeply in the elaborate care involved in changing diapers, controlling the infant's impulses, setting out early boundaries, feeding and not feeding, refusing to hold the infant when they are too tired, and so on.

So the brilliance of our story is that it allows the "Ivan" in both men and women to return in a playful way to those early scenes standing in a crib, in which our grandiosity received its first blows. We suppose that the Ivan inside the girl is just as terrified of the Crib Authority as the Ivan inside the boy is, and small girls suffer from the Mother's blocking of the girl's will as deeply as the small boy does. In his exchange with Baba Yaga, Ivan is able imaginatively to return to his Early Fear, play with it, honor the Big One, and see what happens. He doesn't act the Big Patriarchal Male. Instead, he treats her well and with humor.

The Reply to Baba Yaga's Question

Let's return to our story. Ivan has seen Baba Yaga's hut, knows he will have to talk with her, and his problem is how to get out of the Underworld alive. Baba Yaga now asks him her main question:

> **"Are you here of your own free will or by compulsion, my good youth?"**

As we listen to Ivan's reply, it occurs to us that he must have received some instruction. We do know that the ancient Egyptians memorized appropriate answers that they might give to the fearsome creatures they would meet after death in the Underworld. For example, he or she might say: "I have not done iniquity. I have not robbed with violence. I have not slain man or

woman." We know that the Grave Monster at one point under-
takes to weigh the dead person's heart. The amount of greedy desire still in the person's heart determined its weight. If the heart
weighed more than a feather, the dead person was likely to be
eaten on the spot. So this is an old theme.

Baba Yaga is probably used to seeing dead people standing in
front of her, ready to be ground up. And she must be a bit sur-
prised to see a living human being standing there.

Basically, Baba Yaga's first question is: "Did you come here of
your own free will, or did someone send you?" We know from
many other Russian stories that if Ivan says, "I came of my own
free will!" Baba Yaga will eat him. If he says, "I came by compulsion!" Baba Yaga will eat him. She looks at him with intense,
glittering eyes to see what his answer will be. "Did you come
from your own will, or did you come from someone else's will?"
If he gives a typical or overly simple answer, he becomes food for
her; if he answers wisely, she gets to see a young sage, and so she
enjoys it either way. Her question is a test. If you, as Ivan, give a
simple answer, she eats you, and you deserve it.

Her question reminds one of the question that Fundamentalists sometimes ask a stranger: "Are you saved?" If the stranger
replies, "Yes," Baba Yaga eats him or her. If the stranger replies,
"No," Baba Yaga eats him or her. We could say that Baba Yaga's
area is the territory of truth. The difficulty lies in how to say the
truth about complicated things, which is essential if you plan to
survive her world.

We could also say that Baba Yaga eats whoever is still thinking oppositionally. If you believe that communism is the opposite of capitalism, she eats you immediately. She had a lot of food
during the fifties. If you believe that women are the opposite of
men, she eats you. She had a lot of food during the eighties. She
takes care of cleaning out the garbage of the universe. All either-
or people she eats on the spot with gusto, though it takes a
while for some of them to know they've been eaten. People who

do adversarial and oppositional thinking probably ought to be eaten. It's best for everyone. Nothing much can be done with people like that. Even therapy doesn't help much. It's best for the whole universe if such people are taken out right now. She'll do it.

This scene in which she places her Question about will is not so much an initiation as a test of initiation; it indicates how far the visitor has succeeded in advancing beyond literalist thinking. We can even sense in her question a quandary around our birth. "Did you choose your parents, or did someone else arrange it?" She never ate Robert Frost, because he gave a complicated answer to that question in his poem "The Lovely Shall Be Choosers."[1]

One could even playfully extend the question to readers of these pages: "Are you reading this book on your own accord, or is someone else's will involved?" We know that neither answer is wholly true. If the truth doesn't seem complicated to you, you're not ready to live in her universe, and the best place for your head is on the twelfth stake.

Marie-Louise von Franz, who in her book *Shadow and Evil in Fairy Tales* makes extensive commentary on this story, gives an additional suggestion about the meaning of the question.[2] She considers it a test of how ready Ivan is for change. "Did you come on your own accord or did someone send you?" Marie-Louise takes it as a trick question. It is like a parent saying to a teenage boy, "Are you sure you *really* want to take this dangerous trip down the river?" In the attempt to answer, the boy may lose his certainty or impulse, and begin to brood about impossible subtleties. Who at an early age can see his or her own motivation? The intent of Baba Yaga's question is to pull the hero out of his action mode and into a trance of doubt. So, she doesn't want to deal with any hero who can be distracted from his task.

The two interpretations are not wholly dissimilar. It's clear each of us has been eaten many times by giving an overly simple answer to important questions; it happens to everyone. But for some adversarial people, being eaten becomes a habit, and that's not so good.

What kind of answers can Ivan give so he gets out of her house alive? This is the answer Ivan gave:

"Largely of my own free will, and twice as much by compulsion!"

Who said the percentages have to add up to a hundred? What kind of people are those whose percentages add up to a hundred? When Ivan replies cheerfully, without anger, she knows that she has a live one. It's clear Ivan is not a fundamentalist, or a rationalist, or a perfectionist, but someone who understands the abundance of the universe, how more produces more. The answer is also zany, an appropriate mood for the Goddess. He avoids oppositional thinking by giving a zany answer that nevertheless stays on track. She is satisfied. There should be more humans like this one. His answer is: "I came seventy-two percent on my own decision, and a hundred and forty percent because others made me!"

Well, he's made some progress anyway; he has remained alive. He has answered the big question of hers, and so he has a right to ask her a question. We could phrase the new situation this way:

"Now, Grandma, may I be allowed to ask you a question?"
"Yes," she says, "you may."
"Do you know where the Kingdom Three Times Ten is?"
"I don't know that." Then she adds, "But maybe my younger sister knows."
"You have a sister?"
"Oh, yes, she lives right down the road there. You'll find her. She might know."

"Do you know, Baba Yaga, where lies the thrice tenth kingdom?" "No, I do not," she said, and told him to go to her second sister; she might know.

Well, there it is. On this planet things are never done once and for all. It probably took ten years for him to arrive at Baba Yaga's first house. Now he'll have to use up more time, maybe five years.

While he is walking, looking for the second Baba Yaga, we might talk a little more about Kali and Baba Yaga.

The word "baba" is a word used all over the Asian continent for a teacher, or guru, or wise old person. It is affectionate. So the phrase Baba Yaga brings us closer to Her. The Russian stories praise her wisdom and grandeur. We must note that in the Germanic lands, all that is different. The Grand Queen has been forgotten and has been replaced in the hearth stories by that disagreeable figure widely visualized as the witch. One must say that the Germanic mythology is terrifically deficient in the grandeur and playfulness the figure of Kali or Baba Yaga brings with Her.

When one sees, even in India today, a newly made mask of Kali, one notices immediately the enormous eyes coming right out of the mask toward you, eyes of tremendous consciousness and intensity. This is the real face of Baba Yaga, and why it is wrong to call her a witch. The face of Kali in general is radiant, beautiful, intense.

Kali contains in herself both sides of the Magnificent Mother. The skulls she wears around her neck suddenly turn to chrysanthemum blossoms, and then back to skulls. One side of Her is playful and ecstatic, bringing ecstasy, loving ecstasy, representing ecstasy, encouraging ecstasy, breathing ecstasy, demanding ecstasy, bathing all humans in ecstasy. The other side of Her is dark, Underworldly, lionlike, sharklike, toothéd.

The Hindus, who have been encouraged to see these two sides of the Mother, speak of Her with excitement, fear, great satisfaction, and elaborate joy. For many Hindus, an emotional definition of Kali would be "Terrorjoy," with both emotions experienced in one flash of energy.

The great Hindu saint, Sri Ramakrishna, who lived in the nineteenth century, was given a vision of Kali when he was a young man. Though young, he was already practicing his devotions to Kali. One afternoon he saw a vision. He saw a beautiful woman step out of the Ganges and walk toward the spot where he was meditating. He felt great joy, and then he noticed that she was about to give birth. She did give birth, and tenderly nursed the baby. A few minutes later, fangs came down, the other aspect of her appeared and changed her face, and she now crushed the baby in her jaws and ate it. When that was done, she returned to the Ganges and disappeared into the water.

We are fortunate enough to have the record of a conversation with Ramakrishna about Kali that took place one autumn afternoon in 1882 when Heinrich Zimmer, Ramakrishna, Keshab Chandra and a few others were traveling up the Ganges in a small steamer. Keshab (with a smile): "Describe to us, sir, in how many ways Kali, the Divine Mother, sports in this world." Sri Ramakrishna said, "Oh, she plays in different ways." He mentions Maha Kali, the Great Black One, the Goblin Kali, also Kali of the Cremation Ground. "She resides in the cremation ground, surrounded by corpses, jackals, and terrible female spirits. From Her mouth flows a stream of blood, from Her neck hangs a garland of human heads, and around Her waist is a girdle made of human hands." He mentions also the Tender Kali, and the Protectress, who comes in times of epidemic and earthquake. Ramakrishna compares the Kind Kali to an elderly mistress of the house:

> She is like the elderly mistress of the house, who has a hotch-potch pot in which she keeps different articles for the household use. *(All laugh.)* Oh, yes! Housewives have pots like that where they keep sea-foam, blue pills, small bundles of seeds of cucumber, pumpkin, and gourd, and so on. They take them out when

they want them. In the same way, after the destruction of the universe, my Divine Mother, the Embodiment of Brahman, gathers together the seeds for the next creation. . . . God is the container of the universe and also what is contained in it. . . .

"Is Kali, my Divine Mother, of a black complexion? She appears black because She is viewed from a distance; but when intimately known She is no longer so. The sky appears blue from a distance; but look at air close by and you will find that it has no color. The water of the ocean looks blue at a distance, but when you go near and take it in your hand, you find that it is colorless. . . .

"The Divine Mother is always sportive and playful. This universe is Her play. She is self-willed and must always have her own way. She is full of bliss. . . . She gives freedom to one out of a hundred thousand."

A Brahno Devotee: "But, sir, if She likes, She can give freedom to all. Why, then, has She kept us bound to the wheel?"

Sri Ramakrishna: "This is Her will. She wants to continue playing with Her created beings. In a game of hide-and-seek the running about soon stops if in the beginning all the players touch the 'granny.' If all touch her, then how can the game go on? That displeases her. Her pleasure is in continuing the game. . . . It is as if the Divine Mother said to the human mind in confidence, with a sign from Her eye, 'Go and enjoy the world.' "[3]

Kali is "it." If everyone becomes "it," the game is over. She wants the game to continue, so she gives freedom to one out of a hundred thousand. The rest have to continue the game. So the whole story is concerned with playfulness.

Arriving at the Second Sister's Hut

So Ivan once more walks and walks, and eventually in a clearing of the forest he sees a hut, revolving on a chicken's foot. This must be it. Once more the stakes decorated with the heads of eleven men rise out of the mist. Once more the Toothy One arrives, rolling in from the forest in a mortar, rowing with the pestle, smoothing out her path behind with a broom.

She gives her little song:

> *Oh it's some*
> *Time since I've picked up the yummy*
> *Scent of a Russian boy!*
> *Oh joy, joy, joy!*
> *And now his little bones*
> *Come on their own!*

Glad to have picked up the scent, she smiles with her shiny teeth, and lays out the question most visitors can never answer correctly. "Did you come here of your own free will, or did someone send you?"

In some versions of this story, Ivan is allowed to deflect the aggressiveness of the Baba Yaga's question for a few minutes by the following sentences:

Now, Grandma, you know it's not right to ask a traveler questions before you have fed him. Isn't that so, Grandma?

It's a reminder that even divinities have to obey the laws of hospitality. Some cultural rules are older than the gods, and when Baba Yaga is reminded of the rules of courtesy, she has no choice but to shift into a less aggressive mode. She reaches for food. Now She Herself has been shifted from an Eater into a Feeder.

Of course, after the exchange of food has taken place, Ivan is still obligated to answer the question. But this meeting of Divinity and human being on the common ground of eating has changed the terms of engagement, even if only slightly. Moreover, Ivan, having participated in the traditional age-old courtesies, has a better chance of evading any tendency to reply in a hostile, adolescent way.

The two of them have a little ritual meal together—some Russian bread, found perhaps near the bodies of Napoleon's soldiers while on retreat from Moscow. After eating, Baba Yaga asks the dangerous question again:

"Did you come here of your own accord, or did someone send you?"

"I'd say my own will accounted for about sixty percent, and other people's will about a hundred and forty!"

"Now, Grandma, is it time for me to ask you a question?"

"Go ahead."

"Do you know where the Kingdom Three Times Nine Plus Three is?"

"I don't know that, I'm sorry to say! But it's possible that my younger sister knows."

"You have a younger sister?"

"Oh, yes, I do. She has her own little house down the road. By the way, I must tell you, she is very dangerous. You'll know you're getting close to her place when you hear her filing her teeth. You'll have to be careful."

"If she gets angry at you," she added, "and wants to devour you, take three horns from her and ask her permission to blow them; blow the first one

**softly, the second louder, and the third still louder."
Ivan thanked the Baba Yaga and went on farther.**

Perhaps this new search will take only two years or so. While he's searching, we might return to this matter of playfulness that lies at the center of our story. In general women seem to be more emotionally playful than men. Sometimes you'll see a group of girls and boys singing; the girls will be swaying, and grooving with the music; the boys are standing there stiff as boards. Sometimes, camping with a group of people, one of the loveliest sounds will be the bursts of muscial laughter coming from the women's tents, exquisite as bird calls. From most of the men's tents will come a low muttering at best. Bernadine Jacot and Liam Hudson have some ideas in their book *The Way Men Think* about why some men are playful and some are not.

Jacot and Hudson go back to the difficult matter of the incomplete separation from the mother.[1] When a girl is two or three, she can look up at her mother and say, "That is what I'm going to be." A boy at the same age can look up at his mother and say, "That is not what I'm going to be." Separating from the mother is difficult for both genders; some children have good luck with it, some less good luck. Bernadine Jacot and Liam Hudson offer evidence that for most boys the parting from the mother—speeded up by cries of "sissy" or "mama's boy" from other boys—results in a wound that stays in the psyche a long time. It's important not to mock this wound. Other wounds may be worse, but for young boys this wound is serious enough. The boy achieves a brutal separation willy-nilly, or helter-skelter. But in the "latency period" from five to twelve, the boy has a chance to return to that wound, just as we are doing in this story. It is a place of pain, and some boys return to it and achieve some healing around seven, eight, or nine, and some don't.

If the wound remains inaccessible during the latency period, the man later—so Jacot and Hudson speculate—will tend to be stiff, to become a lawyer, engineer, technician, or scientist, a man obsessed with *distance*. He will keep a distance between himself and others, often by the use of practical intellect. His tendency as an adult, Jacot and Hudson say, will be to treat people as if they were things, and to treat things as if they were people.

Sometimes a man of that sort will spend more time nurturing his theories than his children. It's not unusual. Stories about the physicists at the Princeton Institute center often around this theme. We remember that the behaviorist Skinner literally brought his baby daughter up in a box, treating his daughter as if she were a thing. Many lawyers preserve great distance around them, and some CEOs are able to put employees on a list for disposal as if they were things.

If a boy in late childhood is able to return to his wound, talk it over with his mother or father, experience his separation with more consciousness this time, he may stop being as stiff as a board, and become capable of playfulness in the emotional sphere and remain playful. Such a man, Jacot and Hudson say, will tend to become a painter, a dancer, an architect, a novelist, or a poet.

Among painters, we might think of the playfulness of painting itself. Jacot and Hudson present the male painter as the sort of man who likes some distance, but maybe not as much as the physicist, and the subject of his paintings is often a woman. She enters his studio; he has paid her to be a model, so some distance—five or six feet—is built into the situation. On the other hand, each time he spends an afternoon studying her naked body, he is also "returning" to his longing, to his "wound," and the aim of most painters is to playfully honor the female body. Jacot and Hudson use the phrase "releasing light." An Impressionist painter might work so as to release light from the face of Notre Dame cathedral or work to paint sunflowers in such a way as to release from them their hidden store of light. Bonnard, Jacot and Hudson say, studies the female body, "releasing from it its hidden store of light."[2] It is a lovely phrase. We all know that the work of such painters can be described in a hostile way too, but such descriptions are done mostly by critics incapable of playfulness.

We could say, then, that the Impressionists many of us admire have followed Ivan's route, which is to revive the playfulness by revisiting the scenes of fear. By such means Ivan may also eventually refind the love that the Feminine had for him, which was present once in the form of "the original blissful mother-infant union."

We can see even more clearly now how important our Russian story is for the continuing life of our culture, and for the future of individual men and women. If we can revisit the Large Mother, touch again and again on the pain we felt on leaving that woman we loved so much; if we can remember these early scenes, revisit them, pull "the light" out of them, then we can become playful and pull away a little from the frightful gender war that is paralyzing so many men and women.

Arriving at the Third Sister's Hut

Ivan walked on; his walk took as long as it took. It doesn't take long to say a thing, but longer to do it. Eventually Ivan arrives at an open place in the forest. A hut stands there on a single chicken's leg. This must be it. The Second Baba Yaga has warned Ivan that this one will be dangerous.

Soon the Great One arrives out of the darkest part of the forest, riding in her mortar, rowing with the pestle, and rubbing out her tracks with the broom, in case anyone is following. As soon as She sees Ivan, She picks up a large file—the sort that is used by blacksmiths for horse hooves—and begins filing her teeth. In between the filing work she cries out:

> *Oh, it's some*
> *Time since I've picked up the yummy*
> *Scent of a Russian boy!*
> *Oh joy, joy, joy!*
> *And now his little bones*
> *Come on their own!*

She puts the file down, looks him in the eyes, and says, "Well, worthy boy, did you come to see me of your own accord, or were you sent to me?"

"Now, Grandma, you know it's not quite right to ask a traveler questions before you've fed him." She agrees. Giving him a sharp look, she produces from her hotch-potch pot some bits of matter probably left over from the last destruction of the universe, a bit of dinosaur liver, or the fried wing of a raptor. She becomes a Feeder. Finally she asks, "Did you come to see me on your own accord, or were you sent to me?" He replies, "I'd say my own volition got half of it done, and the other two-thirds went by compulsion!" But this time Baba Yaga doesn't calm down. She is agitated. She reaches for her file again and opens her mouth. He remembers what the Second Sister told him.

"Grandma, I've heard that you have three horns in your house. Could I try one?"

She pulls out a horn and passes it to him. "May I blow it?" "You may." He blows it softly.

"Thank you, Grandma. Could I try the second?" He stands and gives out a deep, resonant sound, as from a seashell.

"Thank you, Grandma. Could I try the third?"

This time all the air he has ever pulled into his lungs goes back into the horn, and an enormously loud and urgent sound comes out, as from two lovers crying out together, or a warrior about to go into battle.

We know from ancient Celtic stories that there was a certain kind of cry that brought on berserk behavior in warriors, made everyone standing around go pale, and caused pregnant women to give birth on the spot. We remember the trumpet sounds that brought down the walls of Jericho. With this cry, we must be in the area of sound as magic.

For thousands of years a powerful voice was a mark of personhood. So we could say that the longer a human being remains in the Underworld, the more powerful his or her voice will become. A man or woman comes back from the Underworld with a voice that has to be listened to.

The cry Ivan abruptly gives reminds us of his abrupt gesture with the sword when he struck off the tutor's head, but this new deed is not reactive. The cry is interior, and comes out in its own time.

Perhaps in order for each of us to have a strong voice, we need to spend time with the dead—or time in conversation with Baba Yaga. Perhaps there has to be an Underworld component in the human voice before a man or woman can reason with the Dark One.

Suddenly birds of all kinds swarmed about him, among them the firebird. "Sit upon me quickly," said the firebird, "and we shall fly wherever you want; If you don't come with me, the Baba Yaga will devour you."

He climbed on the Firebird. And he was gone. Ivan was out of the Underworld. That's the end of this part of the story.

Who Goes to the Underworld?

Many times we—men and women—have descended to the Underworld without knowing it. Another word for the Underworld is depression. The statistics on the number of women who are depressed is enormous. The old reptile that Marion Woodman talks of keeps them on the sofa. Men are more and more familiar with depression, which they traditionally don't want to discuss. In Terence Real's book, *I Don't Want to Talk About It,* he says that every man in the West lives with a covert depression.[1] He adds that the only way out of a covert depression is an overt depression. This means that the only way to escape from Baba Yaga Number One is to go to Two and Three. But that's what our story says as well. When you see Baba Yaga the Bony-Legged, you know your depression is at last overt: "Things fall apart; the center cannot hold."[2]

Lorca beautifully keeps the mood of the Underworld in the poem quoted below:

> *To take the wrong road*
> *is to arrive at the snow,*
> *and to arrive at the snow*
> *is to get down on all fours for twenty centuries and eat the*
> *grasses of the cemeteries.*[3]

Ivan's weeks, months, or years in the Place of Smelly Bones stands for that time of suffering, in which a woman finds herself held fast by a kind of Bluebeard man, and a man finds himself held fast by a kind of Kali woman. Our story suggests that the depressed woman and the depressed man have each, in their own ways, at some earlier time, perhaps out of fear of power, turned away from investigating the wound. Some people believe the descent is natural. The Mayan story suggests that forgetfulness of the Divine is the deciding factor. The insult to the Divine Feminine could mean something as simple as a girl or a boy marrying for advantage, rather than for love. That's what ordinary people, as well as extraordinary people, do. As modern rationalists and skeptics, we insult the Divine Feminine every day, and don't pay much attention to it. But some terror is mythological, and depends—for men—on an awareness that millions of men have, at a crucial point in their young life, refused the ecstatic energies when the boat came toward them, and the payment for that rejection is overdue.

How Kali Belongs in the Malls

In David Kinsley's book, he sets down these summations of Kali's nature:

> These other goddesses, "mother goddesses" in the obvious sense, give life. Kali takes life, insatiably. . . . If mother goddesses are described as ever-fecund, Kali is described as ever-hungry. Her lolling tongue, grotesquely long and oversized, her sunken stomach, emaciated appearance, and sharp fangs convey a presence that is the direct opposite of a fertile, protective mother goddess.[1]

We could say that the teeth of Baba Yaga and the fangs of Kali reveal the insatiable hunger that logically must lie behind the Good Mother's amazing fecundity and liberality.

If we receive from our mother all the good things that we need, we tend to remain infants all our lives: and it is life, food, comfort, nourishment, courage, support, and praise we want from her.

Our mother gave us life. We are all aware how much we have received from our mother. Humanity has gradually developed an image of the Mother of all, the Good Mother, the Universal Mother, the Merciful Mother, the one that stands in a million chapels today, high in mountain villages in Madeira, or Sicily, or Russia, exuding a magnificent calm and holding a child in her arms.

But if all we see when we think of the Mother is the Abundant Mother, then we will never grow up. So the image of Kali as an Eater helps people to become adult. Many observers notice that people in the West, by contrast, are becoming more and more childish, not to say infantile. Some anthropologists working around 1900 found the Eskimos to be the most adult persons on the face of the globe. Surely one reason must have been the limitations so apparent in the Eskimos' world. There were limits to the number of seals Nature brought to the ice holes, a limit to the number of hours one could live in cold wind. The limitations helped the Eskimo men and women to become mature.

The consumer culture we live in promises an abundance almost inconceivable in earlier centuries. The Mall of America in Minneapolis is the largest mall in the world, and it has a statue of Snoopy taller than any statue of Christ in Minneapolis. If we replaced Snoopy with a statue of Kali, with her fangs, her bloody cleaver, her necklace of skulls, her long tongue hanging out, we would see the true face of mall culture. Everyone who saw it would be a tiny bit more adult. They might notice also that our abundance implies insatiable hunger elsewhere in the world.

Many mythologies declare that underneath that Giving of the Good Mother lies an insatiable hunger. We have not done very well in portraying the Dark Side of the Goddess and keeping it alive. I think that is one reason we don't take seriously the impoverishment that is taking place in other parts of the world, brought about by global capitalism. We receive the Feeding, and workers in the "undeveloped" countries receive the Eating.

The Immense Mother then has two sides: the Virgin Mary and Baba Yaga. Some Westerners declare every image of the Devouring Mother to be a patriarchal plot, intended to slander women, to set them up for blame and rejection. This interpretation of the Devouring Mother feels convincing at first, but later we see that the denial that there are two sides is a kind of childlike madness. In fact, it was some early civilizations—often called matriarchal—that brought forward the resonant images of the Devouring Mother. The recent excavations at Çatal Hüyük in Turkey show a supreme instance of a matriarchal-toned society in a contained field. Men were not much in evidence. Women were buried under the floor in the center of the rooms, and men somewhere along the sides. Excavated shrine rooms show sculptures in which a vulture beak rises straight out of a mother's breast. That image is right out of our story.[2]

Psychologically, then, this descent to the hut in the forest set on a chicken's leg is a healthy descent.

Among the English poets, William Blake is one of the few who always insist on lifting discussions to the mythological plane. Ezekiel, the Hebrew prophet, developed during the Babylonian captivity a practice, while on the bank of the Chebar, of lying a long time on one side and then on the other and eating dung. In *The Marriage of Heaven and Hell*, Blake imagines an exchange between himself and Ezekiel:

> I then asked Ezekiel why he did eat dung and lay so long on his right and left side? He answer'd, "The desire of raising other men into a perception of the infinite."[1]

So we can understand that though our story does carry many psychological insights, its main intent is to raise the listener into a "perception of the infinite."

Sean Kane, in his essay, "Wisdom of the Mythtellers," says:

> The definition of myth I follow is pre-agricultural. Myth means a dialogue between human beings and spirit-beings of the Earth, engaged in by the myth-tellers of hunter-gatherer societies for the better part of perhaps 100,000 years, and still going on in some

places. . . . That language is told in stories typically having a top and a bottom level. The top level gives the human side of the picture; the bottom level (often with some irony) gives the Earth's view, and the whole myth, usually without meaning to, constitutes a dialogue. Exchange across this boundary between worlds is the central feature and the whole point of myth.[2]

The top level of our story—the merchant father who marries unwisely and puts a tutor in charge of his son, the stepmother and her interference—gives the human side of the exchange that is always going on between human beings and various earth forces. The bottom level—the Baba Yaga scenes—gives the earth's view, and there are many surprises there for us. Baba Yaga, one could say, *is* the earth.

Myths say that we are not the only beings in the universe with intentions and hurt feelings. If, as Pythagoras said, "Everything is intelligent," that means we have to walk with care. If we can't remain awake when the Divine comes, then we have already opened negotiations with the Goddess on the mythic plane, but disastrously. Probably that is exactly the reckless way each of us opened negotiations with the mythical plane when we were teenagers. We'll have to pay for it sooner or later.

The Firebird

"Sit upon me quickly," said the Firebird, "and we shall fly wherever you want; if you don't come with me, the Baba Yaga will devour you." Ivan had no

sooner sat himself upon the bird's back than the Baba Yaga rushed in, seized the Firebird by the tail, and plucked a large handful of feathers from it.

It's clear that the Firebird has been called down by the Great Sound that Ivan has made. So we are not in the realm of seeing and eyes now, but in the realm of sound.

Blowing the horn is how Louis Armstrong came up out of death. Joachim Berendt, in his book *The Third Ear*, discusses sound as an almost forgotten force. He mentions that there are three times the number of connections between ear and brain as there are between eye and brain.[1]

Oedipus's bless´ed later life, following the gross violence of his earlier years, came when he put out his eyes. Symbolically, his seeing time was done. He spends the rest of his life wandering about, being led by his daughters, and listening.

The company of his daughters suggests a link between the feminine and the ear, and conversely between the masculine and the eye; and Berendt emphasizes those links. The adventures Ivan has had in the Underworld has been associated—as we look back at it—with an increasingly subtle acceptance of the feminine, reversing his early rejection of it by the use of the pin. Ivan's story is in some ways a parallel story to the Iron John story, but this time it is a story of initiation into the feminine.

Ivan is at last learning music. That's one way to put it. He offers to be Sweet Honey in the Rock, or to be a Swiss mountaineer blowing his long horn so as to bring the community together, to be a fiddler who pulls everyone up to dance, an African woman leading field singing, a Jessye Norman who sings out at last the pain of the injured woman, a Bach who brings in sound to comb the tangled hair of the world.

This is the sort of sound that attracts the Firebird.

What Is the Firebird?

The Firebird's descent is a spectacular event; golden feathers fall from its chest as it descends. The stories tell us that when the Firebird descends, all the other birds in the forest grow still. So a full-throated sound calls the Firebird, and the other birds fall silent.

The Russian culture, still so much involved with sound, as Russian Orthodox liturgy shows, has not lost its friendship with the ancient Firebird. The Firebird appears in thousands of Russian jewelry boxes, teapots, folk designs, tapestries, paintings. We might mention that Russian poetry is still recited with a power and verve unknown anywhere else in Europe, and it's possible that the full-throated voice, carried into contemporary times by Russian Orthodox liturgy, is a call specific to the Firebird.

The question becomes: What is the Firebird? We might say that there is something irrevocable about the Firebird; once it has become a part of your life, there is no going back. When the Firebird came to Nijinsky, he could not go back to being an ordinary dancer. We know that one view of initiation is that it means a passage from a mundane world to a realm of dangerous spiritual beings—from whom one will never be free again. For Ganesha, being initiated means losing the human head entirely, and receiving a new head, which in his case was an elephant's head.[1] Mythologically, the elephant represents not the small human world but the Great World With All Its Stars, the Universe itself.

> *Music—*
> *a naked woman*
> *running mad through the pure night!*[2]
> Juan Ramón Jiménez, translated by R.B.

Lorca has much to say about sound:

We know the roads where we can search for God, from the barbarous way of the hermit to the subtle one of the mystic. With a tower like Saint Teresa or with the three ways of Saint John of the Cross. And though we may have to cry out in the voice of Isaiah, "Truly thou art a hidden God," in the end God sends each seeker his first fiery thorns. . . .

Each art has a *duende* different in form and style, but their roots meet in the place where the black sounds of Manuel Torre come from—the essential, uncontrollable, quivering, common base of wood, sound, canvas, and word.

Behind those black sounds, tenderly and intimately, live zephyrs, ants, volcanoes, and the huge night, straining its waist against the Milky Way.[3]

We notice that the Firebird is not associated with the slowness of earth, the healing power of water, the calm clarity of air, but rather with the quick movement of fire. Fire's tendency is to leap out of human control, burn thousands of acres of forest, leap from twig to twig with the speed of Hermes. The speed of fire resembles the amazing speed of wit, when synapses in the heated brain flash and spark until the whole conversation is alive with unrepeatable, outrageous, goldlike, untraceable wit.

The Firebird seems to choose whom it will visit; it will visit ordinary people as well as artists. We sense that it is more likely to visit the renegade Villon than the stodgy Dreiser. But most artists know of it. The last poem Wallace Stevens wrote (just before he left for the hospital) mentions the Firebird:

> *You know then that it is not the reason*
> *That makes us happy or unhappy.*
> *The bird sings. Its feathers shine.*

> *The palm stands on the edge of space.*
> *The wind moves slowly in the branches.*
> *The bird's fire-fangled feathers dangle down.*[4]

All over the world, the sixties in the United States is remembered for the amazing amount of Firebird energy: Janis Joplin, Jimi Hendrix, Jim Morrison. We have the feeling of a human being going into warp speed when the Firebird enters; some bodies survive, some get shaken apart. A proper fear is appropriate near the Firebird.

The elaborate meters and mathematical discipline of great art are actually a nest for the Firebird. The formal brilliance of Rumi's poems in the original Farsi are a fine instance of that nest. It is as if the vehicle has to be an aristocratic construction as intense as the democratic, wild fire. Rumi says:

> *We should ask God*
> *to help us toward manners. Inner gifts*
> *do not find their way*
> *to creatures without just respect.*

> *If a man or woman flails about, he not only*
> *smashes his house,*
> *he burns the world down.*

> *Your depression is connected to your insolence*
> *and refusal to praise. Whoever feels himself walking*
> *on the path, and refuses to praise—that man or woman*
> *steals from others every day—is a shoplifter!*

> *The sun became full of light when it got hold of itself.*
> *Angels only began shining when they achieved discipline.*
> *The sun goes out whenever the cloud of not-praising comes near.*

The moment the foolish Angel felt insolent, he heard the door close.[5]

(Translated by R.B.)

Democracies tend to lose so many great artists early because democracies believe that an artist needs only to be sincere.

The tremendous discipline of flamenco dancing and flamenco guitar has been developed to make a nest for the Firebird. García Lorca admired in flamenco the quality the gypsies called *duende:* the term suggests high spirits in the face of death. García Lorca says:

> Very often intellect is poetry's enemy because it is too much given to imitation, because it lifts the poet to a throne of sharp edges and makes him oblivious of the fact that he may suddenly be devoured by ants, or a great arsenic lobster may fall on his head.[6]

The Spanish bullfight is basically a Firebird event, because the elegantly dressed fighter-dancer is only a quarter-inch from death at any moment. Death in the bullring is an animal, immensely vigorous, muscled, impulsive, and magnificent, whose presence increases the sense of exultation. The human being has been carefully chosen out of all beings in the universe to face death consciously, and it is right and proper that when a human being faces death in such a way, he should be dressed in gold-embroidered vests, because he represents the sun, as the bull represents its partner, the moon, demander of sacrifice.

Lorca said:

> The arrival of the *Duende* always presupposes a radical change in all the forms as they existed on the old plane. It gives a sense of refreshment unknown until then, together with that quality of the just-opening rose, of the

miraculous, which comes and instills an almost religious transport.

In all Arabian music, in the dances, songs, elegies of Arabia, the coming of the *Duende* is greeted by fervent cries of *Allah! Allah! God! God!*, so close to the *Olé! Olé!* of our bullrings that who is to say they are not actually the same; and in all the songs of southern Spain the appearance of the *Duende* is followed by heartfelt exclamations of *God alive!*—profound, human, tender, the cry of communion with God through the medium of the five senses and the grace of the *Duende* that stirs the voice and the body of the dancer.

We could sum this up by saying that the gift of the Firebird lies in the ability to experience the invisible world. Experiencing the invisible world imaginatively is also playfulness. When we see a Chi Quong master moving his or her hands in order to adjust to movement of *chi* in your body, we know that this master has learned to experience the world imaginatively. When we learn to see invisible beings as friends, when we lay out food each day for the invisible spirits who might need some food today, when we've begun to wear the colors that the invisibles may like (instead of what we like), then we come closer to the ability to experience the world. Yeats said:

> We can make our minds so like still water that beings gather about us that they may see, it may be, their own images, and so live for a moment with a clearer, perhaps even with a fiercer life because of our quiet.

The Firebird is a bridge on which we can pass back and forth to the mythological world. Shakespeare in *A Midsummer Night's Dream* says:

The lunatic, the lover, and the poet
Are of imagination all compact.
One sees more devils than vast hell can hold.
That is the madman. The lover, all as frantic,
Sees Helen's beauty in a brow of Egypt.
The poet's eye, in a fine frenzy rolling,
Doth glance from heaven to earth, from earth to heaven,
And as imagination bodies forth
The forms of things unknown, the poet's pen
Turns them to shapes, and gives to airy nothing
A local habitation and a name.[7]

Rumi said:

I am a lover, skilled in the arts of madness;
I have drunk deeply of culture and learning.[8]

The greatest gift of the Firebird, I think, is the ability to raise people into "a perception of the infinite," to use Blake's words.[9] A few years ago when some American men began searching for an image of masculinity different from the view of masculinity dumped on them by the corporations, many found themselves faced with the invisible world or the mythological plane. Mythological thinking proved to be difficult. This little story testifies again that the road from literal thinking to psychological thinking to mythological thinking is a long road, and we are less than halfway down that road now.

The Longing for the Firebird

Everyone longs for the Firebird; everyone wants the "refresh-ment unknown until then." This longing for the Firebird came up vividly one day in Toronto when Marion Woodman and I were acting out the Firebird section of this story for a group of listeners. As storytellers, we had arrived at the point in which Ivan (I was Ivan) receives the three horns from the third Baba Yaga (Marion was Baba Yaga). I blew the horns. Our job was to imag-ine the Firebird descending, and Ivan climbing up on its back. Once the Firebird began to pull away with Ivan, Marion, after she had grabbed a few feathers, found herself falling down on the floor with a long, harsh cry of disappointment and despair. She hadn't planned to do that at all. She mentioned later that her whole body felt abandoned, deserted, left behind in some stag-nant and familiar world.

As the audience discussed this scene, the women particularly had much to say. Woman after woman remembered her mother's grief. They had seen their mothers caught in the concrete world of washing, cooking, laundry, and children; certainly most women in the nineteenth century were trapped there, as most women had been for centuries before that. "My mother never climbed on the Firebird's back." Some women complained that "men get on the Firebird and leave women with the work and the depression."

There was a lot of tension in the room. It took a few minutes before the men in the room spoke up, and reminded the room that their fathers, caught in twelve-hour days at the office, factory work in the thirties, or farm work during the Depression, never got on the Firebird, either, nor even got near it. The idea that men as a whole climb on the Firebird is an illusion. Most men and women, with exceptions as rare among men as among women, are left behind.

The world of most men and women is a flat, horizontal world of wage-earning, driving, child care, taxes, malls, football games, hairdressers, getting by, eating, and working. The vertical world, in which the soul descends to the lower realm of the Dead, or rises to the upper realm of divine energies, is increasingly rare in our day. The Firebird is clearly a part of the vertical line.

The Story: Flying with the Firebird

The Firebird, interestingly, tells Ivan that it can carry him only partway.

> **The Firebird flew with Ivan on its back; for a long time it soared in the skies, till finally it came to the broad sea. "Now, Ivan, merchant's son, the thrice tenth land lies beyond this sea. I am not strong enough to carry you to the other shore; get there as best you can." Ivan climbed down from the Firebird, thanked it, and walked along the shore.**

It's interesting that the Firebird can't go all the way. If he could, every bullfighter would become enlightened. If the Firebird could carry one all the way, Rimbaud would never have become a slave-dealer. There never was a young poet more full of the Firebird than he was. Ivan walks along the shore, and after a long time or a short time he arrives at the house where the Crone lives.

The Realm of the Crone

The Crone traditionally carries all the knowledge of the tribe in her memory. In *Dancing in the Flames* Marion Woodman says about the Crone:

> For most people, it takes a lifetime for the psyche to find its relationship to the Goddess. She appears in the psyche in her three-fold nature, sometimes Virgin, sometimes Mother, sometimes Crone. However, it is the Crone that our culture has so brutally repressed. The wise woman, the healer, the transformer has been one of the greatest threats to the patriarchal world. Ironically, with the founding of universities (centers of *oneness*) in the eleventh century, women's natural talents for counseling, healing, and being a source of wisdom were curtailed; women were barred from attending. Public services could be rendered only by someone with the proper credentials and, since women were not allowed to acquire these credentials, they were effectively removed from the intellectual life of the community. Many who were burned as witches were among the most gifted women of the time. . . .
>
> As a symbol, the Crone had to be suppressed by patriarchal religions because her power "overruled the will even of Heavenly Father Zeus." She controlled the cycles of life and death. She was the Mother of God, the Nurturer of God, and, as Crone, the Slayer of God. While Christianity retained the feminine as Virgin and Mother, it eliminated her role as Crone. . . . The Crone in a woman is that part of her psyche that is not identified with any relationship nor confined by any bond.[1]

Our story has introduced the listener first to the Beneficent Goddess of Ecstasy, then to the Bony-Legged One, and now to the Crone. The Crone in image form is the final sliver of the moon, just as the Virgin or the Girl is the first crescent of the same moon. The full moon represents the robustness of the mature woman; her shape, we could say, resembles the round shape of the full harvest moon. By contrast, the "old moon," the sickle, resembles the woman past child-bearing time; and she is associated with the color black, as the robust woman is with red, and the Virgin with white.

When Ivan enters the Crone's hut, he immediately tells her why he has come. He says, "I am looking for the Ecstatic Woman who lives in the Kingdom Three Times Ten." The Crone, in effect, says, "Are you the one? The one the Ecstatic Woman found, and then you fell asleep?" "Yes," says Ivan. "I'm that one."

The Crone's News

"Ah," says the old woman, and she brings out a crucial piece of information: "She no longer loves you!" There is something astonishing about this news. The fact that She no longer loves Ivan makes an immense change in the story, and the change doesn't feel whimsical. It feels like the inevitable result of some law that we as human beings try to avoid noticing.

C. G. Jung remarked that whatever part of your psyche you don't love in your youth, whatever part you ignore or send away will end up being hostile to you later. If a man puts away sexuality, for example, in his twenties because he wants to be successful, it is possible that when he asks it to come later, in his fifties, it may destroy his life. We see many examples of that.

If a woman puts away her ambition in the world early on, in order to be attractive, it may harm her life when it comes back later.

The question our story asks is: "What happens to a young man who cannot welcome the ecstatic feminine early in life?" There must be a law. The Crone says there is. She tells Ivan that "She no longer loves you!" For all of us alive now, in the late twentieth century, this is a story about "The Goddess Who No Longer Loves You." We have to notice that many New Age practitioners say that if you come to their workshops, you will experience the love of the Goddess. They have no right to say that.

What Can Be Done

"Ah," said the old woman, "she no longer loves you; if she gets hold of you, she will tear you to shreds; her love is stored away in a remote place."

The Crone has offered a second important piece of information. The love the Goddess has for us has been stored somewhere far away from here. There's something promising in that. It suggests a better outcome than if the old woman had said, "She's furious; the love is annihilated; give it up."

The love the Divine One had for us has been hidden somewhere out of reach: the question is where.

The Feminine Divine no longer loves Ivan. Her cooling toward him has gone even further. "If she were to see you now, she would tear you to pieces." We could say that the Goddess's warm, loving mood has been replaced, not by indifference but by active hatred. No one warned us that would happen. "They say such different things at school."[1] And for the United States, which has done so much to destroy Native American religion, or the African divinities of African villages, which has done so much to destroy our own forests and to push global capitalism, what can one say? One has to say that the United States without doubt is in for a string of bad luck. And Ivan, that impulsive fisherman, has a good chance of being torn to pieces.

The Crone's news implies that each of us is in danger of being torn to pieces. It must already be happening to us. Perhaps the increasing hostility between the genders stands as a secret reminder of the Spirit's rage at us—for what? For our lack of courtliness, on both sides, a form of ingratitude among so many in our contemporary culture. There's a shock in this news: Where is the maternal love that we all expect from the feminine, no matter what we, as sons or daughters, do? Forget about it. Maternal love is not for you. "If she were to see you now, she would tear you to pieces."

The increasing childishness of our society is noticeable, both here and in Japan. The Japanese psychologist Takeo Doi says that in Japan the "adult adult" is gone, and all that remains is "the adult-like child, and the childish adult."[2] Such increasing childishness must be connected to the longing for maternal love from our own mothers, from the Feminine collectively, and from the Universe. But it is not coming.

Our longing to snuggle up to the personal Mother deepens with every decade. As the fathers flee the families, encouraged, as we know, by ideas of individualism, their departure makes the children remaining in the house cling even more desperately to the mothers. I recently heard a thirty-year-old man in prison say, "At least when I get out I still have my crib," by which he meant his mother's house. No one knows what to do about the increasing childishness of our culture. And very few people want to talk about it, either.

The Crone implies that some action will be required from Ivan beyond the moping that often takes place when the young man wants more from his mother than she will give. Active and dangerous anger has replaced the missing love, and the missing love has been "stored in a remote place."

Where could that be? No one seems to know. We are struck again and again that each being in the Underworld has a limited amount of information. The first two Baba Yagas don't know where the Kingdom Three Times Ten is; now the Crone doesn't know the place where the old love is hidden. However, her daughter, whom we gather is one of the original thirty women, does know, and the old woman will ask her.

> "Ah," said the old woman, "she no longer loves you; if she gets hold of you, she will tear you to shreds; her love is stored away in a remote place." "Then how can I get it?" "Wait a bit! My daughter lives at the Maiden Tsar's palace and she is coming to visit me today; we may learn something from her." Then the old woman turned Ivan into a pin and stuck the pin into the wall; at night her daughter flew in. Her mother asked her whether she knew where the Maiden Tsar's love was stored away. "I do not know," said the daughter, and promised to find out from the Maiden Tsar herself.

The Crone, we learn, prepares the house for her daughter's visit, and as a part of her preparation turns Ivan into a pin and presses him into the wall. This is a surprising detail; it is as if the pin returns from the early story but now strangely reversed in meaning. The pin that once put Ivan to sleep so that he could neither see nor hear, now enables him to hear all that is said in the room without himself being seen. Ivan gives up activity and becomes someone who listens. Ivan, by this means, has become closer to the state of an infant, or a young child. "All you have to do is listen." In the womb we could not see, but we could hear. In a sense, each of us began as a little pin in the wall of the womb. It's probably true: one listens better when one is hidden.

The Three Mothers

A great contemporary poet has said: "The purpose of art is to re-open negotiations with the mythical plane."[1] It's clear that our story works very hard to do that.

The Mediterranean world has several divisions of the Immense Mother. One distinguishes three aspects: the Sacred Bride, who is Beauty; the Mother, who is deeply loving; and the Bony-Legged One, who is violent. The early history of goddess worship is associated, as well we all know, with many dark events. We could say that a play meant to be a comedy will omit the Bony-Legged One. A play meant to be a tragedy will include Her, and often amounts to a stark conflict between the Abundant Mother and the Bony-Legged One, with the Bony-Legged One winning. The "hero" will be torn to pieces at the end, as Hippolytus was by the Mares of the Sea, or the King by Macbeth and Lady Macbeth.

Our story is not a tragedy. It leaves the steel tracks of tragedy at the moment the Firebird, hearing the Music, flies down and carries Ivan off to the Crone's House. The Crone is a Protector, and she has two pieces of news. The first is that the Ecstatic Goddess "no longer loves you." It's possible that your own mother still loves you; it's even possible that an interior mother still loves you psychologically, so to speak. But on the mythological plane, you are unloved. You may as well become an adult.

The second piece of news is that the love the Ecstatic Woman on the Boat once felt for Ivan has not been vaporized, or annihilated. It exists, but it is inaccessible. Only the Crone's "Daughter" knows where it is.

PART IV

The secret is out now. "There is a Goddess who doesn't love you anymore." I've never heard anything exactly like that in any other tale. The popular attitude today is that the Goddess is always loving. She never kills, like those bad men do; if you pay some money for the weekend coming up, and arrive, the Goddess will be your friend, your health will improve, all your relationships will turn into partnerships, there will be no more Dominator culture. If we love the Goddess, all unpleasant actions, such as teeth-filing, sudden death, murder of infants, and war will end.

It is embarrassing to hear grown men and women say such things. There are several things wrong with this view. Mythologically there is not one goddess, there are many. Some love you and some don't; a few would be insulted if you called them nice or compassionate. Second, the idealization of the Female Divinities is increasing the infantilism already palpable in our culture. The movement to demonize the father gods, and to create a sentimentalized version of the Goddess makes women and men more infantile. Moreover, it is a part of the shame of New Age culture that it confuses this infantile dependency upon the Goddess with mysticism or religious emotion. "The Maiden Tsar" is older, tougher, closer to the fierce intelligence of the adult.

"There is a goddess who doesn't love you anymore."

"What do you mean? Our mother fails us sometimes—our father always—and our siblings—but they are only human. Divinities never fail us; the Mother's love is beyond the human. It does not fail." Dream on. An Eskimo hunter might remark, "If I can freeze to death on Her ice, who is to say Her love doesn't fail?"

The Crone does not report that the Goddess Who Came on the Thirtieth Boat is angry at Ivan. The Crone says that her love has inexplicably migrated somewhere else, and is no longer available. Her love is out of her mind; it is like some formula that she can't remember; the love she had for human beings has slipped her mind, as a dog slips out of its leash, and where is it now? Running around the city somewhere.

This particular goddess once had a love for Ivan—maybe it was a love for human beings—and the love somehow got lost. The Goddess is neither hostile to human beings nor full of love for them. "I don't know where I put it—it was here just yesterday."

As soon as the Firebird arrived it was clear that Ivan would—unlike Hippolytus—not be torn apart. The Firebird's rescue means that Ivan is going to live, and become a sort of test case to see if he can find where the love is.

We could say that atheists really do feel unloved by God. They conclude "God doesn't exist." They might also say, "I've been too busy to look; I have a lot to do."

We understand from all this that the route back to rediscovering the missing love will not be an easy road. The love we want, the story says, can, though hidden, be found, and "on this side of the ocean."

If the ocean is what separates life from death, then the phrase suggests that the search for this love belongs to "the time before death." The fifteenth-century Indian poet Kabir remarks:

Friend, hope for the Guest while you are alive.
Jump into experience while you are alive!
Think . . . and think . . . while you are alive.
What you call "salvation" belongs to the time before death.

If you don't break your ropes while you're alive,
do you think
ghosts will do it after?

The idea that the soul will join with the ecstatic
just because the body is rotten—
that is all fantasy.
What is found now is found then.
If you find nothing now,
you will simply end up with an apartment in the City of
*   Death.*
If you make love with the divine now, in the next life you will
*   have the face of satisfied desire.*

So plunge into the truth, find out who the Teacher is. Believe in
*   the Great Sound!*
Kabir says this: When the Guest is being searched for, it is the
*   intensity of the longing for the Guest that does all the work.*
Look at me, and you will see a slave of that intensity.[1]

We mustn't be fooled by the matter-of-fact tone in our story: the oak, the coffer, etc. "When the Guest is being searched for, it is the intensity of the longing for the Guest that does all the work." One has to be truly desperate in order to find the missing love.

The next day the daughter again visited her mother and told her: "On this side of the ocean there stands an oak: in the oak there is a coffer; in the coffer there is a hare; in the hare there is a duck; in the duck there is an egg; and in the egg lies the Maiden Tsar's love."

We will try to unpack this amazing paragraph. One's first re-action is: "What kind of information is this?" The answer is "metaphorical." Our ancestors often used metaphors in order to make the issue clear. Contemporary newspaper prose, by contrast, deliberately avoids metaphor in order to make the issue clear. We have all been trained in school to think that our expressions without metaphor will be more understandable. Herschel Parker, in his biography of Herman Melville, mentions that in the years just before he wrote *Moby Dick*, Melville discovered three things: metaphor, metaphysics, and Shakespeare.[2] James Wood remarks, "During the time that Melville wrote *Moby Dick*, he underwent a kind of insanity of metaphor. . . . Melville is one of the most naturally metaphorical of writers, and one of the greatest."[3]

For those who find this story difficult because of the step it takes beyond psychological thought patterns, this part of the story will be even more difficult. We will have to walk in metaphor.

The Metaphor of the Oak

Rituals of some sort were acted out under oaks for centuries in the Near East. Isaiah I, 29 forbids oak ritual: "They shall be ashamed of the oaks which ye have desired." For thousands of years before this we know of events that tie the oak firmly to religious ritual around the Goddess. Some ancient ritual energy, one could say, is concealed in the roots of "the oak."

The oak was sacred to Rhea and Artemis among the Greeks, to Diana among the Romans, to Cybele among the Phoenicians. We remember that Circe's island was thick with oaks, and her pigs were fed on its acorns. We know that Diana had an oak grove, and Ovid mentions in his *Metamorphoses* (II, 3) that the Maenads who killed Orpheus were later turned into oaks. The Romans believed that the oak was the "golden bough" that gave access to Hades.

The Mediterranean Great Goddess had a consort ordinarily called the Oak King, who ruled by the Goddess's permission. Sir James Frazer established the ritual succession of that King: Every seven years, the King would station himself under an oak tree with a sword and meet all challengers. If he won, he would remain protected by the Goddess for another seven years. If he lost, he would be killed there, under the oak. Robert Graves says:

> *Water to water, ark again to ark,*
> *From woman back to woman:*
> *So each new victim treads unfalteringly*
> *The never altered circuit of his fate,*
> *Bringing twelve peers as witness*
> *Both to his starry rise and starry fall.*[1]

The Scandinavians still use oak for midsummer bonfires, a hint of its immense ritual age. The midsummer day was known as the Hinge Day; for the Oak King that day was a Door to the other world. The Goddess of the Silver Castle was there, and the souls of sacrificed kings would pass through Her door.

What, then, can we say of this first act of the Search, which goes to the old oak? To search in this way we would have to respect the beliefs and concerns of our ancestors. There is no evidence that we have gone beyond their understanding of things. The deconstructionist or New Historicist attitude, which would describe all practices as some sort of hegemonic plot intended to enslave ordinary people, will stop the process of return dead in its tracks. The oak we are looking for stands "on this side of the ocean," and so it hints at the possibility of which Kabir speaks: some experience of the sweetness of Eternity while still alive. The metaphor says, "Put your head down; go back to the oak stage of religion. You'll have to get down on your knees near the roots of the oak, where the pigs love to eat acorns."

The Metaphor of the Coffer

It turns out that a magic box or coffer is buried in the roots of the oak. This coffer is mentioned in many Irish stories. In one, the giant says, "Have no fear for me. I'll put your mind at rest. In the bottom of the sea is a chest—locked and bound; in that chest is a duck, in the duck an egg," and so on.[1]

Readers who know the Grimm Brothers' stories will immediately remember the story called "The Spirit in the Bottle." A young man—a student—who is helping his father cut wood strolls away one day at lunch, and hears a voice coming from a bottle that seems to be lodged among the roots of a huge oak tree. A voice cries, "Let me out!" As soon as the naive young man hears the voice, he lets the spirit out of the bottle. He expects some reward; instead he is threatened with immediate death. The spirit identifies itself as Mercury, who in Greek mythology would be Hermes. The spirit is furious about being imprisoned so long, and has decided to kill whatever human being lets him out. From that hint we can guess why the energy in our tale is enveloped in so many coverings—oak roots, casket, hare, duck, egg. If it were thinly enclosed, it would kill instantly whoever came near it.

The location of the bottle holding an imprisoned spirit implies, by the metaphorical nature of such details, some energy caught, trapped, in the lower spine of a human being. We do know that Kundalini tradition says an enormous force is caught at the base of the spine, and he or she who releases it will have to be careful. So the bottle is very like the coffer in our story. The way it encloses energy makes us remember the alchemist's retort, as well as a hermit's cell. Wallace Stevens remarked that every great poem is also a container holding dangerous energy. In "Poetry Is a Destructive Force," he said:

The lion sleeps in the sun.
Its nose is on its paws.
It can kill a man.[2]

Care, therefore, is essential. We remember that Jesus said, "Whoever is near unto me is near unto the fire."

In *The Thousand and One Nights* several spirits have gotten imprisoned in a small container; Aladdin met such a spirit living inside an old lamp. That spirit later helped Aladdin. Some commentators regard the Grimm Brothers' "Spirit in a Bottle" as a symbolic biography of Paracelsus. After learning to treat the "dangerous spirit" later without naiveté, the young man receives a gift from Mercurius, a piece of cloth. One end of the cloth turns ordinary iron to silver, and the other end heals people. These are references to the two great themes in Paracelsus's life: alchemy and healing.

What shall we say then about this second step in uncovering the missing love? The first step, finding the oak, suggests a sincerity, a willingness to get on our knees, to go inside a forest, to eat acorns. By contrast, the coffer step suggests something Mercurial, Hermes-like, trickster-like. Lewis Hyde's book *Trickster Makes This World* is a brilliant evocation of serious trickster energy, which is about shape-shifting, imprisonment and release, and the substitution of symbolic food for physical food.[3] In this stage, one has to learn how to feed that part of the soul that has wants, that will steal for those wants, that part of the soul that breaks all rules, crosses boundaries, laughs a lot, filches what it needs, as Hermes stole cows successfully by creating little shoes that made the cows appear to have walked away from his barn, rather than to it. This is the stage of the thief, the sleight-of-hand artist who teaches the trickster arts of imprisonment and release, the art of changing iron to silver, the art of healing oneself. William James gives the mood of the extravagant nature of Hermes:

Man's chief difference from the brutes lies in the exuberant excess of his subjective propensities—his preeminence over them simply and solely in the number and in the fantastic and unnecessary character of his wants, physical, moral, aesthetic, and intellectual. Had his whole life not been a quest for the superfluous, he would never have established himself as inexpugnably as he has done in the necessary. And from the consciousness of this he should draw the lesson that his wants are to be trusted; that even when their gratification seems farthest off, the uneasiness they occasion is still the best guide of his life, and will lead him to issues entirely beyond his present powers of reckoning. Prune down his extravagance, sober him, and you undo him.[4]

We notice that it's hard for fundamentalists to arrive at the Hermes stage in which the spirit escapes from the bottle. Fundamentalists tend to stay with the sincere oak. They thrive on what we could call oaken rhetoric, whose roots are deeply thrust into the ground. The oak has a sturdy trunk that doesn't bend with wind, and the branches hold onto their leaves. So all of this makes it difficult for these sober and good people to move on toward the trickster.

Finally, brooding over this opening of the coffer, one might notice the resemblance the coffer has to the womb, the earliest container we experience. Jesus insisted that "You must be born again," which implies a return for a time to the womb. Nicodemus, the first sociologist, objected: "But how is it possible for us with our big shoulders to crawl back up into our mother's vagina?" Jesus replied, "What kind of schools do you have around here?"

The Metaphor of the Hare

When Ivan opens the casket, a hare leaps out. If we try to un-pack that, we'll find that we've forgotten most of what our an-cestors felt and thought about the hare. The hare carried, one might say, an enormous amount of meaning to ancient people, and the meaning was basically that of sacrifice.

Some dreams recorded in this century reveal very clearly the associations around the hare as they appeared to a modern woman. When the psychologist John Layard was living in En-gland, just before the Second War, he accepted into therapy an Irish woman who was troubled over the behavior of her young daughter. The woman, Mrs. Wright, a Protestant who had an ed-ucation in the elementary grades and no education in mythology, reported the following dream to Layard, who at the time knew nothing of the Hare-egg mythology himself:

> The scene is near my home in Ireland, and I am walk-ing with Margaret up to a square house belonging to a female cousin whom I know very well. The ground was covered with snow. Margaret was in a bit of a fuss want-ing to hurry up and get the place dusted, but I told her not to be in such a hurry, as in any case, with snow ly-ing about, there wouldn't be much dust. . . .
>
> Then I went round alone into the kitchen at the back of the house. Inside there was a great light and every-thing was as white as it was outside, though how the snow got in there I cannot tell.
>
> There were people inside, too, and there, in a white bowl with a little water in it, was a live hare. Someone told me I had got to kill it. This seemed a terrible thing to do, but I had to do it. I picked up the knife (an ordinary kitchen knife) which seemed to have been

placed ready for me and which was lying in the water inside the bowl beside the hare, and with a feeling of horror I started cutting into the fur through to the skin beneath. I had to cut the hare straight down the middle of the back, and I started to do this, but my hand trembled so much that, as I cut down, the knife slipped away from the straight line, and ended up by cutting obliquely into the hare's haunch.

I felt awful doing this, but the hare never moved and did not seem to mind.

Though the ground outside was covered with snow we had left no footmarks on it.[1]

Several weeks later, Layard, who had in the meantime read a bit about animal sacrifice, had a conversation with Mrs. Wright.

[I] told her how in certain primitive religions the animal was always sacrificed before being eaten, and was himself at the same time the willing sacrifice, just as the hare had been. She then told me of the look of extreme satisfaction and trust that had been in the hare's eyes as it looked back at her when she plunged the knife into its back. This made her think of Christ.[2]

Many themes intertwine in Mrs. Wright's dream. We remember the detail of moonlight coming off the snow, though the strange light is also inside the house. That suggests some sort of sacred space. The hare's association with water comes in, and the connection of the hare with the moon. We recall the folk idea that we can see an outline of the hare on the moon. Finally, we notice that the hare in Mrs. Wright's dream carried to her the motif of willing sacrifice.

All these motifs we see repeated in the mythology of many other cultures. A favorite theme in Japanese art is the moon goddess Gwatten, who is shown holding out to priests a dish that is actually a small crescent moon. Inside that dish a white hare is calmly seated, as if it were presented for sacrifice.

In European mythology, the hare is "the moon's own magical love-creature."[3] The hare in many cultures is the mythical animal associated with the menstrual cycle. The moon, one could say, sends down an egg into the fallopian tubes once each month, first on the left side of the womb, next on the right side. The moon accomplishes all this.

The Ojibway call the moon the eye of the hare. We recall that the Nanzibojo, the Great Hare, is the hero of an Algonquin myth cycle. The hare has an association with immortality, which we would suspect already from Mrs. Wright's dream of mysterious light. The hare is shown in China pounding up the herbs of immortality on the moon.

What shall we say, then, about the hare stage of our story? If we look at dictionaries of symbols, we will find the hare, as Mrs. Wright intuited in her dream, associated everywhere with the practice of sacrifice. It is associated with giving up things, letting parts of oneself go, offering something dear to a divinity, not necessarily in order to receive a boon in return, but rather as evidence that you are serious, that you want a change, that you understand that just because you have some object doesn't mean you own it, that you are willing out of gratitude to the spirits and to the universe to give it away. Monks and nuns sacrifice their sexuality—at least, intend to. T. S. Eliot mentions that the writer's life amounts to "a daily crucifixion" because of the sensual life he has to abandon in order to write well. Often a therapist will ask for a sacrifice: I want you to turn off the television for three months, I want you to work Saturdays in a homeless shelter, I want you to come home from work at five every day, and give those evening hours to your children.

Many people feel that women mature emotionally at an earlier

age than men because a woman can be said to sacrifice her blood every month, and she is aware how much she will sacrifice if a baby comes. Some say that the male has to *intend* to become an adult. A writer on myth recently wrote:

> I remember reading what seemed to me a beautiful re-
> mark made by one of the men in the Mandan tribe, a
> tribe up in Missouri. George Catlin, a young painter,
> went out from Harvard in 1832 and painted pictures
> of these Indians and the magnificence of their ritual
> and so forth. The young men who were hung up by
> spikes through their pectoral muscles and beaten said,
> "We have to learn to suffer in order to compensate for
> the suffering of our women." Life brings the suffering
> on the woman, and the man has to match it by im-
> posing suffering on himself.

Sacrifice, then, implies willing sacrifice—we are not talking here about unwilling sacrifice of victims. So the stage of Ivan's search that is described metaphorically as a hare leaping out of the coffer brings up willing sacrifice. Goethe's great poem called "Holy Longing" sums up the mood of such willing sacrifice:

> *Tell a wise person, or else keep silent,*
> *Because the massman will mock it right away.*
> *I praise what is truly alive,*
> *What longs to be burned to death.*
>
> *In the calm water of the love-nights,*
> *Where you were begotten, where you have begotten,*
> *A strange feeling comes over you*
> *When you see the silent candle burning.*

Now you are no longer caught
In the obsession with darkness,
And a desire for higher love-making
Sweeps you upward.

Distance does not make you falter,
Now, arriving in magic, flying,
And, finally, insane for the light,
You are the butterfly and you are gone.

And so long as you haven't experienced
This: to die and so to grow,
You are only a troubled guest
On the dark earth.[4]

(Translated by R.B.)

So the third stage implies an offering of oneself.

The Metaphor of the Duck

The story says that when Ivan finally opened the hare, a duck flew out. How can that be? What a bloody mess! Well, we're thinking literally again. The statement that a duck flies out of the hare is a mnemonic device, so that the storyteller remembers the sequence properly. If we have passed on to the stage suggested by the hare, in which we offer sacrifices out of our own store, then it is possible we have learned "to die and so to grow."

The duck is not tied to the earth, as the raccoon, the wolverine, the bear, the chimpanzee, and the hare are. It lives and moves in all three worlds—earth, water, and air. It's possible that it was this characteristic that led the ancients to associate the duck with spirit, which is not constrained to any of those spheres. We can sense in the swan, because of the cultural associations that have gathered around it in every country in which it lives, the elegance of spirit; the ancients noticed in the beautiful gliding motion, the mating for life, the song it traditionally gives out just before death, its close associations with spirit. Rainer Maria Rilke catches these qualities in his poem called "The Swan":

> *This clumsy living that moves lumbering*
> *as if in ropes through what is not done*
> *reminds us of the awkward way the swan walks.*
>
> *And to die, which is a letting go*
> *of the ground we stand on and cling to every day,*
> *is like the swan when he nervously lets himself down*
>
> *Into the water, which receives him gaily*
> *and which flows joyfully under*
> *and after him, wave after wave,*
> *while the swan, unmoving and marvelously calm,*
> *is pleased to be carried, each minute more fully grown,*
> *more like a king, composed, farther and farther on.*[1]
>
> (Translated by R.B.)

The kingly quality of the spirit is present in the last line. We need to remember to transfer some of these qualities to all water-birds, and then we will be prepared to see the movement from the hare to the duck.

Homer refers to the duck in the name of Odysseus' wife, Penelope. The *Odyssey,* on the popular level, is a simple tale of a man who survives a war, and then goes through various adventures, lively and entertaining, on the way back to his home island. But each ancient work of literature conceals, as we are more and more aware, an occult or hidden meaning as well. Odysseus is moving back toward his wife and his son at the same time his son is moving outward, looking for him. The son's name, Telemachus, "the true aim of our actions," implies that when Odysseus is moving toward his base, the true aim or meaning of his life is moving toward him.

We know that Odysseus' house has become infested, virtually dominated, by suitors, who are eating up all the treasures, and who in the hidden sense stand for the multiple desires still uncontrolled at middle age. Shakespeare says:

> *Poor soul, the centre of my sinful earth,*
> *Foil'd by these rebel powers that thee array,*
> *Why dost thou pine within and suffer dearth,*
> *Painting thy outward walls so costly gay?*
> *Why so large cost, having so short a lease,*
> *Dost thou upon thy fading mansion spend?*[2]

We know that Odysseus' wife, Penelope, has been fighting the greedy suitors as best she can, and cunningly putting off their demands for marriage. Most readers don't realize that the standard word for duck in Greek is *penelope;* it is Penelope who struggles to enable the House to be devoted to spirit. When Odysseus eventually returns, the suitors are properly killed, and the house is no longer "foil'd by these rebel powers that thee array."

The duck lives in water, and yet also migrates, covering vast distances, flying over large swatches of the earth. We are on firm ground in saying that this new "Penelope stage," which implies ending waste of treasure, requires a different sort of intensity than the earlier steps. Many persons who pass through the coffer stage and free the Hermes-like wit, the trickster boldness and subtlety, do not take the additional step toward spirit. Certainly Aleister Crowley, a great trickster of the twentieth century, did not. Crowley is the model for the negative trickster; but many positive tricksters, such as Woody Allen, do not pass into this stage. Spirited jokes are not the same as spirit, as we all know. We sense that Woody Allen, a true striver and an admirable writer, has concretized recently the spiritual in the form of a young woman. But the blue-winged teal, the heron, the flamingo, the swan are intent on flying, mysterious, devoted. They stand as a model for the human being who has broken out of earth fixations, the earth trap. Kabir, praising a life of pure verticality, asks the swan—the soul—to come with him to the place where that intensity is possible:

Swan, I'd like you to tell me your whole story!
Where you first appeared, and what dark sand you are going
toward,
and where you sleep at night, and what you are looking for.

. . . .

It's morning, swan, wake up, climb in the air, follow me!
I know of a country that spiritual flatness does not control, nor
constant depression,
and those alive are not afraid to die.
There wildflowers come up through the leafy floor,
and the fragrance of "I am he" floats on the wind.
There the bee of the heart stays deep inside the flower,
and cares for no other thing.[3]

(Translated by R.B.)

We each want the Heavens now, but Shakespeare did not find those Heavens in *The Tempest* until he had lived for years going over and over the Dark Events that belong in Baba Yaga's clearing.

To rise into the uncompromising energy of spirit is a hard task. Many people—in the sixties particularly—wanted to have the swan life right away during their twenties. I certainly did. I wanted the ascent before I had ever got down on my knees to eat acorns or had agreed to any form of sacrifice. It's possible we used our parents' sacrifices instead of our own as fuel. Now so many forms of personal sacrifice—the scholarship in cold rooms, the learning of Latin and Greek, the voluntary renunciation of multiple delights—have since the sixties virtually disappeared. We have a pop culture now, not a culture of swans.

Blake says:

> *When thou seest an Eagle, thou seest a portion of Genius; lift up thy head.*[4]

The Metaphor of the Egg

The last metaphor in our series is the egg. Human beings have adored the egg since earliest times. There seems to be some genetic match between human beings and chicken eggs. For humans, the flavor is just right. People and chickens live together, feeding and being fed all over Asia, Europe, and Africa. The egg itself is a marvel, whether produced by penguins or chickens or eagles or songbirds. Gerard Manley Hopkins called thrushes' eggs "little low heavens."[1] The egg's shape seems hydraulically and aesthetically perfect. Ukrainians decorate the egg as if it were a Queen; it adapts itself to all geometric designs, all colors and hues; it is a triumph of the simple. And it did not escape the ancients that the yellow ball inside is not merely a "yolk," as we stupidly call it—it is the sun. Any idiot with good eyes would know that. So we have the outer sun, up there, surrounded by the white of the stars, and we have the inner sun down here, right next to our nose, on the plate. What's more, eggs come in abundance, in contrast to the situation up there, where, as Francis Ponge said, "The melancholic old man . . . tosses us with poor grace one sun per day."[2]

So where better for the love the universe has for us than to be stored in an egg, so easily hidden, so much fun to look for?

An Austrian woman described an egg hunt that took place in her village in the 1940s. On Easter Sunday the children would rise before dawn for the hunt:

> Eggs, hard-boiled and colored, chiefly red and blue, but also with other pigments, are hidden in large quantities totaling several hundred, in "nests" all over the gardens, and are searched for by the children when the family returns in the morning from High Mass.[3]

She then reported that "the hare that lay these eggs does not appear, however, until the afternoon, when the children all visit their grandmothers." The emphasis on the grandmothers suggests a Goddess connection or a crone connection.

> The chief figure in the progress to her house . . . is a child dressed in a cape with head and ears representing a hare, who on his or her back carries a small water bucket filled with colored eggs.
>
> The first eggs are given to the grandmother. . . . The children all want eggs, too. . . . But the power is with the hare-child, who dodges here and there, in and out and around about the house and garden, chased by the rest, to whom it gives its eggs at its own sweet will.

How strange! The hare again. We now know that this hare-egg ritual was at one time performed all over Europe. It is still performed—though without any remembrance of its meaning—on the White House lawn each year at Easter, where it appears to be connected to Christianity. I hid eggs for my children without ever understanding what we were doing. A few years ago, scholars reported that there was a Saxon goddess called Eostre or Eastre, still worshipped in parts of Scotland, for whom this ritual was done. We have been performing her ritual for years, without even the church recognizing its pagan quality. The hare and egg ritual is likely thousands of years older than Christianity. So there is a Great Goddess, perhaps not unlike the Woman Who Arrives on Thirty Boats; her name was Eastre and the hare is her ritual animal. We recall that the Norse love goddess, Guda, was accompanied by a hare on her ride into town; she was the Divine Guda, or Godiva.

We know that in Pomerania in the nineteenth century, hares were caught at Easter time to provide a public meal. So we are talking again of a Hare God who is sacrificed.

The hare then becomes, one might say, a model of sacrifice, a theme we continue today by making rabbits out of chocolate for children to eat, so that the "public meal" can continue.

We'll leave this strange reappearance of the hare and turn to the egg itself. The egg will prove to be many things. We have already hinted at some of its symbolic meanings. The fact that the inner egg resembles the sun doesn't cancel the knowledge that the egg on the outside resembles the moon. The moon is a light in the darkness, and it can be found shining in unexpected places, through the branches of trees, just as the brilliant eggs shine in their nests of dark grass. It was natural for the Austrian children to give the eggs to the grandmothers—that is, give them back to the moon. Our story says that only the grown-ups who have gone to the Underworld will ever be able to understand the egg in all its magnificence, and that is probably right.

It is only after the human being's inner house has been dedicated to spirit that we are not afraid to die. It is only after we have learned to move like the duck, the swan, the heron, and all the other waterbirds, who walk on land and fly immense distances through the air, that we can experience, enjoy, give right attention to, admire, deserve, appreciate, be fit for the egg. Once we have had the high flights in air, once we have learned to let go "of the ground we stand on and cling to every day," then we can put our hand down, as Ivan did, and lift the egg. Once he had lifted it, what did he do? He carried it to the old woman's house, just as if he had been an Austrian child.

Carrying the Egg
Back to the House

Ivan took some bread and set out for the place she had described. He found the oak and removed the coffer from it; then he removed the hare from the coffer, the duck from the hare, and the egg from the duck. He returned with the egg to the old woman. A few days later came the old woman's birthday; she invited the Maiden Tsar with the thirty other maidens, her foster sisters, to her house; she baked the egg, dressed Ivan the merchant's son in splendid raiment, and hid him.

Everyone thinks: "What will happen next?" Ivan has returned with the egg to the old woman's house. We do know that the Crone's birthday is only a few days away. It seemed proper to have a birthday party, then, and she decided to invite her own daughter, who was one of the thirty swan-women, as well as her twenty-nine foster sisters. And as long as she was having a party, she might as well invite the Woman with the Golden Hair, the Maiden Tsar herself. All of them agreed to come.

This time the Crone doesn't turn Ivan into a pin and stick him into the wall. She dresses him in elaborate, fantastic clothes that

Russian merchants used to wear—he probably looked like an Easter egg himself—and hid him in a closet.

Ah, she baked the egg! So the egg is not to be eaten raw. Who eats eggs raw? That would be barbaric. All sweet and valuable things need to be cooked. People need to be cooked, eggs need to be cooked, perhaps even gods need to be cooked.

So on that day that was the right day, the *kairos* moment, when silver can change into gold if the tincture is the proper one, on that day when healing of old wounds can take place, the Giver of Blessings, the Being Who Arrives on Thirty Boats, the great female God who isn't sure she loves you anymore, plus the thirty foster sisters, all fly through the window in the form of swans. They sit down at the table with their long wings touching the floor, ruffle their feathers, and become people.

Meanwhile the old woman has been preparing the feast *carefully*. She has gotten from her own chickens—or perhaps her own ducks?—thirty handsome eggs, one for each of the foster sisters. She baked them as they should have been baked. Then she carefully set aside the egg Ivan had brought, and boiled it in a separate pan, just the right number of minutes.

When that was done, she brought the thirty eggs out and served them to the foster sisters in good Russian egg cups, and then served the egg, in a special cup, much blessed by holy women and men, no doubt, to the Maiden Tsar.

The foster sisters ate their eggs quietly, but after the Maiden Tsar tasted hers, she was quiet for a few minutes, then said: "I wonder whatever happened to Ivan. I haven't thought of him for so long."

After she ingested the egg, she asked herself, "I wonder if I still love Ivan? I think so."

And what did the old woman do, listening so carefully? She brought Ivan out of the closet! "Ivan!" "Is it you?" "It is!" "It is so wonderful to see you looking so alert!" "It took so long for us to find each other! I had to go through a lot of grandmothers, let me tell you, to find you"—and so on and so on. We can all imagine that scene and what was said. It's a good scene, and much warmth is there.

Ingesting the Egg

What can we say about this eating? There is a word "ingesting" that seems right here. It is one thing to eat something, and another to ingest it. The Maiden Tsar is eating the egg, but she is ingesting her own love. We have to do this scene delicately, and perhaps ask some questions.

What does it feel like for a woman to ingest her love for a man, or a daughter, or a son, or another woman? How is that different from loving a man, or daughter, or son, or another woman? It's possible that some men love women, but find it difficult to ingest their love, if that man regards all women with contempt. Perhaps some women remain so angry at men that they can love individual men but can't ingest their love for the masculine.

It used to be that very young women would be their good feisty selves, mocking boys and dissing them. Then in their middle twenties, as they became aware of the work men do to support the household or defend a town or work for the common good, often leading a starved life because of this work, a young woman might begin to ingest her love for men. That ingesting did not make her an oppressed being. The sense of oppression came from other sources.

However in recent decades she finds herself still properly feisty in adolescence, but some women later don't find themselves ingesting their love for the masculine.

The boy goes through something similar. One could say that the young man ingests his own love for the feminine less and less. He may remain hard now in the *Seinfeld* mode. *Seinfeld* was really about the inability of young American men to ingest or feel their own love for the feminine. That is a change for the worse. It is easy for men and women to devour each other, but ingesting one's love for the other gender is a different matter.

We might return once more to the astonishing sentence: "I have news for you. She doesn't love you anymore." What does it mean to say: "The Goddess does not love us anymore?" As more and more species become extinct, as the rainforests burn, and the groundwater is polluted, we feel unprotected. People in the nineteenth century experienced a tremendous sense of unprotection, from lawlessness, from fires or storms or plagues; and yet the net of nature seemed to hold them. Nature, in a way, was the Virgin Mary, who held people on her lap.

But we are people pushed off the lap. The younger generation, by and large, does not feel protected by nature anymore. Most of them are urban, and the urban life is to them part of a death culture. When we see a T-shirt that says, "Please Kill Me," we know the wearer does not feel protected. If the Goddess, bruised by our careless treatment of nature, does not love us, we have no firm ground to stand on.

What happens when the chimpanzees leave the forest? That is happening to us now.

Perhaps nature or the universe can ingest its love for human beings only when the human goes through the difficult process the story describes. The human being has to move from a visit to the oak ancestors to the release of the trickster energy, to the principle of willing sacrifice symbolized by the hare, to the flying toward spirit. Finally, he or she has to be present when the Divine One eats the egg.

Is it possible for a Goddess who doesn't love you anymore to change? What must *you,* as a woman or man who feels unloved by the Goddess, do in order to receive that love again? Burning down the rain forests does not seem to be an effective way of ingesting Her. Christians each Sunday practice ingesting the male God in the Eucharist. We ingest the male God, but seem to have no way of ingesting the Goddess. Moreover, in our story, it is the Divine One herself who ingests her love for human beings.

Emily Dickinson offers the ecstasy that happens when a human being ingests the Lord, or the other way around:

> *Wild Nights—Wild Nights!*
> *Were I with thee*
> *Wild Nights should be*
> *Our luxury!*
>
> *Futile—the Winds—*
> *To a Heart in port—*
> *Done with the Compass—*
> *Done with the Chart!*
>
> *Rowing in Eden—*
> *Ah, the Sea!*
> *Might I but moor—Tonight—*
> *In Thee!*[1]

Mirabai, the thirteenth-century Indian poet, describes that mood of ingesting the Divine in the Krishna-Radha tradition:

> *You play the flute well; I love your swing curls and your*
> *earlocks.*
> *Jasumati, your mother, wasn't she the one*
> *Who washed and combed your beautiful hair?*
> *If you come anywhere near my house,*
> *I will close my sandalwood doors, and lock you in.*

Mira's lord is half lion and half man.
She turns her life over to the midnight of his hair.[2]

(Version by R.B.)

About the Goddess, we could say, "If human beings don't ingest Her, why should She love humans anymore?" What is it like to ingest the love one has for another man or woman? To ingest requires a calm scene, such as that at the Crone's birthday party. We sit surrounded by persons devoted to the spirit, and we desire to, want to, intend to taste the flavor of the love we have. It is a subtle practice, and we don't overlook the implication that we are feeding ourselves. So eating and feeding come together in one moment. We will surely find ourselves tasting the flavor of our own soul; moreover, the soul of the other person will be merged with it, the flavors mingling.

After that, we could practice ingesting the Goddess. Dancing may be a part of that, speaking poems, weeping, practicing "remembrance" all night with others, not going to sleep until dawn.

Rumi gives the mood of loving the Sacred Bride and receiving love from Her:

When I am with you, we stay up all night.
When you're not here, I can't get to sleep.
Praise God for these two insomnias.
And for the difference between them.[3]

(Translation by Coleman Barks)

One more poem:

Come to the Garden in spring.
There is wine and sweethearts in the pomegranate blossoms.
If you do not come, these do not matter.
If you do come, these do not matter.[4]

(Translation by Coleman Barks)

There is another step, probably among hundreds we have for-gotten, and that is bringing Her home. Hafez is willing to bring Her—the one from whom we have been separated—into his own house. He says:

> *Send out the criers, go to the marketplace of souls,*
> *"Hear, hear, all you in the colonnade of lovers, here it is:*
>
> *The wild daughter has been reported lost for several days.*
> *Call all your friends! Whoever's near her is in danger.*
>
> *Her dress is ruby-colored; her hair is done in sea foam;*
> *She takes away reason; be alert; watch out for her!*
>
> *If you find this bitter one you can have my soul for dessert.*
> *If she's in the Underworld, then that's the place to go.*
>
> *She's a night-woman, shameless, disreputable, and red.*
> *If you find her, please bring her to Hafez's house."*[5]

(Version by R.B.)

I think we've said all we can now about the story. This image of the Divine One eating the egg that contains Her own love for the human being—that scene passes beyond my mythological under-standing, so I will leave this image to you.

We started in the Underworld. (As Hafez says, "If she's in the Underworld, then that's the place to go.") After Ivan has spent—like each of us—years there, he does a few things right, and the Firebird lifts him out. "Ivan" stands for men but also for the mas-culine element in women, who can get caught too in the Under-world, and stay there, relatively inert, for years, as a man can. After the forgetful human has been lifted out of Baba Yaga's marvelous territory, where he or she has learned to speak truth, as opposed to fashionable adversarialism, it's time to enjoy the company of the

Crone, who is *in touch* with the original Goddess. Now the labor appears, the labor to overcome the Forgetfulness that our culture bases itself on . . . and we pass through the stages touched on—briefly—in this chapter—the oak as the old home, imprisonment and release of the spirited force, the hare's instruction to let go of the earth, and finally the flights asked for by the spirit, and at last, at last, reaching down to pick up the egg and bring it to the old woman's house.

If we get to the eating of the egg by the Maiden Tsar, and Her ingesting of the love that has been missing for so many years, that is good: one could die before that, and it would still be all right.

In our story, all the people are still alive at the end, and one more event takes place.

The Wedding

Well, what can we say? They had a wedding. People in that part of the world had never prepared for a wedding so joyfully. Men polished their boots, and built tables, and brought old wines up from the cellar. Women cooked their best dishes, and great musicians were called in from the whole countryside and even from foreign nations. Yo Yo Ma played at the wedding. Sweet Honey in the Rock gave a concert. Fiddlers played all night; people danced until they fell down laughing. Storytellers came. Marion and I were invited too as storytellers, and when the wedding was over, they gave us a bottle of wine to bring back to you, but somehow the baggage people mishandled it and the bottle fell and broke. And I don't think we'll ever have wine like that again in this world.

Interpretation by

MARION
WOODMAN

PART I

The Maiden Tsar

The intimate connection between fairy tales and dreams can be seen in the bedtime story, told just before we fall asleep, as if to prepare us for sleep, to guide us slowly into it.

Like the more traditional "once upon a time," the phrase **"In a certain land, in a certain kingdom"** establishes "The Maiden Tsar" in that spaceless, timeless world, in which our psyche lives and moves and has its being.

As in the world of dreams, the characters in a fairy tale are the personifications of psychic energies bound to the body and arising from it. The body responding to a fairy tale told as a bedtime story settles into it and is guided toward sleep. The body settles into its own natural unconsciousness where the psyche also originally dwells. Psyche and soma (soul and body) are one in the unconscious.

As we shall see in our reading of "The Maiden Tsar," the story in its natural unfolding restores us to our original state of wholeness. This wholeness is destroyed by the psyche/soma split that is necessary for the achievement of consciousness. In a fairy tale understood at the conscious level, awakening us rather than putting us to sleep, we "arrive where we started/And know the place for the first time."[1] The child settling into a peaceful sleep is arriving where we all "started." The adult reading the fairy tale to the child may finally know that place by seeing in the sleeping child a symbol of the place the fairy tale creates. Tucking the covers around the sleeping body and turning out the light may enact the reader's arrival. The adult fully and consciously awake is at one with the child fully and unconsciously asleep.

In our reading of this tale, I hope our awakened state will not be set up against the sleeping state of the child, as if the two states were in opposition. They depend upon each other, their dependence uniting rather than separating the two realms—the unconscious and consciousness, sleep and awareness.

As in a dream, all the characters in a fairy tale are aspects of ourselves, male and female. The characters in "The Maiden Tsar"— the false tutor, the deceitful stepmother, the firebird, the Baba Yaga, the wise old woman—are all psychic aspects of the questing youth, which the youth, if he is to reach maturity, must absorb by bringing his whole soul into activity. In the unfolding of the story these initially conflicting aspects meet and transform, move on again, and, in new configurations, continue to transform in that life journey toward wholeness in which all aspects of ourselves ideally come together. A fairy tale enacts the process as the eternally evolving pattern that is a paradigm of what, consciously or unconsciously, many of us, women and men, are struggling to achieve. At the core of a fairy tale is a vision of wholeness.

The psychic dynamics enacted in the adventures of the youth in "The Maiden Tsar" spring from the unconscious of ancient storytellers, who remain nameless, as if the real author were the unconscious itself, which the author is. We who read the story recognize the yearning for our perfect love, the loss of all we hoped for, the eruption of chaos, the possible refinding. And we recognize all of this as somehow timeless, as belonging to something universal in ourselves that gives us a larger sense of who we are in the larger psychic meaning of our actions. The very starkness of the detail—a pin in the neck, the cutting off of a head—forges them as patterns in our imaginations. However preposterous they are at a literal level, something in us resonates with their truth. Whether we are five or eighty-five, whether we understand them or not, we feel more whole after being in touch with these patterns because their plot line takes us in the direction of our own potential wholeness. Keats called it a "greeting of the Spirit."[2]

How profoundly we understand these figures from the unconscious depends upon our response to the world of metaphor as the world we inhabit, without necessarily being conscious of it. Metaphor is more easily experienced unconsciously than consciously understood because it is the kinetic or bodily dimension of language. It is language bound to its bodily source in the mother's body, language as rhythm, breath, sound. Metaphor is language at the level of infants who are first learning to speak by making words out of sounds and then attaching sound words to persons and things (ma-ma, da-da).

These sound words, like Helen Keller's discovery of the word "water," which stood for the cold wet sensation over her hand as she stood at the pump, release the infant from its total dependence upon physical sensations while maintaining at a different level a binding to them. The sound words of an infant are its unconscious way of bringing itself to a world other than itself without cruelly confronting it with its otherness.

Words at this primitive level have, therefore, a magical power. Uniting the person or object named with the name itself, the infant maintains a fusion with the person or object. Language at this primitive level is the carrier of bodily energy, transformed through sound into psychic energy. Language operating at this energy level, where psyche and soma meet, is what, in essence, metaphor is.

Thus, when we were children, we felt metaphor; we didn't care what metaphor meant. We clenched our jaws when the wicked witch arrived with the poisoned apple; our bellies rolled when we heard, "The better to eat you, my dear"; we clapped our hands when the fairy godmother finally came to the rescue. We experienced what was being read to us in our bodies; without our knowing it, the language was the psychic transformation of bodily energy. This huge conversion of energy from the physical to the psychic state, a conversion that constitutes metaphor (*metaphor* means "a carrying over") is experienced without being understood. Too often, later in life, the reverse may happen: we understand without experiencing. What the adult carries consciously, the child affirms bodily. Joined in the reading of a fairy tale, child and adult enact a fusion essential to the wholeness of life that the fairy tale embodies.

Our bodies love metaphors because they join our bodies to our soul rather than abandoning them to a soulless state. The ancient alchemists called this bodysoul state "the subtle body." They believed that the deeper we go into "the subtle body," the greater the soul treasures it contains. At its core is a "diamond body." This "diamond body" is a many-faceted wholeness like the one waiting to be discovered in our reading of "The Maiden Tsar."

If we are seriously searching for insights into our own psychic dynamics and those of our culture, we cannot read fairy tales as we did when we were children—though to lose touch with the child in us in the reading would cut us off from those very dynamics. In childhood we could project all our own pent-up fears onto the little match girl, our jealousy onto the stepsisters, and our rage onto the giants, and then go to sleep in peace. We did not have to deal with these fears, jealousies, and rages as our own unabsorbed states. We could simply, like Ivan with a pin in his neck, go to sleep. But Ivan in the story has to wake up and absorb what is going on in his own unconscious. The story is telling us that as adults we can no longer project out of ourselves what is in us and belongs to us. Our task is to wake up and try to understand what is going on in our own unconscious, because its dynamics are controlling our outer behavior. We have to claim our projections. That is the true meaning of Ivan's fishing trip with his tutor—and the message of the fairy tale as a whole. "The Maiden Tsar" is about going fishing—deep-sea fishing—on a very small raft.

The relationships that are present at the commencement of the tale are painful to look at consciously because we know they are destructive, as a child unconsciously recognizes them to be. We are immediately facing parts of ourselves we prefer not to see, even cannot see, because they have been so deep in our unconscious. We may, in fact, be trapped in them, even as Ivan is trapped in the triangle formed by his relationship with his stepmother and the tutor. The story gradually transforms these unnatural dynamics, particularly the interplay between masculine and feminine energies, until wholeness is reached. Thus, by the end of the story, the unnatural relationships are resolved in accordance with the dynamics of a healthy psyche.

What are these two energies in their natural relationship to each other? Recently, I watched the sun rise over the beautiful farm on which I was staying. At the same time, I saw the full moon riding the silver clouds in the dark sky. I heard the cock crowing, geese cackling, saw the cows and horses outlined in the darkness. "How gentle night is!" I thought. "How exquisitely it 'knits up the ravell'd sleave of care.' "[3] Golden sunbeams were radiating on the horizon, even as silver moonbeams caressed the landscape. The two energies—feminine night and masculine day, complementary energies, both essential to life—were in love with each other.

Cultures close to nature, to the natural dynamics of the psyche, have no trouble honoring this love affair. Ancient Hinduism, to use another metaphor, holds Shiva and Shakti at the center of its faith. Shiva, the Great Spirit, the Mystery beyond our understanding, and Shakti, the exquisite Body, manifesting that Mystery— together are always in divine embrace. To think this way is to abolish theological wrangling over the gender of God. Spirit without form is invisible; matter without spirit is dead. Matter and spirit love each other. They live through each other. To separate masculine and feminine—as they are at the beginning of "The Maiden Tsar"—is unnatural. Their struggle to come together is the struggle toward consciousness, a process in which we come slowly to understand what, in the unconscious, *always already* is.

Because my own life work is rooted in dreams, I am very much at home in this always already world. In dreams—my own and my analysands'—the complementary energies are imaged as men and women. If I want to understand how the two energies are relating in body and psyche, I look at the relationships of male and female in the dream as the embodiment of these energies. I do not look at them biologically in terms of gender. Whether we are in homosexual or heterosexual relationships, the two energies, masculine and feminine, are present in both men and women. Their inner complementarity, in its fulfillment, becomes what is called the "inner marriage," like the marriage of night and day.

"As within, so without" is a psychic reality. The energetic process attempts to bring the inner complements, masculinity and femininity, into the inner marriage. On that journey to wholeness we become nature conscious of itself rather than abandoned and treated like an unconscious body that is exploited like a brute animal. We meet and leave strangers and loved ones, depending on where we are inside. When we find an equilibrium between the energies, a soul mate (who may have been there all along) sometimes arrives and affirms that equilibrium and gives it an outward form. Fairy tales have stood the test of time in revealing the inner and outer psychic dynamics between the complementary energies of masculine and feminine. These dynamics, as they emerge out of the unnatural constellation in which a fairy tale begins, can be very painful, especially if we are not acquainted with our own unconscious characters.

Until we recognize the power of the unconscious to sabotage

our conscious endeavors, we can change nothing. This story, ancient as it is, speaks directly to the deepest disappointments at the core of our personal heartbreaks, and to the raw wound at the core of our culture, as we enter the new millennium. It pinpoints the power drive at the center of our culture, a drive that respects neither femininity nor masculinity as it bludgeons our bodies and our feelings, separating us from our souls. "The Maiden Tsar" taps our unconscious roots and connects us to the beloved wholeness within ourselves that is our birthright. The Maiden Tsar has loved Ivan since the foundation of the world. Their love *is* the foundation of the world.

Positive Mother vs. Stepmother

In our story, the first detail establishes **"a merchant whose wife died, leaving him with an only son, Ivan."** The key to a fairy tale is what is missing at the beginning. What is missing in our story is the natural or positive mother as a bodysoul presence in the life of her child. Ivan has been deprived of this presence and, in its absence, been subjected to the unnatural, deceitful stepmother, the shadow side of the natural mother. To grasp what is missing in what is present we need to understand what the psychic energy of the natural mother, if present, provides, and what, if absent, her deceitful substitute imposes. And to do this, we have to recognize the necessity of the shadow.

By "natural mother" I mean a mother who lives happily in her own body, loves her femaleness, experiences her menses as her feminine relationship to the phases of the moon. In nourishing and cherishing her children, she is confident in her own feminine identity and is, therefore, able to be a mirror for them. They are psychically and physically fed by the unconditional love she bestows. They can look into her eyes and recognize themselves as they are, without any sense that there exists an agenda as to what they ought to be, should be, must be. She sees their individuality and honors its becoming into being. She provides a powerful vision of wholeness that is fully embodied in her affirmation of herself. She therefore becomes a home for her children, a home they will go in search of when, in the process of growing up, it is inevitably lost.

Children raised by such a mother will not spend their lives frantically searching the eyes of others for applause. They will not have to deny their own desire in order to please others just to survive. They are not in terror of being annihilated if they are not what they ought to be. Exaggerated as this terror may sound, I have repeatedly discovered it not only in sons, like Ivan, abandoned to a deceitful stepmother, but also in daughters whose true womanhood is held captive by a figure not unlike Ivan's stepmother. Many of the women who enter analysis with me arrive in the grip of a deceitful stepmother. Their natural mother, like Ivan's, lies dead within them. In many fairy tales, dead mothers are reborn as an immense shift in psychic energy, bringing with it a new perspective.

Psychic energy, like physical energy, can be neither created nor destroyed. It can be transformed into what may be experienced as a series of deaths and rebirths. Ivan's feminine energy, for example, appears in a variety of forms: the dead mother who becomes the stepmother at one pole and the Maiden Tsar as Bride at the other. Between these two poles there will appear a series of female figures who mark Ivan's rites of passage from one pole to the other, until he finds a new integration.

In analysis, I have watched both men and women move inwardly over a period of years from one pole to the other, from a deathlike, dismembered state to an abundant wholeness of life. This inward movement is not linear, one step after another. It is like the movement of a snake: the forward movement is propelled by a coiling or circling back as a gathering of energy to move ahead. Their dreams and the accompanying associations, coilings, and circlings that propel them, mark the various stages of their rites of passage. Ivan's life-renewing adventures mirror the unfolding inner life of many people who, feeling initially cut off from life both physically and psychically, gradually are able to absorb what their unconscious is telling them.

As they attend to their dreams, what may emerge is a realization that each time they go round the circle they are in a new place. They are spiralling, finding new meaning and new resonances in each round. The image is releasing more and more of its mystery. As they move up and down on the spiral, they may find themselves periodically lost; then, on the next round, they may feel themselves resonating right through their spiral. They are circling "the diamond body." To see all its facets is to look at it from every angle, including from above and below. At some point, it may radiate in its totality, if only for a moment, as in a Cubist painting by Picasso or Braque.

Ivan's life-renewing experiences are stuck by the pin in the neck that cuts him off from his inner feminine. It cannot be removed until his ego is strong enough to absorb the pain of his unlived life. This unlived life dwells first in Ivan's dead mother and then in the fleeting presence of the Maiden Tsar.

As the unfolding action of the story will demonstrate, the psyche is kind. So long as it is not pushed beyond the capacity of expanding consciousness, it will not create a psychotic episode. "Eternity," writes Blake, "is in love with the productions of time."[1] The psyche waits for the fullness of time, what the Greeks called *kairos*. Ivan's expanding consciousness is gradually able to absorb and transform the terrors of the deep.

I've watched a woman struggling to confront these terrors. I've seen her attempt to raise her arms to express her own empowerment, attempt to speak, only to collapse in a shuddering heap on the floor. Why? Because her mother's voice, like the step-mother's pin, introjected from infancy as the false voice of her own unconscious, still batters her in the guise of love: "Who do you think you are? You don't want your mother to be ashamed of you, do you? Be a good girl, now, and do as I tell you."

Often the words are not spoken. They are subliminally understood between mother and daughter. They feel like a given in daily experience. Only when a woman begins to contact her inner natural mother, bringing to life what she had experienced as dead in herself, is she strong enough to recognize the inner voice of the shadow stepmother that is putting her down. When her ego is strengthened by the reemergence of her natural mother, she can forcefully respond, "You are not my voice. You never were. You never will be. I will no longer be undermined by your poison." In absorbing the pain, she experiences the transformation of the negative mother into the positive one found in the depths of her own unconscious terrors. Energy cannot be destroyed; it can only be transformed. That is the first law of the psyche.

As she gains consciousness, the woman learns to contain anguish. She knows that the life-denying voice did not belong to her mother, either, nor to her grandmother, nor to any of the long line of women who had no way out of their bondage. They accepted the judgment that was placed upon them in the Book of Genesis and many never even heard it as a judgment. They accepted that they are earth; they are connected to the serpent that crawls on the earth; they consort with Satan. Earth, serpent, Satan are evil. Mother Earth is second-class to spirit; therefore, feminine is second-class to masculine, and born to serve. As John Milton so succinctly summed it up in *Paradise Lost:*

He for God only; she for God in him.[2]

In "The Maiden Tsar," this culturally embodied negative experience of the feminine is personified in the stepmother. Wanting, in her sexual greed, to possess Ivan, she cuts him off from his own inner feminine, which thrice presents itself to him momentarily, only to be obliterated by the pin stuck in his throat on the stepmother's orders. What Ivan does not yet know is that, in contrast to the unnatural jealous sexual love of the stepmother, the natural inner feminine just beginning to emerge has genuinely loved him all his life, from his very conception in his mother's womb.

The negative voice that tells us we have no right to experience joy may come from the human father as well as from the human mother. At a deep psychic level, it is associated with the negative side of the Great Mother, whose children we all are. If our human parents were cut off from their vibrant life force flowing in their blood, then that damper is in us. When our fire would flare into full flame, that damper closes us down. The Mother carries the life force that flows in our blood.

This painful awakening to the lost feminine demonically parodied in the stepmother contains, as pain, the beginnings of recovery. The pain contains a blessing. The awareness of the blessing expands as consciousness develops. It is a psychic process that we all undergo if we are consciously to arrive at wholeness. Paradise must be lost if it is consciously to be found.

As they read this story, men may recognize in Ivan's engagement with his own feminine the painful process of their awaking and maturing masculinity. Men need to be firmly in touch with their own masculinity before their path opens to their inner feminine. Robert Bly developed this theme in *Iron John*. His concern there was with men who had opened to the feminine before they had established their firm connection with the masculine.

Women may recognize a similar process of maturing in their own inner masculine as they struggle to reclaim their lost femininity. In their dreams, most women find their roots in a strong feminine container with a strong bond to the Good Mother before they begin the phase of the journey that will take them to the inner masculine. As the inner relationship grows, both energies, entwined like the two snakes in the medical logo (the caduceus) are enhanced as they relate back and forth with each other, each gaining strength as the relationship constantly shifts. This back-and-forth relating will resonate with early parental relationships, good and bad.

Two people living in the process together are in a constant dance. Like lovers' "eye-beams twisted . . . upon one double string,"³ they have to be constantly on the alert to subtle shifts in each other. They need to remind themselves that each of them, as partners in the dance, has a lifetime to reach the inner marriage. Are both partners willing to put in equal work? Was this relationship created by Destiny as the work of the unconscious or was it a human mistake? "All—is the price of All—"⁴ and one partner cannot do the work of both.

Many women do point out that they seem to be doing more than their share in bringing consciousness to the relationship: "Why do I have to carry that responsibility?" Well, my only answer is: "That's the human story. Eve brought Adam to the Tree of Knowledge of Good and Evil, though little thanks she got, and now she may be bringing him to the other tree, the Tree of Life, for which she is likely, at least in the short run, to receive even less thanks."

The process we are discussing is a dialogue between consciousness and the unconscious as a divine mystery that reveals each of us to ourselves and to each other. The outer marriage depends for its human success upon the inner marriage forged out of the archetypal materials of the unconscious. It becomes the human expression of two individual inner marriages relating to each other. It's the outer expression of an inner divine life. If there is in the relationship no awareness of this divine life to which in a crisis they can turn, the couple may settle for patchwork solutions. That is not a judgment. "The fullness of time" is a fact in the unconscious. Nature has its own laws of maturing. If the time is not yet right, some temporary solution has to be found.

I recognized the divine mystery that reveals each of us to ourselves and to each other in my own marriage when, after twenty-five years, I looked up from the armchair in which I was enjoying my morning coffee and saw, for the first time, my husband with no archetypal projection. He was standing in the kitchen. He was a man garbed in an old Black Watch plaid housecoat with two spindly legs sticking out below. He was attempting to crack an egg into a flimsy poacher. "I could have done better than this," I thought, "much better than this." As I mused, the man put his hand on a loaf of bread, picked up a knife, and before me was a human being concentrated on feeding himself. "This is the hand I know so well, the hand that plants tulips, types, makes love to me. I have put him through hell; he has put me through hell. Here we are on the seventeenth floor of an apartment building in Toronto with a schizophrenic world outside and an unholy mess in the kitchen. We're still here together. He walks his path as courageously as he can; I'm walking mine as honestly as I can." Suddenly a wave of love welled up in me. I loved this human being who was so totally different from my inner Bridegroom—so totally, gloriously human. "Do you want some more coffee, Marion?" "Yes," I said.

Viewed in the context of the divine marriage in both men and women, the subordination of the feminine to the masculine, outwardly enacted as the subordination of women to men, is a horrendous lie. For at least three thousand years women have carried, whether consciously or unconsciously, their culturally determined role in relation to men, an inferior role that has left their masculinity wounded by patriarchal training. As a result of the inferior role assigned to the feminine, men are culturally and personally crippled by a weak feminine every bit as disabling as the weak masculine in women. As complementary energies, masculinity and femininity require each other for natural balance in relationships. A weak feminine in men produces a distorted, one-sided masculine—the militarist, the corporate robot; a weak masculine in women produces a distorted, one-sided feminine—the baby doll, who pretends to be everything any man imagines her to be, or a Gorgon, who reduces others to stone.

The result is our present situation: a collapse in the relations between men and women that is extending to a breakdown in the normal operations of the natural order. Consciously or unconsciously, this is the lie that has cut off our Judeo-Christian culture from the positive mother. In physical terms, this lie has distanced both men and women from their first chakra, their survival chakra, the energy center in the perineum that shouts, "I love life. I desire color, shape, texture. I desire sexuality. I desire the luscious possibilities of all life has to offer. I accept life. I accept life with its imperfections that work together toward wholeness. I love life in its constant state of flux. I accept death as part of life, contributing to growth. I trust renewal in the abundant life of the soul." Sure, this is a manifesto, but I have to seem to exaggerate in order to make a clear connection to the flowing blood of the Great Mother.

Herein lies the tragedy at the core of our culture: many contemporary men and women do not know they are cut off from their own life source as Ivan is cut off by the pin. In working with this dark period in his process, I find myself longing to move beyond it while knowing I have to remain with it until its repressed energies have created in me, as in the story, their own release. I have to work my way through it again and again, as Ivan has to work his way through it. A fairy tale requires more than a casual bedtime read. Children unconsciously know this; they insist that it be read over and over, night after night, without changing a single word.

Many people are undermined by the loss of connection to their own life energy in their own body. Patriarchal judgment in mothers and fathers has cut them off, leaving a trail of wounding in both sons and daughters. If their natural desires were met by a constant "No," they gradually disconnected from their own "I desire" in the survival chakra in order to please. In infancy, "I desire" is indistinguishable from "I need." As adults, they look at other people who seem to love life and wonder why they themselves do not. They pretend, even as children, to be reaching out from their own desire. Their place of desire is false; their desiring is not coming from *natural* instincts; therefore, those instincts cannot be satisfied. Because their bodies are not expressing desires that come from natural instincts, they fall into unnatural desires, driven desires that overwhelm them with stupor and manifest as addictions. They crave food that brings them no nurturance, drink that brings them no spirit, sex that brings them no union. Because their culture worships matter and minimizes soul, they concretize metaphor and literalize life. Their hunger *is* for food—*soul* food; they are starving for sweetness—Mother food that will reconnect them to who they were born to be. Their thirst is for spirit; their longing is for union. They yearn for connection to their own "I desire" that springs from the waters of life within their own pelvic bowl. This terrible denial of who they are is present in the image of the fraudulent stepmother who personifies the absence of the natural mother.

The natural "I desire," repressed in the unconscious, makes itself known in dreams as it makes itself known in fairy tales. In dreams, a beloved dog repeatedly bites the dreamer, an elephant trumpets fiercely in a postage-stamp backyard, a tree sickens and dies. Nature, like Hamlet's court of Denmark, is awry. The dreamer cannot understand its "bizarre" behavior.

If the dreams are ignored, they eventually cease and the conflict drops into the unconscious where it may be somatized, psyche converting to body even as body converts to psyche. Ivan's failure to respond to the Maiden Tsar drives the story into deeper levels of the unconscious. In their psychic reality, his adventures are the unfolding stages of the soul's journey toward wholeness. Far from being mere torture or punishment, they are a healing process. Much that might otherwise remain unconscious (a death wish, for example) is brought into a consciousness for which the psychic adventures as symptoms of imbalance have been crying out, "Release me. Bring me into your consciousness." This cry is now resounding around the globe as the planet's plea for the recognition of its one life.

Eventually, as in all fairy tales, Ivan must awaken and recognize the truth in his own unconscious. In life, we can be so overwhelmed by what is happening that, like Ivan, we do not know whether we are driven by compulsion or by our own free will. To be asked the question in the midst of our apparently irrational behavior, is an invitation to look at our behavior as a way of finding within it what has remained hidden, as the Maiden was hidden from Ivan. The drive that remains hidden is compulsion; the drive that is revealed is freedom. In the question, Ivan is being invited to enter his own freedom, which is his own authentic life. The authentic life is the transformation of compulsion into freedom without the loss of the energy contained in the compulsion.

Men's relationship to the positive mother is somewhat different from women's because they are in male bodies. From my experience working with men, they are as deeply cut off from their *mater* (the Latin word for mother) as are women. Many of them have spent their boyhood being "the best little boy in the world," trying to "measure up." Now, because they have kept their bodies so rigid, their shoulders so straight, they are unable to let go and lie flat. Their muscles are so locked that they do not experience their feeling values in their viscera. They are literally cut off from their own experience in their own body. Like the pin-struck Ivan, they say, "I tell her I love her, but I've got no feeling of what I'm saying below my neck." I think of Ivan as I think of the impotent Fisher King with a javelin through his testicles as the Holy Grail passes by, even as the Maiden passes by Ivan.

The loss of connection to the positive mother is at the core of this emptiness. Let me make it clear that this is in no way mother-bashing, nor father-bashing for his lack of femininity. Most of us had parents who did their utmost to give us the best possible life. They couldn't give what they had never received, nor could their parents, nor theirs. If we work to find our own connection to our own life force in our own body, something may transform in the unconscious of our parents. Sometimes, to our immense surprise, we become their brothers and sisters, all of us wounded children of patriarchal judgment.

Without the security of feminine love that trusts life in the body and is, therefore, open to trust life, we learn to fear life itself. Even as children, we build a false foundation often enacted in nursery rhymes in which London Bridge is falling down, or Humpty Dumpty is falling apart. As adults, we seek further security through opulence of possessions.

We are a society famous for our greed. Without a loving connection to the Great Mother, we literalize her. Mother becomes *mater*. We accumulate mounds of matter in an effort to blind ourselves to our own yearning for the Divine Mater. Ironically, we are materialists, essentially a *matriarchal* society worshipping the Golden Cow at the center. In the absence of the natural mother, the greed of the stepmother, including sexual greed, takes over. Ivan under the control of the stepmother is a metaphor for our contemporary society.

Loss of the Positive Father

Ivan has no connection to his positive mother, and his positive father is about to leave him at the mercy of his stepmother and a
tutor. To be left without a father who can honor his soul is to be
forsaken with no masculine model, no inner ordering principle. A
man who has not found his "at-one-ment" with his father may
fear older men, fear their authority, or remain forever a rebel
against all they stand for. In either case, he is judging himself
through their eyes or through the eyes of his patriarchal mother.
He is not maturing through his own authenticity—a loss Robert
dealt with from the man's perspective in *Iron John*.

An equally huge gap opens in the daughter's psyche. While this
gap does not yet appear as a core issue in this tale, it is a sublim-
inal problem in Ivan's femininity. Without a father, his feminine
side may act like a fatherless daughter who idealizes masculinity;
his projections then may fall on a perfect, unattainable woman for
whom he yearns. A woman whose masculinity is damaged
through the absence of a positive father (either through alcohol,
or divorce, or death, or because he could not see her reality) may
find herself fearful of being forthright, especially with men who
represent paternal and patriarchal values. Shakespeare's Ophelia,
for example, when her maturity is put to the test, blindly obeys
her father, unlike Ivan, who uses his sword to cut off the destructive patriarch's mother-bound head. Ophelia thus betrays
Hamlet, the man who might have loved her had he not been
equally bound to a ghostly father. Gradually, she founders "as one
incapable of her own distress"[1] and drowns in the muddy waters
of her own unconscious.[2] Such a woman may accept her role forever playing Daddy's little princess and/or Mother to her little
boy husband. Her own reality is nowhere near consciousness in
such relationships because she lives in a fantasy world of radical

opposites. In fairy tales, she is the swan maiden, exquisite in her beauty, cursed with wings.

One of the deepest wounds for the woman with an absent or ghostly father is her idealization of Daddy. Without Daddy to give realistic masculine ground to balance her childish idolization of men, she may fantasize, "If only Daddy were here, all would be well." In adult life, the fantasy poisons her relationships because, when Daddy does come home (in her husband or lover), he is not the perfection she has yearned for all her life. In her dreams she belongs to a fantasy Dad and any man who does love her has to be aware that sooner or later that Dad will say, "He's not good enough for you." If that doesn't cool the living relationship sufficiently, another dream may come in which the father figure actually kills the lover. Unless the woman can bring that to consciousness immediately, the relationship is in imminent danger of breaking. Once again, she will be left wondering why she is always alone. Translated into the psychic action of "The Maiden Tsar," Ivan's unconscious idealization of the Maiden may be a combination of his yearning for his positive mother and his projection of Daddy's little princess. Had he not consciously confronted this idealization in the momentous struggle to bring it into consciousness, a struggle repeated in the Maiden Tsar herself, Ivan's fate might have been that of Ophelia.

The deepest loss for the fatherless daughter is in her wounded sexuality. A little girl cut off from playful flirtation with her father, as Ivan's inner feminine is cut off, misses the gradual acceptance of her erotic life. Moreover, she is cut off from daily intimacy with her father's unconscious and, therefore, from a loving familiarity with her own inner masculine.[3] While that intimacy can lead to psychic incest, it can become the connector between her femininity and her own inner masculinity.[4] It is the strong bridge to her own creative spirit, strong enough to dare the ferocity of creative chaos. It is also the strong bridge to a loving spiritual guide, a daimon (rather than a demon), who becomes her Bridegroom in the inner marriage. If she can flow with this transformative process, she will one day celebrate her father complex.

The fatherless daughter is an important component in this story because, in her search for spirit, she can so quickly sprout wings, slip away from earth and become a swan maiden. That very quality would attract a youth yearning for the perfection of divine womanhood. Somewhere in himself, Ivan holds the feminine out of life, idealizes it on one side, demonizes it on the other. Either way, it can tear him "to shreds." We have to see what this undeveloped feminine in Ivan looks like in order to understand what he must undergo to be released from its limitations. So long as he idealizes the feminine by denying her a human life, the Maiden Tsar must remain in hiding in his unconscious. His task now is to let his dead mother go, and out of her death give birth to his own Bride. The Maiden Tsar, the feminine in both man and woman, has to find her own ground in *mater* and in the masculinity that honors her.

Loss of Both Positive Mother and Positive Father

Ivan, in the absence of the positive mother, is dependent on her unconscious presence, darkly embodied in the stepmother. It is this familiarity with the unconscious that makes him unusually susceptible to its enchantment, an illusion that can destroy him or, in accordance with the laws of the healthy psyche, settle into a genuine human awareness.

His father has left him in the charge of a tutor who is in the service of his stepmother. Left without a positive outward model of either masculine or feminine and forced outwardly to submit to parodic substitutions of both, Ivan must rely entirely upon what Jung calls archetypal figures, belonging to the collective unconscious. Ivan's situation reflects the status of much of the human race at the end of the twentieth century.

Denied guiding models of both masculine and feminine in the temporal world, Ivan must compensate by moving into a timeless world, the "once upon a time" that announces our entrance into the fairy tale realm. This descent, which Ivan is forced to make after he has exhausted the possibilities of his temporal state, is the realm of "faerie," the realm of realized human nature that from earliest childhood needs to be ceaselessly explored. The "diamond body" is to be found there.

In this realm, the stepmother as we have been discussing her may take on violent proportions—a great maw that threatens to devour the emerging masculine ego.

The masculine struggle, then, becomes a struggle to break free of the devouring mother as the force that perpetually threatens manhood. As a result of their own cultural conditioning many men are, in relation to their feminine, in the position of Ivan confronted by his deceitful stepmother. Which is worse: a dead mother or a deceitful stepmother? Somewhere between the two, many men remain precariously suspended, their feminine either dead or treacherous. Their perilous journey cannot end in the inner marriage because they experience their feminine as too treacherous to be embraced.

The individual relationship to the feminine has extended into a collective attitude to the planet. Technocrats have raped Mother Earth, filled her with toxins, distorted her natural rhythms, until she can take no more. She is retaliating with outbursts that are forcing her blind assailants to open their eyes to what they are doing to her in their frenzy to appease their own greed. This disturbing situation is in large measure the result of a flawed solar myth that confers upon the masculine a heroic status, which now threatens us with extinction.

Dark and disturbing as this picture of the absent parents is, "The Maiden Tsar" offers us an uncompromising yet hopeful confrontation with where we are. This is not light entertainment, nor the escape from reality so often offered in modern cartoon versions of the classic fairy tales. If we choose, we can accept our unique place in history. We have reached the point where men and women no longer want to fight against each other. By waking up to our inner dynamics, we can transform our relationships, our environment, our children's future.

A Vulnerable Triumvirate: Power Without Presence

Both fairy tale and dream convey their insights through a pattern of images. While the pattern is not straightforward, it does have its own coherent infrastructure. For example, in "The Maiden Tsar," the tutor, the stepmother, and Ivan are personifications of three different energies in destructive relationships with one another. As the tale develops, the destructive pattern becomes more dangerous, until the tutor is killed. Then the stepmother also disappears into the unconscious. Gradually, as Ivan pulls the repressed energies out of these two complexes, their transformed energies strengthen his conscious ego. Changing imagery vividly depicts inner shifts taking place within the psyche. In them, we see the natural pattern of death and renewal being enacted in the realm of the collective unconscious to which the fairy tale belongs and of which we are a part.

As in a dream, the tale instantly presents us with the characters who will enact the conflict that arises out of the initial situation. The conflict builds to a climax. A startling turn moves the action toward a new place of wholeness. Jung believed that a natural movement toward wholeness exists within the psyche.[1] If we follow the dream process and try to comprehend the messages from the unconscious in other possible ways, we are guided to people and situations that help us, or force us, to deal with parts of ourselves that we need to integrate. If we conduct dialogues with our inner cast of characters, we just might become whole human beings.

As in a dream, everything in "The Maiden Tsar" is part of the whole; each character and thing represents an energy in our body and psyche in relation to other energies, physical and psychological. Energies can attract each other; they can repel. The unconscious tends to pair partners who share wounds that complement each other and at the same time carry possible healing. We think we marry through our own choice, but our ego has minimal choice when the fierce energies of the unconscious magnetize each other in our most wounded and most healing hot spots. What goes on at the unconscious level in individuals and in the constellation between them determines the outcome of the relationship. Unconscious collusion is often the dynamic that both attracts and repels.

In "The Maiden Tsar," in the absence of his positive parents, Ivan colludes with the surrogate parents by responding to them as if they were his genuine parents. He thus becomes their victim by acting as if he were their son. In his psyche, he becomes an orphan in the power of surrogate parents who do not love him because they have never experienced love themselves. This void is what makes the triumvirate vulnerable.

We need to focus for a moment on the word "unconscious," because many of us, even after years of therapy, cannot see the mote in our own eye. We cannot understand why people we dislike the most are in our dreams. We deny they are part of us. Some people even deny the unconscious exists; indeed, they mock people who know it does. Believing they are masters of their fate, they are confident that their willpower, if only they can make it strong enough, will wipe out all difficulties. The more they go into the power principle to gain that control, the more hostile they are to their own unruly unconscious. It is a collusion of denial, denying both the vulnerability of willpower and the strength of the unconscious.

Any addict knows that when he butts out his "last cigarette," that's exactly the moment he wants a cigarette more than ever before. Facing an addiction head on is facing a black wave of killer energy. The addiction is a symptom of an unconscious death wish that has to be brought to consciousness if the individual is ever to be free to live. The unconscious is part of our organic totality. Dismissing it, in either physical or psychic disorders, is like putting a Band-Aid over a malignant mole. The vitality of the cancer cells that are living their own autonomous life will eventually make itself known. Collusion in denial does not change the situation.

Unconscious means unconscious. When we act unconsciously, we literally do not know what we are saying or doing. When, for example, we suddenly hear ourselves blathering to our children the exact phrases we hated to hear from our parents, we may suddenly wake up to our own unconsciousness.

At the core of the unconscious collusion in our tale is the stepmother. In this story, she is the greedy, lustful, power-driven part of our femininity that most of us do not want to recognize or fail to recognize because it is unconscious. She has lost connection to her own male partner and turned that energy, a loose cannon, toward Ivan, believing that she is "in love" with him. Pity the young man who falls into the machinations of power in this version of femininity! Pity, also, the soul of the feminine incarcerated in that ravaged and ravaging energy or complex! She is a soul cut off from her own body and, therefore, from her own passion, lusciousness, and life. Lust with power she may be able to contact in herself; lust with love she will not comprehend.

Stepmother is dangerous because she is vulnerable, vulnerable because she is not grounded either in her own imagery or her own musculature. No point in talking to her about soul or dreams or subtle body or imagination. Her energy is expended in trying to control everything and everybody around her. She finds her identity in power over (sometimes called love of) her body, her family, her friends, her garden. Without that control, she is nobody. She may have a nightmare about her childhood pet bird buried in a shoebox in the attic. When she lifts it out on the palm of her hand, the tiny skeletal creature looks into her eyes and whispers, "I only wanted to sing my song." She may wake up to the song her soul once sang. Or she may simply add singing lessons to her overstuffed agenda.

Stepmother energy is rampant in our culture. For all our delight in physical fitness, many people relate to their body as a machine that they drive very well. Listening to its wisdom, honoring its imagery, living that imagery creatively—these are not part of their vocabulary. As a result, life becomes a mire, a two-dimensional mire, cut off from its own deep sources of love.

The dark side of the mother tends to say, "Shame on you! Shame on you for enjoying life. Shame on you for desiring to create anything." That kind of thinking activates unconscious jealousy toward those who do have healthy desire. When she projects that jealousy, along with unconscious lust and rage, especially onto a young person, that person is pierced by a poisoned arrow. He or she begins to act as if in trance, unable to be present in any situation, unable to make decisions, unable to take hold of life.

Ivan is gullible, uninitiated. In the absence of his father, he has for his model of manhood a tutor who is the puppet of his stepmother. She sees her stepson as a substitute lover. In a dream, the situation might appear as a mess of cobwebs created by a mad spider.

Yet, it is not an uncommon scenario in many contemporary homes. The father has lost his masculine strength and sunk into his shadow side, turned his responsibility over to his wife, who feels herself no longer loved by her husband, moves out of her frail feminine eros into patriarchal power, holds that power by anesthetizing her impotent masculinity with alcohol or whatever kind of anesthetic suits their collusion, and pours her fantasy hope onto her young masculinity (son), into whom she unconsciously projects a poisoned erotic arrow, then consciously sticks a pin into his tunic with the help of her impotent puppet, who does what she tells him because he is drunk on his own unconscious rage.

That last sentence is deliberately too long. I want it that way. It expresses the meaningless tangle of cobwebs insidiously twisting.

A psychotic spider that won't dare to go near the dissociated hot spot dwells somewhere in that tangle. Not the kind of functional family or functional culture we would choose to live in! Most of us have to look no further than our dreams, our jobs, our homes to see some version of this dysfunctional spider.

Again, let us be clear. There is no judgment or blame in this analysis. We are where we are in history. Two world wars that sapped the ideals of at least four generations, the splitting of the atom, unprecedented scientific advancements, technological leaps, electronic miracles—all have left us spiritually on scorched ground. Most of us are microcosms of the macrocosm that is our culture. As we move through the darkness of this transition into a new millennium, we need to have our ears wide open.

A shortwave radio cannot receive the full range of frequencies. Our experience limits our perception. An article about some aspect of our dysfunctional culture is easily understood. However, an article about the absence of the positive mother in our culture, which is destroying itself because it can't hear Her, is apt to be dismissed as "psychobabble" because our antennas are set to pick up a different wavelength.

At a very deep level, however, such an awareness can stir up considerable fear, which comes up to the surface as anger. When confronted with the absence of one's own positive mother, an absence too painful to be consciously absorbed, a person may fall into total unconsciousness, identify with the rush of negative energy, and in defense of the personal mother (who is, in fact, an unperceived fairy-tale stepmother), move into rage, even violence. By speaking of the absence of the positive mother, we not only make room for the negative mother, we invoke her. Even as I write this, I can feel the quaking in my belly that erupts in my office when the negative mother is invoked. Belly understands what head cannot.

In an intensive workshop, where soul is being given free expression and body is being cherished in a positive mother-child relationship, participants often find themselves crying uncontrollably because their soul is being recognized as it has never been recognized in its own beauty before. Or sometimes they block, and reject all this "touchy-feely crap," and flee because they dare not allow anyone past the stepmother armoring that protects them from their own yearning. Often we need to ask ourselves why we are so focused on our partner who is so afraid of intimacy. Are we in collusion? Is it possible that we are projecting our own terror?

We all have our own reasons for blocking. There is no point, however, in going deeper into this story if the cornerstone is lost. That is precisely what this story is about: living with stepmother because positive mother is absent. Put the pin in the neck, cut the feeling off from the thinking, take enough drugs to go to sleep so that we won't have to face the emptiness at the center and the unconscious suicide drive at the core of the addiction that is destroying us. So long as we reject that deep connection to our own life force—Nature Herself, our Positive Mother—how can we know our genuine *I am*? How can we know we've lost it?

Positive mother is not a concept to be understood in the head; it is an experience felt in every cell of the body. Children who have been cherished in a womb for nine months have cell memory that trusts life. If, when we are born, our environment mirrors who we are without judgment, we don't develop a built-in assumption that we have to justify our existence. Nor do we expect to be critically judged every time we attempt to do something.

Many of us unconsciously project critical judgment onto every teacher, male or female, who marks our papers, every parent, every audience to whom we speak, every partner with whom we try to live. Unconsciously, we are living with a pin in our neck. Our own voice is strangled. In dreams, our mouths are fixed in metal cages, our head sits at least an inch above our neck, a snake head fills our mouth, our tongue has been cut out. And worse, our body is numbed, has been since childhood, and therefore we don't know what we as adults want to say.

If, for whatever reason, we were unwanted in the womb, if we were the wrong gender, if we survived an unsuccessful abortion, we carry that knowledge in our cells. We know that our mothers carried the power of life and death over us. We know our cells were not resonating with her. In adulthood, these cell memories cause a bodysoul to "numb out," become petrified, when it suddenly realizes it is no longer pleasing someone and is thus no longer lovable, and therefore even in danger of being annihilated.

Fear of annihilation reduces adults to infantile behavior—they may go out of their way to please others by never disagreeing with them so as not to make them angry. For them, anger means rejection, and they will fall silent or lie rather than be rejected. By whatever means, they hold on to the pulse beat in their own body by resonating with the pulse beat of those they love, or hate, however tenuous that resonance may be.

Thus, lack of resonance with the mother's body creates chronic fear imprinted in the cells of the child. This is *body* fear—the body fear of people who have experienced a very bad earthquake with all its aftershocks. Without solid ground in the Great Mother, the body is in perpetual fear of yet another aftershock, leading to God knows what kind of extinction. That fear at the cellular level has a destructive impact on the psyche. If the physical or psychic container is in any danger of shattering, the capacity for play is crippled. The exuberance of the creative imagination delighting in its own extravagance becomes unthinkable. Ultimately, body fear and psychic fear are one.

The outcome of this combined dismantling of body and psyche is that the positive mother, absent and therefore unable to provide the security she would give to the body, flips into stepmother. Stepmother says, "Life is not playful. Life is not to be enjoyed. It's a deadly serious business." Deadly serious business means we have to have money to pay taxes and we have to keep up with the Joneses and we don't waste money on useless luxuries like opera, dance, music, drama—unless the Joneses do. We keep our nose to the grindstone. If we have little escapes, at least we're not into airy-fairy flaky stuff like soul and imagination. Stepmother abhors change. She turns everything to stone. And the child/adult who is not embodied, and therefore not empowered, dare not disagree with her, regardless of whether the body she speaks from is male or female. Chronic fear swells into fear of annihilation without *mater.* One tiny detail can ignite a panic attack that paralyzes action. A headline about an event in Russia may trigger blind terror over the possibility of a third world war. The headline is the pin that annihilates consciousness, leaving a vulnerable abyss.

Ivan is momentarily annihilated by the stepmother's pin. The pin enacts the killing of soul. Ivan is stabbed by the stepmother's greed, her selfish possession of him. He buries his soul in opaque matter in an attempt to absorb her. The fear of annihilation, carried in the cells of the abandoned child in many of us, makes us cling to matter as if that were the *mater* we have lost or never had. This is the root of addiction. Addictive objects appear to offer us the comfort and security of the positive mother, when in fact the greed that governs addictions actually deprives us of them.

Moreover, the pin in Ivan's neck is the stepmother's fear of scarcity, fear of life. Cutting Ivan off from his own soul abundance, she stockpiles it, literally, for her own miserly use. The result is poverty in the midst of abundance. The brutal literalization of the soul's abundance leaves both men and women cruelly raped and robbed. To literalize the Great Mother as material wealth is to slay her. The stepmother, similarly, literalizes her desire for Ivan's body as sexual greed, and, to satisfy her lust, she must put Ivan's soul to sleep by sticking a pin in his neck. Her psychic desire for union she can perceive only in the flesh, and she seeks to gratify it literally.

To reduce to the literal level of material wealth the abundant energy that supports an ever-expanding universe is to reduce Nature, the Great Mother, to her material body, matter *(mater)*, and then to take possession of it. Materialism run rampant is wonderfully personified in Freud's Oedipus complex: the mother's body as the child's sexual object.

In our story, the appearance of the Maiden Tsar gradually transforms the profound despair caused by this materialism into life-renewing energy. Ivan's true wealth does not lie in the lasciviousness of the stepmother, but rather in the creative transformations of feminine energy originating in the Great Mother. The outward form of these creative transformations is the endless transformation of matter called the "subtle body."

In the dreams of contemporary men and women, there is appearing with increasing frequency the image of a sensual, sexual, earthy Black Madonna. This is not an idealized, chaste, detached Madonna, high up on a pedestal. This is a Madonna who loves her own body, her own flirtations, her own compassionate presence among human beings. She is an aspect of the feminine that is as yet unknown to Ivan, and perhaps even to the Maiden Tsar. That she is beginning to surface in contemporary dreams suggests that as a race we are at last beginning to find in ourselves a vision of the feminine that has been buried in the unconscious for too long.

The Fishing Trip: Deep-Sea Collusion

I am not suggesting that this little fairy tale has all the answers. I am suggesting that its universal wisdom can tell us a great deal about our shortcomings and our potential for shifting our thought and action. Nothing will change so long as we wait for the absent fathers of government to do something. Their fathers, too, were absent, and most of them have no idea what to do or where to find the vision that would guide them. Nor can we look to the stepmothers, whose mothers and grandmothers too were stepmothers, because somewhere they lost touch with their genuine desire. Without a fundamental love of life at the center of everything, children learn from infancy that they are being judged. That judgment restricts every desire, thought, action. The less conscious the judgment is, the more it is projected, the more the child unconsciously lives it out, and the more the parent is appalled by what he or she is forced to live with in the child's reaction, or lack of reaction. Until the shadow is recognized on both sides, forgiveness is impossible. Without forgiveness the heart does not break, and the love does not flow.

The intelligent way to deal with a projection is to step out of the trajectory of the poisoned arrow. For example, you may have lived your life in a bland household. Your mother never said to your father, "You're an irresponsible baby brat," as she heaved her martyr's shoulders and lugged the garbage, muttering something about no commitment. Perhaps you need to look at why the very furniture was sodden with rage, why the cells of your body are sodden with rage. Perhaps she beamed arrows of sunbeams on you to redeem her broken hopes. Perhaps those arrows were so bright with flattery, even seduction, that you smoked dope or drank alcohol to fill the gnawing gap between your reality and her hope. And still do. Then you are in collusion with her.

If you can wake up, you can step out of the arc of the poisoned arrow. If you have the strength to do that, your living stepmother, or your introjected dead stepmother, is depotentiated. The arrow does not hit the bull's-eye. Immediately, a new dynamic is in operation. If you physically and/or psychologically remove yourself, you are no longer a receiver of energy that does not belong to you. You are in a totally new place in your life, a precarious place. The projected energy that you have carried has supported you, even as it undermined you. Now your dark crutch is gone and you are ready to find your own strength inside.

Ivan is moving into that position. He is stepping away from his stepmother's arrows, but he blindly trusts his tutor. Together they go out on the sea to fish. Universally, the sea represents the vast unknown of the unconscious, whose contents may be caught and maybe landed. Those fish and sharks and whales are the bridges between the unconscious and consciousness. They are the dreams that we are sometimes lucky enough to pull onto our raft. If we have the courage to ingest these fish—that is, bite into them, chew them, swallow and digest them—then their energy enhances our conscious life. Gradually, we contact our own creativity and recognize how we have been incarcerated by unconscious material, both ours and what does not belong to us. The devils and angels are in our depths.

On the raft, the collusion of devils and angels coalesces. The pin that the stepmother gave to the tutor as she poured more alcohol into him, alcohol he cannot refuse because his unconscious forces him to please mother even if he hates her, is the pin for which he takes no responsibility, the pin with which he does as he was told to do. He sticks it into Ivan's tunic at the very instant Ivan glimpses his angel and his own mature potential. It is stuck at the neck, splitting connection between head and heart, thinking and feeling, severing throat from life energy in body. The throat is the chakra of creative expression. Like Sleeping Beauty, Ivan is silenced by a weapon so tiny it is invisible.

If we think of Ivan as a developing masculine ego in the psyche, he is endangered by two immense negative energies that are colluding to destroy him. To understand this in ourselves, we need two Jungian words: complex and archetype. If we imagine these words as images, this jargon is not difficult to understand.

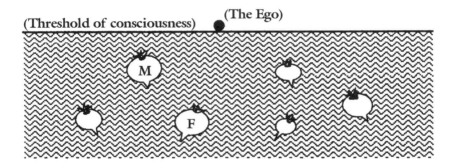

In the diagram, the straight horizontal line represents the threshold of consciousness (the surface of the sea). The ego, the filter through which everything passes into consciousness, sits precariously on this surface. Energy fields float like onions in the sea of the unconscious. Like onions because they are layers of associations that have been built up through our personal associations in conscious life. Jung calls these "complexes." Two of the largest are the mother and father (M and F) complexes. If something happens in daily life that activates a complex (someone shouts at you the way your father used to do), it floats up (metaphorically speaking) and disturbs the ego—creates Freudian slips, bloats the body, makes it blush, creates diarrhea, all those irrational things. The ego in our story is Ivan, the small light of consciousness that is trying to keep afloat. With a stepmother and a tutor like his, Ivan's task is daunting.

It is daunting because at the core of the complex is the archetype. It is invisible. It is an energy field, like that of a magnet, onto which we project images. If, metaphorically speaking, the complex is carrying 1,000 volts of energy, its core, the archetype, is carrying 100,000 volts. The archetype is more than everyday human energy. It is energy that bursts through us from some sacred place—demonic, angelic. It is the Divine Maiden who suddenly ignites the lonely Ivan. It bursts into flame from someplace within us, someplace that manifests imagery shared by human beings from many cultures and many eras. The images change because as cultures change, energies shift and their images automatically change, except when people are stuck. An archetypal image that does not change becomes a stereotype—dead energy.

Right now in England, for example, the Queen (an archetypal image) has realized that the old image of the monarchy, aloof and perfect in its regal isolation, no longer stirs the hearts of her subjects into a consolidated country. It has become a stereotype. She and her family are attempting to create a warm, connected relationship that can act as the crown that holds the nation together. Without an archetypal image that resonates with the magnetic field, the monarchy is nothing—worse than nothing, because there is created in the psyche a counterpole, which flips the Queen from Great Loving Mother into Stepmother (negative side of archetypal image). History is full of such reversals, as are relationships. Consider Louis and Marie Antoinette in France, or Nicholas and Alexandra in Russia, or Henry and Anne Boleyn, and all the countless marriages that end in divorce today.

Ivan finds himself in such a reversal because his archetypal natural mother has flipped into stereotypical stepmother. Moreover, he is a young man in the care of surrogate parents: a woman who, rather than serving life, serves her own selfish goals; a tutor whose energy is not his own—no fire, no creativity, no trustworthy feeling, not trustworthy because his body is "numbed out" by alcohol, disconnected from its own resonances. He has no way of evaluating whatever it is he represents. Rather, he colludes with the stepmother and, like the Nazi leaders called to account for themselves at the Nuremberg trials, obeys orders and takes no responsibility for his actions. He is a puppet of the matriarch.

The tutor is a pathetic creature. Like Lady Macbeth, his "eyes are open . . . but their sense is shut."[1] He is so unconscious he cannot see the crime he is committing in killing his own soul and the soul of the young masculine in his trust. Psychologically, he and Macbeth are in similar bondage to a very strong woman. But unlike Macbeth the tutor is not a tragic figure.

Macbeth, from the beginning, is conscious of his potential, conscious of himself as a warrior in service to his real king. He attempts several times to use his own voice to protect himself against Lady Macbeth's taunts. He is well aware of her treachery. He is also well aware of the power of his own imagination to destroy him. Once he accepts his collusion with his wife, he *consciously* makes his decision to kill his king. Gradually, he falls into the clutches of his own feral shadow and savagely destroys himself. Macbeth's relationship to the woman who was once his "dearest love,"[2] yearning to be queen, and the three "secret, black, and midnight hags"[3] provides an interesting contrast to Ivan's relationship to the Maiden Tsar and the three Baba Yagas.

This weak male figure in thrall to a powerful woman or to an alma mater, or Mother Church, or powerful corporation or institution, is not uncommon in our culture. Even as I write this, 126,000 of my former teacher colleagues are "renegade revolutionaries" in an "illegal" strike that has closed every school in Ontario for almost two weeks. Why? Because the tutors in our provincial government are conducting a "Commonsense Revolution" that will remove upward of $1 billion from our educational budget and so improve the system. More of their "commonsense" ideas include minimizing, probably ultimately removing, the arts—"unnecessary luxuries"—from the curriculum. The teachers are in fact standing up for their rights as teachers to teach children what and how they need to be taught. Recently the government officials announced the need for more money to build more "boot camps" for young offenders. Television gave us images of adolescent boys being kicked out of cars into boot camps. Pin their imagination. Keep them asleep. Keep the high voltage deep in the sea. Have to teach these kids discipline! As we are treated, so we treat others. Power is the name of the game.

In many universities, moreover, Shakespeare is no longer considered a prerequisite for life, even in the Honors English Department. John Milton is impossible to read because his sentences do not stop at the end of a line. What can the elders teach the younger generation in their initiation rites if all the great stories are forsaken? Immense voltage buried in the sea!

Ontario, Canada, is not the only place where the arts are becoming frills in the eyes not only of the government but of many citizens as well. As budgets are being balanced, the arts suffer because so many tutors are so far away from the soul they simply don't care. The pin that is in Ivan's collar is in their collar. Their head is separated from their heart. What these pathetic tutors who pass these laws do not realize is that young people do start out with imagination, with enthusiasm. Take away their disciplined outlets and they are birds without wings. Moreover, their frustration at not being able to soar results in rage, which they have no idea how to contain. Any one of the arts can give them a container strong enough to hold their natural frustration until it distills into paint, or dance, or song. Any teacher knows how much energy is required to teach a student how to hold the container solid until the emotion has time to resolve itself into an art form. This is what culture is.

Our tutors are passing laws that will destroy what has taken centuries to build—a civilization that can contain its own vision. Without the arts, the principal is shot in his office instead of Julius Caesar being massacred with yardsticks in the classroom. Raw instinct runs rampant in the streets, imagination is ciphered into primitive behavior, spiritual and moral values cease to exist, and the millions that are saved are spent in building boot camps to try to contain thugs.

Tutors and stepmothers belong together because together they make an unholy marriage in the psyche. As the shadow side of the true father and true mother, their collusion traps them in delusion. Their imagination is pinned. They think literally. People living in their fiction sense emptiness and assume emptiness needs literal food to fill it; they sense fury, fury needs to be controlled, build a prison; spirit needs to fly, get the bottle. Without recognition of the soul that is always at play with metaphor, healing addictive behavior is almost impossible because the meaning of the metaphor at the core of the concrete thinking is not addressed.

An image—a white rose with a thorned stem—speaks to our emotions, our reason, our imagination. When it rings true for us, our Being resonates in unison, sometimes with the healing of benediction, sometimes with the healing of fearsome truth. To be in touch with our own imagery is to play, dance, fight, sing, love, live, and die with our whole body and soul.

Tutor and stepmother believe in perfection—their perfection—and power that will be so perfect it will never change. They will establish the laws and institutions that will keep it so. That concept curses life. Life is always changing in every cell. Imagery is always dancing with the sheer delight of an imagination at play—imagery that we make our own as children make imagery their own. Because it originates in instinct, it animates body, mind, and spirit.

I cannot stress enough how disastrous it is to go to sleep with tutor and stepmother in charge on our new millennium raft. In giving over our sense of responsibility to them, stoned in their own power, we lose our psychic strength. We fail to see the great moments that happen upon us and fail to grow to our true stature. The more we project onto these betrayers, inner and outer, the more power they take on, the more we are reduced to victim.

The Pin

For it is important that awake people be awake,
or a breaking line may discourage them back to sleep;
the signals we give—yes or no, or maybe—
should be clear: the darkness around us is deep.[1]

Without his roots in the life energy that would open him to his elemental "I desire," Ivan is asleep without knowing it. He is not alert to his own passion for his own life. His father has turned him over to collective values. Metaphorically, he falls into sleepy dependence on the corporations (stepmother) that control the status quo (tutor)—none of them connected to their natural life energy. They wrangle for money, over who will own the waterways they will pollute, the forests they will clear-cut, the salmon they will destroy. As they vie for cyberspace or whatever ideal acts as a cover-up for greed, Ivan falls into a trance.

If he moves deeper into trance, Ivan won't be able to think anymore. His attitude, his postures, his voice will convey victim. "I can't do anything about anything anyway—the violence in the streets, the abuse of women and children, unemployed fathers. Nothing."

The depth of the sleepwalking can be understood only if we

look deeper into the collusion between tutor and stepmother. In this story, we have no King and no Queen. We have only the shadow side of father and mother. That leaves us with no positive parental figures. The King in the psyche is an archetype personifying the dominant collective principle of ordering, authority, civilization. The Queen personifies the feeling value that brings life to the King.

In the Grail Legend, a strong virile King is essential to the fertility of his lands, animals, and people. The king calls up associations to the kingpin, the center point, the center around which everything turns. If there is no King, nor even a wounded King, the solar ordering principle that radiates throughout the land is absent, so also is the spirit, the wind, the *pneuma* that fires the imagination. Without a Queen, the love for the King that brings purpose and blessing to the individual is absent. Psychologically speaking, a person may be a staunch Roman Catholic, for example, believe in the ordering hierarchy of the Church, take the communion, and give a solid donation. Still, if there is no love in the commitment, the person is "as sounding brass or a tinkling cymbal."[2] The King is present, the Queen is absent. Ivan, like many contemporary men and women, has neither King nor Queen in his psyche.

Another way of seeing that dynamic would be through Shakespeare's *Othello*. He has a strong King, but no Queen. He does not see that if he kills his soul (his Queen) his King will become a bombastic liar or a rank sentimentalist. When Othello enters their bedroom to kill the sleeping Desdemona for what he imagines is adultery, he dramatizes himself, "It is the cause, it is the cause, my soul."[3] Overwhelmed by her beauty, he argues with himself:

> *Yet I'll not shed her blood;*
> *Nor scar that whiter skin of hers than snow,*
> *And smooth as monumental alabaster.*

Yet she must die, else she'll betray more men.
Put out the light, and then put out the light.[4]

He snuffs out the candlelight, and then places his fingers on Desdemona's throat to snuff out her light. He knows he is putting out the light of his soul for a cause—patriarchal prerogative—and like Macbeth, when he casts away his feminine feeling, he becomes a raging tyrant.

The vacuum created by an absent family, archetypal and personal, is in danger of being filled by an impersonal collective—by bureaucracies in which nobody takes ultimate responsibility. Without the spirit of the father and the ground of the mother as base, citizens are in danger of being taken over by tutors who control by pinning—cutting off head from heart, leaving people no longer acting from their own values and emotions. The bureaucracy itself goes to sleep, pretends to be virtuous, covers up where it is protecting the very values it despises. The hysterical sobbing of the president of one of the largest corporations in Japan as he announced his company's collapse, along with the stunned faces of the employees who were dependent on the morality of that bureaucracy, is a recent image of what our world is increasingly moving toward.

Some bureaucrats are puppets of the billionaires who, in the name of a fast-growing economy, create slave labor in Thailand to make the shoes Westerners wear on their feet, shoes that are made in Asia because high American wages have forced factories to close down. How long will we remain pinned into believing that such a displacement of power is creating a booming economy? That lie boosts the polls for the existing puppets of billionaires who are the tyrants behind the great gates. It is a society based on lies, with pinned-in-the-neck citizens who can hardly bear to hear the truth, and, if they do hear, rarely act to cut off the tutor's head. Our tutors keep their students quiet by telling them lies about how much they value traditions, and the lie goes into another level of trance, because few citizens value or believe in those traditions anymore.

In dreams, traditions are often broken by the birth of a Divine Child. Whatever the religious belief of the dreamer, that child is radiant with light, intelligence, love. The dreamer is astonished by its beauty, and its capacity to talk with the wisdom of an elder. If that child is nourished and loved and brought into conscious life, the life is turned inside out. Marriages cease or transform, jobs disappear and are recreated, countdown is rampant. The old life dies; a new life is born. The soul is finding a new world. In "Journey of the Magi," T. S. Eliot expresses the anguish of the wise men when they realize the gap that now exists between them and the wasteland around them because they have experienced the Birth that is "[h]ard and bitter agony,"[5] forever separating them from their friends who are now strangers clutching their dead gods.

The pin blinds Ivan. He cannot see the ordinary; therefore, he cannot see the extraordinary when it is right before his eyes. He is cut off from his own base and trapped in trance. Until he reads the letter from his soul connection, he is not free to act. When the extraordinary finally penetrates his human awareness, the trance snaps, and Ivan cuts off the tutor's head.

The Sword

Every dark thing one falls into can be called an initiation. To be initiated into a thing means to go into it. The first step is generally falling into the dark place and usually appears in a dubious or negative form— falling into something, or being possessed by something. The shamans say that being a medicine man begins by falling into the power of the demons; the one who pulls out of the dark place becomes the medicine man, and the one who stays in it is the sick person. You can take every psychological illness as an initiation. Even the worst things you fall into are an effort at initiation, for you are in something which belongs to you, and now you must get out of it.[1]

When Ivan recognizes that he has been betrayed, he acts instantly. This is a dangerous action because it is coming from fury. He cuts off the tutor's head. That, too, is dangerous. To cut off what has been our only source of security leaves us in limbo. However, if the trance is deep enough, sometimes the instant sword is the only way out.

"Cut off the tutor's head." Five words. What might go off with that head? Again, the image severs head and heart so that feeling value is cut off from intellectual understanding. Such a cut could be very cruel in relationship. A woman, for example, is angry with her partner. She explodes. Suddenly, her anger is charged with the rage of centuries. She is no longer present, no longer capable of controlling her sword. The cut may destroy the relationship. Or destroy a job. Many men who have been in top executive positions, never imagining they could lose their job, are now suddenly finding themselves on the street. They are so heartbroken they can't cry. They have lost their tutor. The total organization of their lives is gone.

Using the sword wisely will require a lifetime of discrimination, discernment. As the patriarchal frame collapses, men and women are finding themselves in many roles. Without finely honed decisions and a sharp sword, they begin to realize their psyches cannot tolerate the pressure and their bodies are breaking down, often with autoimmune disorders. The body is becoming enemy to itself!

As tutor and stepmother are removed, as the old frame collapses, painful decisions arise in personal relationships. The rotten foundations of the psyche are being dismantled. The psychic incest at the core of the marriage is being dismantled—the mother-daughter bonded to the father-son is no longer acceptable to the body. A profound sacrifice is going to be made if both partners are going to grow up into mature relationship. New boundaries are established. Psychologically, mother will give up son; father will give up daughter, whatever the dynamics in the particular relationship have been. This will change the dynamics between the actual parents and their children. What does it mean to give up the son? What does it mean to give up the mother? Yes, the sword is a sacred instrument.

In using the sword with this speed, Ivan's unconscious is putting him through a profane ritual. He does not know what he is doing. He has not created sacred space. His instrument is not sanctified. Still, the Maiden soul within him is crying out for union. It is she who learned of the stepmother's ruse and the tutor's treason. It is she who wrote to Ivan telling him to cut off the tutor's head, and, **"if he loved his betrothed, to come and find her beyond thrice nine lands in the thrice tenth kingdom."**

Ivan's masculinity springs into action to defend the new life his femininity is offering. Suddenly in touch with his own life force, he acts from his own desire. Whereas he was lost, now he is found.

The sword must be respected, perhaps cherished, and polished every day. I like to think of it with a golden blade and a silver handle, the metals of masculine and feminine balancing each other. Men and women need the concentration to discern, discriminate, and cut. All must be done with love. Ultimately, we hope that the rose that is our soul will blossom in full flower. If we strike in haste, the sword wounds our rose as surely as it wounds the other's. Ultimately, wound and sword are one.

A beheading in a fairy tale usually releases a buried-alive child. That's true for Ivan. It can be true for the reader. The feminine that is too often imprisoned in a masculine head-trip can be released. A beheading releases the imaginal hidden in the literal.

This is a point in our storytelling when the listeners are becoming tense. What power heads would they like to cut off? We need fresh energy, fresh air. Robert suddenly picks up his bouzouki and says, "Time for some Jiménez."

I have a feeling that my boat
has struck, down there in the depths,
against a great thing.
    And nothing
happens! Nothing . . . Silence . . . Waves . . .

—Nothing happens? Or has everything happened
and are we standing now, quietly, in the new life?[2]

The Conscious Virgin

So far, our journey has taken us downward, into the depths of the psyche. Patiently, arduously, through rung after rung of the spiral, we have moved as in a dream. In this relatively simple story, our ground has been split through—personally and culturally—to our primal center, the missing life force.

Now we are about to continue the journey from a different perspective. We begin to travel through the healing spirals. "Thank

God," you are probably saying, and so am I. And so, I'm sure, is Robert. He always tells our audiences that as soon as he begins to fly, really enjoying his flight, he turns around and there I am drilling away into the earth. The audience laughs in recognition. And sometimes, like a lark, I fly straight up to heaven. Then I look down and there is Robert nesting on the ground. The masculine and feminine energies are continually interchanging.

Ivan is finding his masculinity, not through the masculine heroic journey, but through the feminine. Many contemporary women and men find the path of the hero killing dragons increasingly archaic. For Ivan at this point in the story, the path curves suddenly from stepmother to beloved maiden. **"[S]he told Ivan that she loved him passionately and had come from afar to see him. So they were betrothed."**

How many of us have been so lucky! In those bewildering days of late adolescence when we are living in possibility, taking leave of our parents, stepping into our own shoes, suddenly a shining one crosses our path. Whether that one comes in vision or in flesh, for one moment we are whole as we have never been whole before. We love. We carry the possibility of being loved. We are all the tulips in the park, the pink in the peony, the gold in the rising sun. We stride naked in our jeans and pour blessings on those who dare to behold us.

Ivan is granted this moment, but he is so pinned by his stepmother and tutor he can barely wake up to it. Psychologically, the maturing energy bursts through, attempts to move out of the prison of the complexes, and, at the very moment of possibility, drops into unconsciousness. Three times Ivan sees the Maiden Tsar and her thirty foster sisters sailing in on their thirty ships. He recognizes his soul. And although he loses her at this moment, she initiates in him the warrior energy to fight for what is precious to him. Those "Moments of Dominion/That happen on the Soul"[1] change life. In a flash, all the best that is in us connects and flashes through and, especially when we are young, is projected outward onto that One who carries our soul. All that we never imagined within us is born. The archetypal voltage, turned up full, flows through us so that ordinary life suddenly has beauty and meaning.

We are alive. Many of us can remember such a moment—a moment that shone and was later lost, but never quite lost. Perhaps, gradually, we were able to recognize the treasure we had projected out of ourselves, and very gradually were able to claim it as our own.

Diana, Princess of Wales, carried in projection something of the shining Maiden Tsar for millions of people around the world. Many who "didn't like her all that much before she died" suddenly felt sobs lurching through their bodies when they heard news of the violent crash on the thirteenth pillar in the Place de l'Alma tunnel in Paris. They could not understand what was happening to them. Divinity in its feminine guise seemed to be crossing the human path.

Now, long after her funeral, many people are still bewildered by the depth of what went through them. "I want to understand what it was about. I don't want such an experience to simply pass away and life go on the same. I cannot believe she is dead." If we are going to keep such an experience from simply passing away, we need to take the pins out of our collars and bring to consciousness what we were projecting onto Diana. We need to look carefully at the projection and take responsibility for carrying what she carried into ourselves.

I will discuss Diana's story in depth because it encapsulates so much of what we have been looking at in our culture. Fairy tales are not divorced from life. They portray the mythic dimension of historical events; that is, the meaning of those events. What we witnessed on television was the world's mythic response to the historical event. That innermost dimension is always alive and ready to go into action—ordinary or extraordinary. Thus, the universal is always present as the meaning in the particular.

In our tale, the hero is male. In the historical event, the hero is female. The unconscious is not gender oriented; masculine and feminine are not male and female. Clearly, one fundamental difference exists between Diana and the Maiden Tsar. The first is human, the second divine. However, in a period of a few hours, Diana, the human being, was catapulted into archetypal femininity. Not woman. I stress femininity because her story intertwines with Ivan's story. He is a masculinity initiated by six feminine figures in the tale. Diana is a femininity initiated by the patriarchal structures into which she was born. Together they might represent the maturing of masculinity and femininity in many of us.

As you read this story, allow images from your own dreams to drift through. They are images of unconscious contents that might be carried out on a projection. Consider an image of an abandoned tiny girl or an adolescent pretending to be smaller and dumber than she is, or a seductress or betrayed wife, cherishing mother, hesitant rebel, tongueless beauty, confident benefactress. As you think of these images, imagine them all being lived in one person, and you have some idea of what the new archetypal image of the feminine looks like as it arises spontaneously from the collective unconscious of millions of people.

People on this side of the Atlantic experienced the historical event of the death in a way most English people did not. Britons woke up on a quiet Sunday morning to find their princess dead. In North America, our Saturday night programs were interrupted with breaking news of a car accident involving Dodi and Di in a Paris tunnel. Ten minutes later, came news that the police had arrived. Fifteen minutes later, Diana had been taken to the hospital in fair condition. Then the regular program was discontinued. Pictures began to appear of the crumpled car inside the tunnel with news that Dodi was dead, the driver was dead, the bodyguard in hospital, Diana in grave condition. We were being gripped by the archetype of death. How could anyone come out of that car alive? Surely, she'll be all right. Then the statement: Diana, Princess of Wales, is dead. The staggering minutes afterward, the restless night, and the recognition on Sunday morning that an era was over.

At a time of such rapid and radical transition, the whole population tends to move into the "once upon a time" world. Most of us will always remember exactly where we were when we heard the news, as we remember where we were when John Kennedy was assassinated. Diana was an imperfect human being before her death, answerable to the literal. With her death and the starburst of images and music that exploded in the media, we were transported from our literal body into our subtle body. It became our mode of perception.

Diana, huntress and hunted, died in what became almost a ritual killing, a sacrifice made for the people, a death that would release new feminine life. The life that we could not read except imperfectly suddenly became an open book. The imperfect human Diana became an icon. Even the literalists were powerless to stop the transformation, as the once scattered pages of her life spontaneously came together into a meaning that none could have guessed. The extravagance of her dress, like all of her publicly displayed behavior, suddenly assumed a different meaning. It was as if she were offering herself to us for a purpose not even she could detect. Like a princess in a fairy tale, the imperfect human being took on divine attributes. All that was swiftly projected onto her called forth grief and awe and mystery that surged around the world, surged with archetypal imagery.

In Hyde Park, giant television screens were set up to transmit the funeral to thousands. In Kensington Gardens, circles of candles burned around every tree, chrysanthemums and daisies cascaded from the branches. Lilies and roses were spread like immense fans before the palace gates. Love poems to the beloved princess blessed her on her flight to Paradise. Handpainted pictures, teddy bears, and unabashed outpourings of love and grief appeared on a scale never before seen in the streets of London. Somewhat lesser scenes took place all over the world.

The voltage of repressed energy that was instantly released was nothing less than archetypal. To use an image from later in the story, the pin was blown out by her death. Its suddenness was real, frightening. Her reality instantly became a spiritual reality that revitalized something around the world. People who had never understood ritual or pageantry as a transformer to shift energy from one dimension to another, from the physical into the subtle body, for example, had some sense of it during the week of mourning and the funeral for the fairy-tale princess.

Even through television, most of us could feel ourselves being lifted into limitless space not only by the facts of what we were experiencing, but by the images and silence that were carrying the metaphorical meaning. What we saw with our physical eyes was what was literally going on. The literal was carrying a larger psychological meaning—for some, a spiritual meaning. Surely, for almost no one was it merely literal—the sudden extinction of a body and its burial. The archetypal flow of spontaneous energy was coming from one mysterious center, centering citizens of the planet in wholeness.

To understand the intensity of the response, we acknowledge first that it is archetypal energy far beyond our personal capacity to release. We are the instruments through which it flows. If, however, we are to keep the pin out of our necks, we have to bring the images to consciousness, insofar as we can, to keep the new energy flowing through. What are we projecting onto Diana? If we look at the total picture of her life and death (as we know it) as if it were a dream or a fairy tale, we will be able to recognize what we are projecting and thus recognize what we need to integrate into our own lives.

Since the word "projection" is the key here, we need to take a moment to recheck our understanding. A projection is like an arrow. Unconscious content in ourselves sees someone or some-

thing in the outer world to which it says Yes or No. The arrow
flies to its target. Part of us is then hooked into that person or
thing. (Other names for the phenomenon are "falling in love" or
"adoring my guru" or "mad about Bombay Sapphire.") The ego,
unless it is very conscious, has no control over the content or the
direction of the flight. If the arrow carries big voltage (archetypal
projection) the dynamic between arrow and target may be elec-
tric. Here is the electricity Emily Dickinson discovered in herself
when she experienced the flight of the arrow.

> *He touched me, so I live to know*
> *That such a day, permitted so,*
> *I groped upon his breast—*
> *It was a boundless place to me*
> *And silenced, as the awful sea*
> *Puts minor streams to rest.*
>
> *And now, I'm different from before,*
> *As if I breathed superior air—*
> *Or brushed a Royal Gown—*
> *My feet, too, that had wandered so—*
> *My Gypsy face—transfigured now—*
> *To tenderer Renown—*
>
> *Into this Port, if I might come,*
> *Rebecca, to Jerusalem,*
> *Would not so ravished turn—*
> *Nor Persian, baffled at her shrine*
> *Lift such a Crucifixal sign*
> *To her imperial Sun.*[2]

If the arrow is rejected by the target, such rejection has created
some of the greatest love poetry, music, art, drama, ballet in the
world.

Individuals who are attempting to find themselves by withdrawing a projection and mining its resources write in their journals, paint, dance, compose, until they bring to consciousness attributes of themselves that are being sent out in the arrow onto someone else.

Reclaiming projections involves reclaiming demons and angels and redeeming them. In the early 1980s, when Ronald Reagan was president, Mikhail Gorbachev said to him, "I am going to do something terrible to you; I'm going to take away your enemy."[3] He did. Without Russia to project its own aggression and subterfuge on, the United States is being forced to look at its own filthy backyard. Analyzing projections is the best possible way to know ourselves in our light and darkness, especially since we are now being shoved into new territory in our psyche. When our dreams are taking us into pitch black scenes, we know we are in unconsciousness, where we have never been before, even where our ancestors have never been. There is no psychic map. The better part of wisdom is to study our projections. In recognizing them outside, we may transform them inside.

What then did we project onto Diana? When she married Charles in the fairy-tale wedding of 1981, the shy nineteen-year-old Cinderella whose prince had come carried the hope, faith, and love that most brides yearn to carry. Moreover, her prince would one day be King and she the mother of Kings. Thus, she carried the dreams of a nation. The pomp and pageantry in London sparkled with hope for a new dawn in depressed England.

The fairy tale continued, and Diana became the ideal cherishing mother who chose to travel with her young son rather than leave him at the palace in the charge of strangers. Here was genuine feminine feeling breaking the royal coolness of the Queen and her severe Prince. As time went on, the media gave us delightful images of the laughing mother on a roller coaster with her handsome princes, whom she hoped would "sing their song." Her obstinate husband was missing. He preferred to work alone in his garden, perhaps because he had grown up pinned in royal privacy.

Increasingly, rumors spread of the princess's lonely childhood in the family castle at Althrop. She, too, was born of aristocratic lineage. Her family, indeed, was known as the great king-makers of England. They made and broke dynasties, as now a dynasty was being threatened. This princess was not blessed with parents who loved each other. As children, she and her little brother traveled repeatedly back and forth between their stepmother and tutor. Much later, her subjects who loved her would look into Diana's eyes and see their own abandoned child, even their own divine child, mirrored in those sparkling vulnerable depths.

Whisperings were not all friendly toward the beautiful princess. Indeed, many suggested that the fragile woman knew well enough how to climb the rungs of patriarchy, knew exactly how to manipulate the hierarchy of the palace in order to have her own way. Her ways were not her prince's ways, and sadly they went different ways, she into the arms of James, an untrustworthy horse trainer, and later Gilbey, who called her by the delightful epithet "Squidgy."

Now, natural as shadows are, many of her subjects had husbands who had a Squidgy in their lives, or wives who had a James, and knowing their princess was as unhappy in marriage as they, united them with a velvet chain. Their suffering was no longer hidden under the rug; their suffering was the suffering of the royal princess.

Even as I write this, I can feel myself being taken over by the fairy-tale language, entering the fairy-tale world. Like so many others at the time of her death, I began to recognize my projections onto Diana, began to experience the unreality of the world she found herself in. Everything in her childhood prepared her for a life of isolation that would either destroy her in aloneness, or temper her into an aloneness that would bring out the shining essence of who she was. Having borne two princes, heirs to the throne, she was no longer necessary as a womb for the monarchy. Her husband, Charles, was almost thirteen years older, very introverted, and in love with another woman, Camilla, who had been present even on the day Diana walked down the aisle. Rumor has it that he had a private telephone line to Camilla from his grandmother's palace, the grandmother who conspired with her lady-in-waiting, Diana's grandmother, to bring about this marriage in the first place—two fairy godmothers with pins in their pockets.

Psychologically, Diana was alone. She was Her Royal Highness because she was married to the heir to the throne, not because she was true royalty. In the eyes of many, she was a simple, sweet girl, simple enough that anything could be projected onto her. Like the Maiden Tsar, she shone at the center with her thirty foster sisters around her.

However, Diana was not simple, nor was the Maiden Tsar. She could have remained silent, carried her own guilt and shame and disillusionment in silence, as women have done for centuries, and appeared as the perfect princess, mother, lover of good works. The latter part of the story reveals the true nature of the Maiden. When she was about to meet Ivan again, she **"and the thirty other maidens flew into the house."** In other Russian stories, this figure and her entourage are, in fact, swans.

The word "swan"

> has the same root as the Latin word *sonare* meaning sounding . . . referring to the singing swan. . . . The strange cry made by the old swans when dying on the ice is probably the hook for the projection of the swan song. The beauty of the swan with its fascinating feathers has also given rise to the idea that it is supernatural. . . . Because the swan is the bird that knows the future, it is holy

> to Apollo in Greek mythology and to Njödr in Nordic
> mythology and plays a big role in the famous mytholog-
> ical swan-maiden motif. . . . The swan can be said to rep-
> resent an aspect of the unconscious psyche. Like all
> birds, it has its timeless analogy and demonic qualities
> which represent intuitions and hunches, sudden ideas
> and feelings which come from nowhere and go
> again. . . . The feather garment has to be grasped, and
> the deed is to restore the bird to its human quality.[4]

Diana could have become a swan. As in the Russian ballet *Swan Lake,* Odile could have split from Odette and a pinned world would have gone on pretending that this beautiful woman was not an adulteress, knew nothing about the shining of sexuality, cared little or nothing about the infidelities of her husband. No, Diana rejected that split. She cut off the tutor's head. She found her own tongue, expressed her own feminine values from her own heart, came out of her swandom and became an empowered woman speaking for the women of this century and for the feminine in men, the anguished split-off whore and the equally anguished perfection, both crying for life in a human body.

Diana rejected the projection of perfection. In this she was aided by the media. The hundreds of photographs kept us in touch with both sides. To the degree that individuals identify with an archetypal projection, they experience themselves as dead. As human beings, they may cease to exist. In our story, the Maiden Tsar later hides her love in a coffin.

In putting on her black widow's weeds and extra-black eyeliner for her November 1995 post-separation interview with the BBC, and speaking with her head somewhere between shy tilt and de-fiant set, she spoke her truth. All her pinned listeners were so shocked they didn't speak much about it. But they heard, and their unconscious heard, and the anguish that poured out at her death was the repressed anguish of centuries that was punctured open that night. Many of the women interviewed at the funeral had brought their young daughters because they wanted them to remember they were here. They were at the funeral of the princess who gave them a tongue. "Maybe I'll never know freedom," they said, "but I hope my daughter will."

Diana took on the dynasty of Windsor single-handed. She married into a household with no King; the creative masculine, bathed in sun energy, was not present. The loving side of the Queen was pinned by her respect for patriarchal law and protocol. The radiant charm that once bound her to her people rarely shone. The ancient robes of duty that tradition decreed she must wear to open Parliament were becoming too heavy for her aging shoulders. The final blow to the House of Windsor in the *annus horribilis* was the burning of Windsor Castle. Something had to change. The liberated Diana arrived.

Perhaps I need to say here that I was one of those who did not particularly like Diana. I didn't trust her seductive ways with the media, especially her flirtations with the camera. I was always interested in her psychology, however, because she was for a time bulimic and did make attempts on her own life. Any addict who has that kind of courage and the kind of energy that dares that place of the opposites interests me. Here was a princess desperate enough to ride the undercurrents of the collective values in the palace, her body refusing to digest what was poison to her, her psyche willing to go to the edge in her attempt to realize herself.

She refused to be pinned. She refused to be the Prisoner of Wales. She used a sword, neurotically at first, but gradually with the conscious decision necessary to allow consciousness to move ahead.

As a father's daughter, she probably tended toward the fate that would separate her from life. I watched her valiantly attempting to humanize the swan that would take her out of life. I saw her more and more at home in her own body and in the values that she honored. I heard her voice quietly proclaiming that she would be true to her own heart rather than to a patriarchal arrangement. As one woman said, "Was there ever before a woman in history who gave up her Queendom because she would not accept a fraudulent relationship?"

She lived on the razor's edge between life and death. She died on that edge. She gambled for the whole of life—beauty, wealth, fame, happiness. In the crowning moment of her gamble, she trusted. She failed to ask, "Who is driving this car?" She died in a tunnel in Paris on what was probably the happiest night of her life. Personally and culturally, she was at her peak. Something in her shadow must have been shouting, "What a way to go!"

And how another fairy tale might have ended had the "pair of star-cross'd lovers,"[5] Dodi and Diana, like Romeo and Juliet of the enemy houses of Montague and Capulet, been buried together, and "with their death [buried] their parents' strife,"[6] even the strife of the Christian and Muslim worlds. Such was not yet to be, although many letters hanging from the palace fence, as well as two large pictures in Harrods' window, sang them together to Paradise.

The unconscious will out; all it takes is a crisis to release it. What was the crisis that released countless dreams of Diana? What lay in the unconscious of millions who didn't know they cared about her? What is absent at the beginning of her story that provides the key to its meaning?

Like the tutor and the stepmother, the House of Windsor, indeed England itself, is pinned at the beginning of her story. New blood, new spontaneity, new voice, new feminine values are necessary to bring in new life. A nineteen-year-old *un*conscious virgin is brought in to fill the gap. She bears two sons. At first she complies with the patriarchal protocol. When she introduces her own feeling values, the palace walls begin to shake. As she finds more of her Conscious Virgin strength and begins to live her differentiated feminine and differentiated masculine, London Bridge begins to fall. The androgynous Diana is both exquisitely feminine and courageously bold. Then the crisis strikes. Diana is violently killed. The pin is pulled out. The cultural unconscious responds not only with the answer to what is missing in the House of Windsor but what is missing in the world.

And when her brother in his eulogy (rebuking the Queen) recalled Diana as "someone with a natural nobility who was classless and who proved in the last year that she needed no royal title," the clapping, at once approving and rebellious, began in front of the big television screens in Hyde Park, swept across Green Park into Westminster and into the Abbey itself, where the House of Windsor sat in the midst of a revolution that was happening right there before our eyes. A dynasty without the vibrant feminine was being dismantled. In that moment, the yearning for the feminine burst out of the unconscious of the grieving nation. The consciousness of the world shifted. Whether the pin remains out or we go back to sleep depends on what we do with this new feminine that is now released from the unconscious. What was missing was in the coffin at the center. What was not missing was the living image of a new feminine—mother, lover, seductress, humanitarian, with strength to articulate her values, and courage to defend them. Diana was never more alive. Death released her into an abundance of life, and the crowning glory of millions of archetypal projections yearning for embodiment.

In rereading my story of Diana, I am aware that many readers may say, "But Diana was a very flawed human being. The Maiden Tsar is divine." In my effort to find a new balance between human and divine in the feminine, I perhaps have not clarified both sides, and you perhaps have not heard with both ears. Let us both try to avoid the patriarchal either/or and move into the feminine both/and. In that paradox, the mystery of being human lies. We are both animal and divine. In our essence, the opposites are not in opposition. In an electromagnetic field, same poles of a magnet repel each other, opposite poles attract, creating a tension that is attempting to pull them together. To me, this is the place of the Maiden Tsar in our tale. She is beautiful, yes. She is divine, yes. And she carries both sides of the archetypal energy, as we shall soon see in the Baba Yaga. That, too, is paradox that keeps us growing. If we drop either side of the paradox, that side hardens into ice. If we can hold at the center of the tension, our hearts will open, will be opened, by love greater than we have ever known. As I understand it, that's what this journey is all about: being strong enough to hold the tension until the love that can contain the paradox breaks through. Yes, there's suffering, but it doesn't feel like suffering when the love is divine on one side, human on the other, and one in the loving heart.

"What did thy song bode, lady?"[7] Diana's song brings to a sleeping world at this moment in history the release of a femininity that has never been integrated into the culture.

Whether or not Diana embodied that femininity is not what is important. What is important is that we recognize in her tragically brief life the unrealized potential in the femininity that burst into cultural consciousness through her death. If we look around us at the upheavals in relationships, surely there can be no question that a tidal wave is being released from the unconscious that is sweeping out the archaic paradigms of relationship that are now impossible to live. The feminine has disowned the old paradigm of male/female relationships as well as the inner relationship between masculinity and femininity in both sexes. The old psychic order has now outlived its usefulness and can operate only in a self-destructive way. We are at a new stage in the evolution of consciousness, called to move into our individual and cultural maturity.

Through one confrontation after another, men and women are being released from dead stereotypes, whether they like it or not. The feminine in both genders is undergoing painful initiations in order to achieve what for so long has been culturally denied.

Women are finding their identity as women; men are recognizing that their masculine identity can no longer be grounded in a false view of the feminine. Patriarchy flourished on a crippled masculinity rooted in split femininity. In the present chaos of relationship, masculinity and femininity are releasing themselves from the paradigm that was equally damaging to both sexes. This initiation is not through matter or spirit, but through both.

In our contemporary situation, Destiny arranged events so that Diana was the spark that ignited the smoldering fires of the unconscious in the collective. In our story, the Maiden Tsar is the spark that ignites the unconscious in Ivan. What is now incubating in the unconscious of millions of people is what was incubating in Ivan. Like the Maiden Tsar, Diana bodes the coming of the Conscious Virgin, she who is one in herself.

While this Virgin was still in its birth pangs in Diana, as it is still in its birth pangs in Ivan and the Maiden Tsar in our tale, we need to hold it now as intuitive possibility in the rest of our story. What we are looking at is the image projected from the collective unconscious of the millions focused on the death of an exhausted psychic order and the birth of a new one, not only in September 1997, but now as a released energy in consciousness. The drive that is still hidden in our compulsive society could become a release into freedom, freedom from a shackling fusion with other people and things. We are being called to live our own identity.

The feminine side of this identity is what I call the Conscious Virgin. As in the phrase *virgin forest,* the original meaning of the word *virgin* had to do with the natural state of an organic life form, a state that is always in touch with its own inherent resources without human interference. Psychologically, when I think of Conscious Virginity, I think of the natural state of an organic soul that has reached a consciousness of itself without that consciousness interfering with its natural evolution. What distinguishes our human state from other forms of life is the consciousness that illumines it to make it what it is. That illumination is inherent within the soul rather than imposed upon it. The Conscious Virgin is the conscious natural human state of Being.

In this state, soul is not a prisoner waiting to be released from a body in which it is a stranger or a victim. Rather, body and soul are friends, maturing together, constantly interchanging messages. Consciousness naturally arises out of the five senses in images, that act as the creative connection to soul. Body thus becomes the instrument of soul's consciousness. Soul and body resonate together so that divine and human are continually informing each other. Soul is at one with body now conscious of itself.

Conscious Virginity is Being, *I am* that reflects the eternal *I am that I am*. Like a lily of the field, the Conscious Virgin has no need to justify her existence, no need to fear aloneness. Her Being is present in the present moment. Her presence affirms its continually evolving wholeness through its continually evolving creativity, not only with herself, but with the whole natural universe. She knows the sacredness of matter. This uniquely human consciousness of the totality of all things is the mystery that connects us to the divine body of love that holds creation together. Whether we are male or female, one moment of Being in that mystery is the birth into Conscious Virginity.

Ivan has to experience his own depths before he can even conceive of such a feminine. And we need to journey with him and absorb more of his experience in order to experience in our bodies rather than conceive in our heads what Conscious Virginity might be. To embody that archetypal image, Ivan has to integrate the idealized swan maiden and the lusty Baba Yaga.

· PART II ·

The Descent: Journey into the Unconscious

I put new Blossoms in the Glass—
And throw the old—away—
I push a petal from my Gown
That anchored there—I weigh
The time 'twill be till six o'clock
I have so much to do—
And yet—Existence—some way back—
Stopped—struck—my ticking—through—[1]

"The Descent" is a mythological term for the period during and after a powerful event in which the ego has been overwhelmed by a wave from the unconscious. Energy that is normally available to consciousness falls into the unconscious so the person is often disoriented, exhausted, perhaps in a trance state. This is known as journeying into the underworld, a state in which creative energies are going through transformations that the unaware ego may know nothing about until big changes begin to happen in the outer world, or the studio begins to shine with totally new pictures, new music, or new sculpture. New images grow in the darkness of the creative mother. The goal of the descent is a new connection between earth and spirit. People often fall into this realm when they are about to be taken into a new phase of life and they have to die to the old in order to be reborn into the new. This often happens during a period of mourning for a loved one lost through death or separation.

If you read aloud the above excerpt from Emily Dickinson's poem, written during her descent, if you stop at her dashes, and slightly exaggerate her flat monosyllables, you will experience the mechanical, somnolent Death-in-Life of the Underworld.

Striking off the head of the tutor is Ivan's commitment to his own life. Yes, he wants to know who he is. He wants to find the beloved woman. He wants to find purpose in his life. The instant he makes connection to his feminine soul, he has something to live for, and he acts.

At first, Ivan shines with the exuberance of freedom. He cannot know the submerged resistance that he has also released. As soon as that new energy begins to come together, new voltage builds up in his inner stepmother, especially because he does not go home to say good-bye to her. It's as if her voice is in his gut snarling, "You think you can be free? You're mine and you always will be. You can journey **'onward, straight ahead, a long time or a short time—for speedily a tale is spun, but with less speed a deed is done.'** I will be always with you."

This is the natural law of action/reaction in the psyche. Think of an energy pendulum swinging back and forth. We can feel it swinging further into trust, hope, faith, but as it swings further on one side, it will balance that new reach with a corresponding reach on the other side into fear and vulnerability. The psyche that has protected itself from annihilation all its life will feel totally unprotected in this new act of free swinging trust. The dreams are often nightmares, especially in a situation like Ivan's, where his faith is so utter and his beloved so idealized. The depth of emptiness is in ratio to the depth of love, although the love is total projection.

A person in life in a situation like this is suffering immense grief for life never lived; equal rage against the tutors and stepmothers who are now perceived as betrayers; bewilderment, loneliness, guilt for allowing the treasure to be lost when it was just found; bouts of low self-esteem often related to an addiction; failure to honor the new values. All of these are potential situations for more pinning. And each of us has our own individual points of vulnerability that we have to bring to consciousness.

In this period of descent—one, three, seven years, less or more—genuine courage and strength are required. The more the ego strives for consciousness, the more the resistances on the other side of the pendulum claw us down into the black pit of paralysis, especially if an addiction is involved. Again, the intensity of idealization will be uncannily balanced by the depth of the black hole, which the dreams keep repeating until they are brought to conscious understanding. The addictive object is holding magnetic power because it represents life itself. After all, what is a party without alcohol, or New Year's Eve without cocaine, or reading without a cancer-caressing cigarette?

Anyone in the twelve-step program of Alcoholics Anonymous knows the crises that occur in this time of descent. There is a yearning for what I call pig consciousness—wallowing in mud and loving it. Mud, mud, glorious mud—totally unconscious matter where no discipline is demanded. At the same time, the opposite pulls toward impossible perfection. Repressed energies begin to surface from the shut-down body. And they have to be released if the new energy is going to rise rich and free from the pelvic floor.

Here again, psychic laws have to be acknowledged. In normal circumstances, the psyche moves in its own time to protect itself. It does not, for example, bring up a severe trauma until the conscious container that has to receive that painful material is strong enough and flexible enough to contain the material without shattering. So long as no one is attempting to engineer the process, the psyche will ebb to and fro until the ego is strong enough and the body is strong enough to deal with the early pain.

The problems that can come up in this period are as many as we are individuals. This is the end of performance between partners and the beginning of terrifying risks. Most people have been performing since they were tiny children. They don't know there's any other way to live except for the voice inside that's saying, "If this is it, it's not worth living." One of the saddest cries I ever heard came from a woman I met in a workshop. She suddenly jumped up and cried out, "My husband of twenty-five years left me. As he was going out the door, I realized he never knew me."

The values you have lived by are taken away. You don't know the new questions, and certainly not the answers. Partners feel they don't know each other, maybe don't like each other, certainly couldn't make love to each other. Sexuality is totally awry.

As projections are pulled back, the sense of loss is breathtaking. A man who has projected—and given away—his soul to a beloved woman may find himself alone. He has created a symbiotic relationship with her and in her leaving he experiences loss of soul. He will experience himself as a zombie until he pulls back the projections and realizes what he has projected is the beloved within himself.

This is a time of hard, slow work, a time of aloneness. Projections are being pulled back, forcing us to look at our own forsaken shadow. We wonder if we were stark mad to let so much go. Still, sometimes in these days, we give ourselves over to our imagination, let it live, let it play. We paint, we dialogue with our journal, we dance, we make music—all those things the soul loves. New things are being given. And we do go on.

In the Descent, the two worlds—conscious and unconscious—do not freely interact unless particular attention is paid. Some people in descent tend to fear and reject the world of their unconscious and, therefore, fall right into it. Others work very hard to capture their dreams. They are a source of light in the darkness. Their imagery brings the feast the soul so desperately needs. A theme that brings great comfort is replayed in many different images. It brings comfort because it says to the dreamer, "You are not alone. I am working as faithfully as you."

In dreams of descent, the setting may be a jungle through which the dreamer has to cut his way, leaf by huge leaf, with no idea where he is going. He passes black hole after black hole. Eventually, his clothes torn, his body bleeding and exhausted, he arrives at a river. He rejoices, but then he sees a jungle on the other side. He knows he can go no farther. Then he notices a path just like his own through the forest on the other side. Someone who knows far more than he, Someone who greatly loves him is working very hard on the other side. All he has to do is build the connecting bridge.

Most of us go through "The Descent" more than once in our lives. At different ages, different power-heads are dismantled with very different results. Since this is our hero's first descent, let us look more closely at the adolescent initiation. Ivan, like most young men in our culture, has no spiritual heritage into which his elders are going to welcome him. On his own, he does glimpse the treasure three times.

The Maiden Tsar is the golden maiden who initiates Ivan's journey. At this stage, naturally, he projects divinity onto her, a plutonium-charged energy of sexuality and spirituality. However, he is pinned, his body is numbed, he has no support and no strong container of his own. The Maiden Tsar is too radiant for him. The repressed energy is released too fast; he cannot integrate it. All he can experience is the sense of betrayal of his love and the accompanying shame. The energy falls back into his unconscious. Similarly, many contemporary adolescents who have had a glimpse of what love could be, or what freedom from a rigid system could be, cannot deal with the loss of possibility. Their energy has surged for a moment and they have failed to rise to it. They are alone in overwhelming conflict. Chaos is not balanced with creativity. Their despair carries a very serious death wish. Their radiant soul has been abandoned in a waste land.

In my experience teaching adolescents and working with anorexia, I have felt the adolescent despair. With no understanding of ritual, they have no way to create sacred space. They are imprisoned in literalism and, therefore, many cannot tell the difference between actual death and ritual death. They want things as they are to end. From some primitive depth, they understand transformation requires a sacrifice. It is no small task to convince anorexics that their life is not the sacrifice necessary to move from stagnation into new life. Without connection to their own soul, their dreams incarcerate them in concentration camps. Until they find the connection between consciousness and the unconscious, they are in the grip of their tutor guards.

I have seen similar dreams at the midlife initiation. A man dreams that he and his son are driving together and his son begins to tell him of being thrown into jail at the age of sixteen. The father knows nothing of this. At the age of sixty, he has to try to figure out what part of himself was jailed at the age of sixteen, befriend him, dialogue with him, and initiate him into manhood. Grief for his own lost life is released and contained within a container strong enough to perceive and receive the rejected rebel. The dreamer is now able to take responsibility for unpinning the energies of his sixteen-year-old.

This jailed rebel often appears in women's dreams as well. Arrogant as he is, he still carries primal energy because he went to jail very young, determined never to bow down to a patriarchal structure he did not respect. If this fellow can be loved into civilization, he may become the most creative energy in the woman's psyche. Even the Christ within.[2]

The dark night of the soul can descend at any age and release very young energy, depending on when stepmother and tutor pinned it. A woman in her fifties realized she was feeling totally incompetent. At the same time she knew from her dreams that she was connecting with her own life force. The newest character in her dreams was a three-year-old girl determined to take over mastery in her psyche. The woman was raging with anger, toxic in her cells. Her primitive shadow was a feral animal. "I annihilated myself at three," she said. "I tried to please everybody else. My life still depends on people liking me. If they do not receive what I have to offer, I cease to exist. I annihilate myself. I try so hard to give the right gift. Even my dog knows its own desires. I do not. Nobody related to me when I was young. Though I was with them all the time and accepted their expensive presents, they did not see me. I feel myself now in exquisite torture. I am drooling and lubricating. I am nothing; I am everything. I am concentration. I am rage. I am a sexual woman." Her inner child whom she annihilated at the age of three, reentered her dream life on Christmas Day. That child is no Barbie Doll.

Ivan's descent is completed in less than a sentence in our story, but he has accomplished a great deal in constructing a strong container for himself. When he arrives at the nadir of his descent—the little hut of the Baba Yaga—he has learned how to conduct himself in order to survive, and he is not afraid.

The Baba Yaga

If only it were all so simple! If only there were evil people somewhere insidiously committing evil deeds, and it were necessary only to separate them from the rest of us and destroy them. But the line dividing good and evil cuts through the heart of every human being. And who is willing to destroy a piece of his own heart?

Alexander Solzhenitsyn

Ivan's wanderings through ten or twenty, perhaps thirty years take him to the hovels of three Baba Yagas, the three-in-one Dark Mother, the dark side of the Good Mother. In so far as possible, our culture avoids what these Babas personify, but Eastern Europe and the Far East use the honorific "Baba" to mean "Reverend One" or "Grandmother" or "Holy Teacher." Ivan meets these three when he has lived his own isolation and searched long enough to undergo what might be called a midlife initiation. Of course, each of us moves at our own time on our own journey with the "divinity that shapes our ends,/Rough-hew them how we will."[1] Sooner or later, we meet the Baba Yaga, and how we deal with her will determine whether we remain frightened children or mature into adults, or even whether we live or die.

Traditionally, one Baba or three sisters eat naive people, people who think life should bring them only happiness. To the uninitiated, suffering is not acceptable. Their thinking is dualistic—white or black, good or evil, science or religion. They can't hold opposites as complementary energies. Their masculinity and femininity are nowhere near the inner marriage.

Meeting the Baba Yaga is the test in which all that we have accepted is challenged. She has certain rules of behavior: she has to be honored; her food has to be eaten. We are suddenly thrown out of our own milieu into the darkest corner of the forest in order to recognize who she is and who we are in relation to her. Dealing with her requires that we be in touch with our own life force, or that we find it very fast. Her ferocity does not allow for namby-pamby behavior.

Anyone who has been brought to her little hut, turning on a chicken leg and been able to stay awake knows that this meeting is the pivotal point in life. In this place, there is no cover-up. Either we look her in the eye or we go to sleep until we meet her uglier sister. If we are able to stay awake, look her in the eye, and answer her questions without being gobbled up, we may continue on to the ugliest of the three and there we meet death/life straight on. Either we stay awake and face our truth by accepting what food she has to offer—biting into it, chewing it, swallowing it, incorporating it, and making it part of ourselves, knowing in our bones the meaning of her questions—or she eats us up. What does that look like? She possesses us and we eat or drink or smoke or drive ourselves to death.

Why does she have to feed her guest and why does he eat her food? There are laws of civility in dealing with these sacred energies. They expect companionship (taking bread with), a sharing of energy that becomes forever a part of whoever partakes. Persephone, for example, after she has eaten a pomegranate seed in the underworld, can never go back to stay with her mother. While this energy belongs to the archetypal world, it enhances the human one.

The Baba is interested in the bones and the blood, key symbols for the life force. In the shamanic tradition, the initiate fasts until he or she is almost skeletal in an attempt to go back to original purity. This symbolism is very important in anorexia nervosa, in which the patient is blindly attempting to find his or her own *I am,* free of the too-much-matter Mother. The blood corpuscles are made in the bone marrow, so that the life energy, the authenticity, the soul level is in the bones. The concept of incorporating the god or goddess by taking in symbolic food is a most sacred ritual in most religions, and fundamental in the compulsive drive of an addict in perverted eating rituals.

Why is an understanding of this dark goddess of creation so important in our culture right now? Essentially, we do not want to deal with the dark side of the feminine—none of us, men or women. We do not want to feel ourselves being pulled into her devouring maw, swirling and being swirled deeper and faster into her vortex, with no way to control the chaos through which we are plunging. Yet as we face the end of the millennium, we are faced with her activity in every dimension of our lives. Individually, our relationships are in upheaval and our health may be precarious; culturally, our moral and ethical frameworks are collapsing, throwing us into stress; environmentally, we are dealing with the wrath of the Mother in earthquakes, floods, hurricanes, as well as global warming, the hole in the ozone layer and the many other manifestations of her rage at our transgressions. So long as we pin ourselves in the neck, the chaos is either numbed out or becomes less endurable because it is more meaningless. If in our arrogant innocence we can learn from older cultures that respect the Baba Yaga, we can find some meaning in the chaos that is erupting at our very center.

Moreover, our willingness to face the Baba is our chance to grow up. Until she is encountered consciously, the values she teaches cannot be learned. We are facing her unconsciously in addictions, for example, but because we have no cultural myth to understand what we are dealing with, most of us are obliterated or obliterate ourselves through our compulsion. We come out of the experience either angry or asking, "Why me?" We try to believe that she does not exist, that we are miracle babies born to be happy, never to die, and prosperity is our right to life. Nothing ugly, destructive, death-dealing exists, and, if it does, we dress it up to look alive.

The Death Goddess does exist. We are meeting her every day in the parts of us that need to die in order for new life to come in. We meet her in our lost job, our lost marriage, our lost loved one, our lost youth. So long as we are hostile to her, she is hostile to us. Our either/or thinking exacerbates our agony because we are trapped with no third possibility able to arise unless we can hold the tension of the opposites until they transform. Courtesy, accepting the hospitality of the Baba Yaga, eating what she offers is a third possibility.

Perfection polarizes the world, makes life impossible to live. Our ideals, including our ideals of swanlike beauty, keep us constantly projecting anger onto our imperfect bodies, her territory. Women and men increasingly focus on body as enemy. That attitude constellates the energies of the Dark Mother (Dark Mater), making her retaliate with symptoms that may force us into dialogue with her. That dialogue can bring her sufficiently into our consciousness that we are not obliterated by fear of death.

In a relationship, all may go well until the power of "I desire" of the Great Mother surfaces, and the partners are exhilarated by the energy of the new sexuality. Once the primal energy begins to swirl them into the vortex, they may panic and project onto each other the gaping maw that will swallow them whole. People with a stepmother and/or absent-father complex have to be especially careful at this point. Their personal experience of having to fend for their life will quickly swirl around them. They fear being sucked alive into the vortex. The Death Mother is capable of doing just that if consciousness is not present. So long as that potential for terror is at the center of a relationship, no solid base exists. The closer the intimacy, the deeper the "I desire," the more the Baba files her teeth. Conscious willpower and counseling cannot stop the unconscious terror. Until partners can see what they are projecting onto each other and begin a dialogue with their own inner Baba—paint her, dance her, even fight with her—the relationship cannot move onto a deeper level.

Allowing the imagery to come through us is allowing the new energy to come through in a contained way. If our own ego strength is not strong enough to contain it, then we need to find someone to give us temporary support. Connecting with that energy is going to open all the instincts. Jung understood the instincts to be creativity, religion, aggression, sexuality, hunger (easily remembered by the mnemonic device "CRASH"). Anyone working with this energy understands why Baba is the "Revered One." In painting, for example, her energy begins to pour through our body and paint, until the swirl we were so afraid might devour us becomes the swirl that is moving our arm, choosing our colors, creating what we were afraid to see. As our body and psyche become stronger, we can dare to surrender more and more to her creative chaos. There we find multitudinous seeds of possibility. The energy begins to move from the unconscious into our conscious totality. We no longer need to project terror and blame onto our partner. Our focus is on transforming the terror and blame in ourselves.

That doesn't mean there won't be skirmishes. Of course, there will be. As two people are casting off their illusions and performances, both are in for great surprises. In surrendering, tears will flow for the unlived life, the partner, the tutor, the stepmother. Out of the rage and grief and fear comes the forgiveness. And the love.

What does that look like in life? Here I am compelled to forsake theory and speak from my own experience. I know these Babas well enough to recognize when their 100,000 volts are rumbling in my body. That's when they will be obeyed. Do I come to this place of my own free will or do I come by compulsion?

In 1968, I decided I had to get out of the warm comforters of my sleepy Canadian city to find out if I was alive underneath their coziness. I was secure in my schoolteacher efficiency and my theater arts creativity; I was equally secure as the wife of my husband professor. Part of me clung to the sweetness of that gentle Our Town I knew so well. "Will Charlie be invited to the wedding? Will June go, if he comes? Will Mrs. Davis be pouring at the minister's reception? George isn't handling his alcohol well at all." No, I did not want to leave any of that humanity. But I couldn't breathe my own breath. I didn't speak my own voice. Everything in me wanted to live before I died, whatever that meant. Did I leave of my own free will or did I leave by compulsion?

And did I arrive at my destination, the ashram in Pondicherry where I hoped to be surrounded by spiritual teachers who would guide me to Reality? No. Instead I collapsed with amoebic dysentery and had to stay in the hotel focused on my own excrement and the dozens of monsoon-drenched black crows on my balcony. In the silence of my room, I lay for days on a cot reading aloud my passport, repeating my own name, my birth date into this world just to be sure I wasn't in the other. And when the death messengers on my balcony seemed to be coming into my room, I recited Shakespearean sonnets or the New Testament to the cockroaches. I had to live in the poetry I loved to bring some meaning into the chaos or go stark mad. "And Death once dead, there's no more dying then"[2] echoed contrapuntally with "Peace I leave with you, my peace I give unto you; not as the world giveth, give I unto you."[3]

As the raw truth in those exquisite lines cascaded over my body, I could feel a new order exerting itself. I could see hope even in the macabre crows. I could feel peace—the peace that passeth understanding[4]—and I could trust the love of God would either let me live or let me die. In surrendering my fears of annihilation, I entered my own life.

And when I got up from my cot and dared the streets of Calcutta, beauty had a new meaning. Beauty was now stark Reality—the beauty of the children's tiny fingers clutching my skirt, the buzzards in the black trees at sunset waiting to descend on a dying cow, teeming life thrusting in every direction. Barbers shaving genitals, aged ones dying on the six feet of sidewalk they shared with their family, eight-year-olds carrying dead babies—all of this in the midst of emaciated cows, pariah dogs, furtive monkeys. Was I "led all that way for/Birth or Death"?[5] This was life being lived from the blood, from the bone, and death within it.

I never saw anything in luxurious Canada the same again. Life here was buried under layers of makeup, too many gadgets, too much niceness, too much bureaucracy, too much too much too much to take care of. And life itself was slipping away in petty quarrels, longtime diversions—in the light of eternity, meaningless bric-a-brac. Did I come back of my own free will or did I come by compulsion?

I journeyed to my second Baba Yaga as I midwifed a dear friend into life beyond this one. After years, months, weeks, of watching the gradual ravaging of cancer, we were in the final days. We had an excellent hospital room—every amenity, clean warm sheets, several machines. We had arrived at the place where pretense was sacrilege. Love pulsed in the silence of swabbing parched lips and gently, so gently, changing soft diapers on the skeletal body. Love pulsed too in the silent prayer we prayed as we watched the ugly tumor growing hour by hour around the beloved neck. In words that "lie too deep for tears,"[6] we prayed for whatever mercy existed that Death would come before strangulation. That's the ugliness of the Baba Yaga. And the glory. Never before had I experienced love so shimmering, energy so pure, life so precious. Here, at the center of the best that science could offer, the best that human compassion could give, was the murderous tumor that nobody could do anything to control. Here was the mystery the two of us dared, as Blake's Tyger burned bright in the forest of that night:

> *What immortal hand or eye*
> *Dare frame thy fearful symmetry?*[7]

Were we surrendering to Birth or Death? Did we come all this way of our own free will or did we come by compulsion?

I came upon my third Baba Yaga in my own encounter with death-in-life, cancer. Looking the Death Goddess in the eye, experiencing the cold terror of annihilation in the same breath as the exhilaration of release from human agony, I stood by the window in the darkness of night breathing in the fragrance of our garden, aware that death would end my ever smelling roses again, end my seeing white lilies by moonlight, end the gentle love calls of the doves. End me. Or release me into what mystery? Knowing—yes—knowing I had come all this way of my own free will. I was exactly where I wanted to be, needed *to be* in this exact moment. And yes, I was compelled to be here. Life/Death, God/Nothing, Faith/Doubt had stripped me. Yes, stripped me into the freedom of cronedom.

The Baba Yaga's stripping releases our essence. "Essence" is from the Latin verb *esse,* to be. Essence is our Beingness, our *I am,* our soul. We all meet the Dark Mother sooner or later and she wrings from us our essence. We wonder, we really wonder, "Is there a God? Is there a loving God? Is there an all-loving, all-powerful God? If there is, how could such a God allow this?" Yet, here in the heart of matter, she, Goddess, *is.*

Encountering her is an initiation into wholeness, into a maturity that burns away infantile baggage. In dreams we cross the border into a new land. We leave behind our clutter, our father's old car, our mother's sweater, our childhood licorice-framed glasses, and our overflowing toilets. Having passed customs, we may find ourselves operating a nuclear power plant or controlling a laser knife. If we do not cross over, we are suddenly dealing with nuclear bombs, plutonium fallout, and laser-guided warheads. Such images suggest that in consciousness, we have not been able to leave behind our old habits and cherished complexes. The new energy has come in and been blocked, creating anger, bitterness, rage in the unconscious. At this point in body work, powerful releases may occur. It is important to recognize whether anger, for example, is coming from childhood release or from blocking new energy. So long as we cannot bring to consciousness what energy our scream or dream is, old patterns and old images continually repeat.

If we are able to connect with our inner world, we grow up and find our true parents in the great Mystery, no matter what name we give it. Growing up is accepting the darkness within us, as it is in everyone. Until we can accept that responsibility, we will go on blaming the other sex, our parents, other countries, other religions, the environment, the dog.

In our story, Ivan in his search for the idealized feminine is confronted with the reality of matter. The Baba threatens him in his head, heart, body. At this threshold in life, people trained in patriarchy who idealize intellectual order, controlled passion, physical hygiene are thrown into terrifying chaos. People like Ivan, women and men, who idealize the perfection of the feminine are faced with its opposite. The archetype has two sides, and if we blind ourselves to the side we don't wish to see, it paradoxically appears before us in compensating horror or beauty.

Ivan sets up that polarization. It must also be said that he was working hard on himself during his descent or he would not have escaped so easily from the Baba's maw. What might have been going on during those fifteen or twenty years, yearning for that perfect Maiden Tsar? He was probably embroiled in impossible relationships because he expected too much. His body was probably shut down or playing Don Juan as he attempted to pull his own masculinity out from the negative stepmother. Because he never said good-bye to her, she was still sitting like lead in his cells. He has no doubt been through loss, loss deep enough to pull him out of polarization. He knows better than to speak from a polarized either/or when he is talking to the feminine, which abhors polarity. Both/and is her vision. He has let go of the tutor's philosophy before he arrives at her hut.

Hopefully, my beloved Canada will pull out the tutor's pin before it is too late. We are known as the best country in the world to live in, but we are stuck in polarities. And we are asleep there. During the Quebec referendum vote of 1995, most of us were glued to our television sets writhing in terror as the little dial went back and forth between *Non* and *Oui,* just over fifty, just under, and finally settling just over. We all woke up for a few days, but we have gone back to sleep. Two magnificent cultures enhance each other, cannot live without each other, complement each other exquisitely, and yet archaic thinking and bombastic rhetoric never cease to point out the seeming oppositions. If the citizens fail to hold the complements as one, we will lose our country. Is it not blind stupidity for two cultures at the end of this millennium with planetary consciousness in the wings, two cultures whose citizens love and respect each other, to break apart because the feminine both/and is too futuristic?

Canada, like so many other countries, is struggling to enter a third possibility in which polarization becomes an opening to otherness that contains within it the realization that the acceptance of otherness, including our own otherness, is the essential condition for the global unity upon which our very survival now depends.

Ivan's both/and has taken him into the Baba Yaga, the creative matrix that holds diversity in unity out of which new life comes. In the fullness of time, when we are strong enough, we are taken to her in one way or another. Dealing with her gives us our life, if we stay conscious. No sense in pushing it. The soul has its own time. *Kairos*, it is called, when divine and human paths meet at the crossroads. Any ritual before that is melodrama. Our task is to hold the tension of the opposites, allowing the transformation to happen. Even as the caterpillar is in constant transformation in the chrysalis, so we are moved into a new place of possibility. From this perspective, time with the Baba Yaga is grace.

Initiations always produce thresholds in dreams. As we move from one room into another, we cannot know what is on the other side. Thresholds in hospitals are awesome. Knowing that life as we have lived it is over and something unknown is to be born is the threshold of growth.

The Baba questions, "Are you here of your own free will or by compulsion?" If that question is falling on patriarchal ears, it will resonate with old splits that deny her existence in the world and in the psyche. That throws her into devouring rage. She wants our thinking head on a stake. She wants more, more, more, which we unconsciously act out. If, on the other hand, we are sufficiently mature, we answer honestly, "I'm here partly because I lived my life the way I wanted to live it (maybe by compulsion), and partly because God and you grabbed me by the scruff of my neck and pushed me here (maybe of my own free will)." She loves paradox. Her lesson is to surrender to what looks utterly irrational to a linear mind. She makes no allowances for lying, self-pity, sins of omission. Our ego has to surrender consciously to her divine plan.

Many contemporary parents find themselves on that razor's edge of growth with their young adult children. Suddenly they are perceived as devourers and, therefore, unworthy of communication. They know that if they attempt to speak to their children, they will be rejected and fall into a pit of grief. If they don't speak, they will be consumed by their own aloneness and their children's. The unconscious devourer is devouring the whole household. Hearts are being eaten out as the impasse holds adamant.

The catalyst for possible transformation is the Baba Yaga. She would have them recognize that, whether it makes head sense or not, both have to surrender their ego positions, go into their own human heart, accept their own human imperfection, and sacrifice their stubbornness or whatever it is that is cutting them off from their own bloodstream. That transition has to come from the heart, or the ego will yet again puncture the soul. Quantities of Baba Yaga's food will be bitten off, swallowed, and digested before such a transition can happen because the tension is bewildering and terrifying to experience. Giving up ego desire and willpower feels like choosing powerlessness, and surrendering to soul is a leap into some unknown dark. Mad self-destruction! The negative complexes are clinging to the past: the new energy is forging ahead. Without that tension, the old bottles will never be shattered by new wine.

The ego's power stance has to be sacrificed by parents and children. The Baba Yaga demands the surrender of willpower. When that is acknowledged, she is no longer perceived as good or evil. When the rage has been expressed and the tears shed, she can be recognized as the life force that is forever renewing itself, life moving through everything. What does not move dies. Death in the service of life. That is the Baba Yaga. She *is*. She burns us in her hottest flames to purify us of all that is not us. She can bring parents and children to the place where they can look into each other's eyes and see their own shadow, often the very best that is in them, unlived.

She can do the same thing in women's groups where the energy that has been so supportive begins to turn hostile, so hostile that the members have migraines or nausea before every meeting. As women begin to find their own empowerment, the stepmother in some will raise her pointed finger and snarl, "Power. You are trying to take control. You are falling back into patriarchy." Then everyone in the group has to look at her dreams to check whether the new energy is coming from power or empowerment, from free will or compulsion. The Baba Yaga is requiring stark honesty from everyone. Without it, the Stepmother will destroy the burgeoning new feminine just when she is about to step into her own magnificent strength—the Conscious Virgin uncontaminated and strong enough to live her truth. This can happen in mixed groups, or among men attempting to experience their femininity in balance with their healthy and secure masculinity. It is sad to see men and women who have worked so hard to transform stepmother energy tricked into betrayal of one another at the very moment of birth into their authenticity. The Baba Yaga energy would strip them to the gut level, pushing with nature in labor to release that new baby into life.

The Baba Yaga strips Lear on the heath and tears him to shreds in the fangs of his wolf daughter, Goneril, and his fox daughter,

Regan. And as he labors to distill his sanity from his insanity, she returns the soul child he once exiled in a fit of rage. He takes his daughter in his arms and says,

Upon such sacrifices, my Cordelia,
The gods themselves throw incense.[8]

And every heart that has ever trembled on that heath beats with anguish and forgiveness for human folly. Tears of love fall.

The Baba Yaga is not the same as the Stepmother with a different voltage. It is true that in trying to bring these energies to consciousness, we may experience both as directionless. Even the Baba's house moves in a circle balancing on a chicken leg. It is a frightening time because the very energy we have developed in order to survive is the same energy we are being asked by the Baba to surrender. We experience her voice and the voice of the Stepmother as the same voice enticing us into a swirl. "You're never going to be free. How did you get yourself into this mess? There's no way out. It's your blood and your bones that I want." If, however, we listen with more discernment, there is a subtle, crucial difference. The Stepmother does not serve life. Her motives serve selfish goals; they block creativity and end up in paralysis. She is life in the service of death. The Baba Yaga is death in the service of life. She is impersonal. She does not care what lives, what dies. Her motive in her decisions is to serve life. The Stepmother is the pitch-black side of the negative mother that annihilates. The Baba Yaga is the light in the darkness, the life force that is always transforming, always evolving, always sacrificing for the new that will be born.

Once we begin to honor her, we begin to move our ego position from a subjective to a more objective view of life. So long as we are totally in life, we feel ourselves involved in the tragedy. Once we move to a more objective position where we can both be in life and look at ourselves being in life, we can hold the perspective of the clown. Then we can see ourselves as part of the Divine Comedy.

Ivan is able, in part, to hold an objective position. He can eat her food, answer her question, and engage in dialogue with her. He can have reverence for her mystery. If, like Ivan, we can stay with the soul position in relating to her, we can gradually let go of the ego position whenever we wish. We can face her paradox and hold a position of waiting. The longer we live, the more we accept her mystery, or we become bitter and reject life.

Sometimes in workshops, I become too intense describing the blows the Baba Yagas can aim at us. Robert chirps from behind, "Nothing personal, you understand." Everyone laughs with relief, including me. Still, I've noticed recently, when a fearsome blow comes my way, I hear that little chirp, "Nothing personal, you understand." And I know that I am not singled out for punishment: I am simply part of her larger scheme. "Nothing personal" moves me from victim caterpillar to acquiescent butterfly.

The Three Horns

The number three in relationship to the feminine has to do with life, death, rebirth. The Goddess herself usually appears in threes—the wyrd sisters in *Macbeth;* the three horns; the Mother, Virgin, Crone trinity. The number three in dreams usually means something is going to cross the threshold into consciousness. One, two, three, go. Something happens.

Perhaps with the first Baba we are paralyzed with terror. Maybe with the second we play victim a bit. But then we begin to realize we are playing victim and, if we're ever going to get out, we're bloody well going to take responsibility for ourselves and move. On the third chance, we're ready to blow, ready to blow the pin out of our neck. And we're going to blow with our own voice if the firebird is going to come. Of course, when we blow we have no idea what may come. Because Ivan has already been through two initiatory preparations, he has the courage and strength to deal with what emerges. We have to remember the divine is not necessarily kind and supportive. It can be terrifying as well.

Now Ivan can blow the horns. We need to note that it is the Baba Yagas who have made his journey to the third Baba possible, and the third Baba does not refuse him the horns. He does as he was told to do and blows gently in the beginning. When we're finding our voice for the first time it is the better part of wisdom to open our throat gently, let the energy from our body come forth gently into the outer world. Remember, he is in the creative matrix, supported by the Baba Yaga, but he is not sure of his connection to the life force.

Like Ivan without that grounding, people in a body workshop have no idea what is going to come through their open throat when the pin is out. All they never said, the grief of their body, jealousy, anger, and shame, plus the grief of generations and the planet's grief may be in there—everything the Baba Yaga symbolizes. More than that, when the throat chakra opens, the sexual chakra also opens. If too much is released too fast, psychosis is a real danger. The breath of life reaching deep into the body opens the closed-down resonators, bringing the bodysoul back to life. The soul is in the anguished cries. The feminine side of God is crying. At the end of the session, painting, dancing, or sculpting embodies the image that may have appeared in the voice work. In this way, what has been going on in the body is brought to consciousness. Without that final concentration, the energy would fall back into the unconscious and repeatedly come forth, until sufficiently integrated. The dreams that come following the workshop are invaluable in revealing the connection between the complexes and the pinned jaw.

⋆ PART III ⋆

The Firebird

In the meeting with the third Baba Yaga, by blowing the horn, Ivan finally opens his whole Being to the breath of inspiration. By reconnecting to the Baba matrix, Ivan is strong enough to blow out the pin. He opens his connectors right through his body. **"Suddenly birds of all kinds swarmed about him, among them the firebird. 'Sit upon me quickly,' said the firebird, 'and we shall fly wherever you want; if you don't come with me, the Baba Yaga will devour you.' "** The firebird is aroused from chaos.

Let us imagine this magnificent bird. In Russian pictures, the firebird is red with flaming breast and wisps of flame coming from its head and tail—living fire energy. Like the phoenix rising from its own ashes, it comes out of the devouring maw of matter as the rescuer of spirit, the indestructible energy that is the essence of matter. This theme is echoed in the story of the Medusa, the Gorgon whose ugliness and writhing-snake locks turned those who looked upon her to stone (the pitch-black shadow of the Baba Yaga). When Perseus struck off her head with his sword, two horses flew like firebirds out of her neck: Pegasus, the flying horse of creativity, and Chrysaor, he of the golden sword. Medusa had been pregnant and part of her rage may have been her inability to release these horses into life. Her inability to give birth came from being locked in her head, cut off from her body, as Ivan was locked in the head of the tutor before he beheaded him. In both cases, release was brought about by the act of beheading.

As the newly released form of pent-up energy, the flaming bird is the transformation of "I desire" as instinctual energy into "I desire" as spiritual energy. The coming of the bird is comparable to the first time the explosive energy locked up in the atom was unleashed, an event that permanently transformed our understanding of matter, and our relationship to life on the planet.

The transformation of instinctual energy into spiritual energy does not involve the sacrifice of instinct, but rather a refinement of instinct. By means of his flight on the firebird, which brings him ultimately to the Maiden Tsar, Ivan's instinct begins to be refined beyond the level of sexual greed that might have kept him bound to his stepmother.

We all relate to a fairy story from where we rumble the most as we read it. That's probably where we are in life. It's like a Rorschach test. Am I pinned by the tutor? Am I possessed by the stepmother? Am I in descent? Am I in the hut of the Baba Yaga? Am I flying on the firebird?

If you are on the firebird, you may have already discovered some of its shadow side. Like the pendulum swinging, the firebird is going to carry Ivan further into the positive side than ever before, and, therefore, open him to a greater possibility of despair. So long as he holds his connection to his body, he can find a place midway on that swing where he remains still and allows the pendulum to swing through. Then he may say to himself, "Despair is in me. I am not despair. This shall pass," or "I am in love. I am madly in love. But I am not love. This too shall pass."

I don't think Ivan has reached this stage of maturity yet, because the firebird is not able to take him the full way to the thrice tenth kingdom. To me that three times ten suggests a tripling of the unity of the one, which implies a profoundly well-balanced body and psyche. Can you imagine the presence in the body that is required to support the influx of spirit, when spirit is the firebird? Saul, on the road to Damascus to kill Christians, was knocked down and blinded when the firebird visited him. Many artists, poets, and musicians are visited by a firebird and some do not survive: Emily Brontë, Sylvia Plath, Dylan Thomas, Mark Rothke, Janis Joplin.

Having worked with the psyche/soma connection for years, I have seen many people dealing with both firebird energy and kundalini energy, which is the snake energy coming from the core. This topic cannot be dealt with adequately here, but it may be of value to point out that when these energies are activated in the body, a profound shift occurs, as if Rolls-Royce energy were suddenly racing through a Volkswagen. When this happens, the receiver needs to honor it and ask some questions that she or he has never asked before. The body parts will respond to questions. Lower back pain, pain in the chest, pain in the hip joint—any of these can be engaged in dialogue and their answers can bring understanding of what is happening in the cells. This is what I call bringing the body to consciousness—becoming the energy released by the firebird that as conscious *mater* (mother) carries the soul. These answers may be like the feathers clutched from the firebird by the Baba Yaga as Ivan is flying off on its back, feathers clutched from spirit into matter. We have to be careful not to hold on to one so hard that we miss the next one drifting by. This would be returning to the old pattern of being compulsively driven by will power into a life that is no longer a birthright, a gift to be enjoyed. Life keeps opening and changing, but if we have come from a place of being "numbed out," this process seems miraculous, something to be clutched.

Thematically, the story deals with freedom and compulsion, the flight to freedom out of compulsion. The three horns are the instruments of the transition. The paradox still holds in the clutching of the feathers: freedom is not flight, if it remains, in part, bound to compulsion. The Baba Yaga does catch some feathers. Full flight without any compulsion would be pure spirit. As in life, the unconscious feminine is bound to nature, and nature is bound to the laws that govern it; the masculine as spirit would fly out of life. To fly off on the firebird would be to fly into death.

The danger lies in hubris, ascending beyond the human limit by sacrificing instinct to pure spirit, like Icarus flying too close to the sun and falling into a bottomless ocean of unconsciousness. If we think of pure spirit, symbolized by the sun, as masculine, we can see that, released from the feminine, the masculine spirit is death. The feminine is what holds the masculine in life.

This conflict/paradox becomes clearer with an illustration. We can speak of the healing of an addiction as the rescuing of the soul from the dark womb of the chthonic mother. The chthonic mother is the purely instinctual mother imprisoning her child in physical bonding. It is her energy that takes possession of the ego in the addiction. The rescuer is an infusion of spirit, which, far from robbing the feminine of its chthonic ground, is bringing it to consciousness. The freeing of the soul from addiction is the birth of the Divine Child, the second birth. The soul free of addiction, inhabiting its own body, is matter living its own released energy, the partnership of conscious feminine and conscious masculine. From this perspective, the treatment of an addiction is an initiation rite, the archetypal image of which is the Conscious Virgin, impregnated by Spirit, giving birth to the Divine Child.

When either partner in a relationship taps into these huge energies, a time of crisis will surely erupt. The one who is in the midst of the transformational experience is desperately trying to hold to sanity and does not need criticism or anger or fear from the partner to compound the difficulties. Energy released from the toxicity of the parental complexes, from the drugs of addiction and inertia, is not energy for immature people. This is energy that can tear oneself and other people apart. It doesn't necessarily come out as rage. It is more likely to be a stark statement of truth that quietly cuts through to the heart of everything that is dishonest in the relationship. This is the place where the truth can set us free if we can hear it and if we can be free. Grief and shame and guilt will out, and, in the releasing, unite splits that previously we had been unable to heal.

One of those splits that is deep in our culture and deep in our story is the Virgin/Whore split. Men and women raised in the Judeo-Christian tradition find living both the idealized feminine and passionate sexuality in one relationship difficult. It is easier to keep the Virgin Mary and Mary Magdalene living in two separate houses. However, when this fire ignites the flesh, the Maiden Tsar energy and the Baba Yaga are no longer polarized. In dreams, the Virgin and the Whore can look into each other's eyes and not only love each other, but be each other. What a shock this is in a relationship! If one partner has moved further along the path than the other, this may be a time of required celibacy. Both have to hold fierce patience and keep their eyes on the ultimate goal.

Psychologically, the profound shift that has taken place is the release of the son from the stepmother complex. This applies not only to men, but also to women releasing their masculinity from the inertia of passivity. In our story, Ivan has faced the pitch-black aspect of the Baba Yaga energy. He has been able to engage it in dialogue without being possessed by it. He can *relate* to it without *identifying* with it. Now he knows what freedom can be, and while he will have to fight to maintain it, he knows what he is fighting for—his own manhood. This is the masculine that can be a partner strong enough for the Maiden Tsar, the Conscious Virgin. Most men and women have to free their young masculine from its infantile yearning for security in order to release it from its passivity into its own creative power. Too often in a relationship, an unconscious collusion is holding the couple in a mother/child symbiotic bond that prevents either from moving into mature empowerment. Dependency is not love. An encounter with the Baba Yaga releases us into totally new dimensions of love.

The firebird is not strong enough, or perhaps too strong, to carry Ivan over the broad sea to the thrice tenth kingdom on the other shore. Ivan thanks the bird (the civility of honoring the unconscious) and walks along the shore. He has more work to do before he can find his Maiden Tsar.

The Crone

Ivan **"walked and walked till he came to a little hut."** How many years are in "walked and walked"! During that time, he has civilized the energy of the Baba Yaga into crone energy, not that the Baba will never again appear, but in the crone her wisdom is less volcanic. Taming that energy takes years of conscious living and conscious sacrifice. To be able to speak directly from center with an honesty that clarifies even as it horrifies is the genius of the clown, who is very much a part of the crone. Many aging people have this quality, sometimes consciously, sometimes unconsciously. Robert and I sometimes launch into singing this greatest of crone songs with the sheer exuberance of two old crones:

> *An agéd man is but a paltry thing,*
> *A tattered coat upon a stick, unless*
> *Soul clap its hands and sing, and louder sing*
> *For every tatter in its mortal dress.*[1]

The journey to cronedom begins with a commitment to finding one's own life. It has nothing to do with a fast leap into enlightenment. Cronedom is based on the solid work of a lifetime. Gradually, over the years, the commitment loses its push-pull quality. It no longer comes from ego desire. Rather, it comes from a place deep inside that lets go. As Christ said, "My yoke is easy, and my burden is light."[2] In our core we know who we are and what path we are meant to be on. We know that when we're on the path, we don't need to focus on the future goal. The goal is here in the present. This moment *is*. The process is all in the pleasure of the journey—this face before me, these lips, these nostrils flaring, these eyes. This concentration and surrender. This intensity without tension. The crone knows she's in the right place, and knows that place requires all the strength she has, all the courage she has, all the common sense she has to stay on the road. No need to be striving toward a goal.

The crone appears in our dreams when we have surrendered our ego ideas of where we are going and what we should be doing to reach a goal. Discipline has become a part of fine-tuning our bodies and perceptions. We are surrendered instruments being played by the Mystery. Receptivity is being still, alert to what is coming to us from inside and outside, listening with inner ear, seeing with inner eye, knowing we no longer know everything, if anything.

The day we know that in our bones is a birthday—New Day. The young feminine that we were in our late teens, early twenties, often appears in dreams in her full embodiment, glowing with energy, hair flying, striding like a gypsy into her own life. As her energy meets crone energy, physical strength may pour into the aging body. Delight shines in the crone who feels the freedom of young womanhood united with the freedom of letting go. Challenge is opportunity to wake up, to recognize whatever pins (bits of denial) are still blocking energy. Her soul is singing.

The crone knows the truth has set her free. She believes it can set others free. She is not willing to please for the sake of pleasing. "I can say what I think, be who I am. If people think I'm a funny old thing, no matter. I'm glad to be who I am." Nor is she looking for applause. Because she has no expectations, she suffers few disappointments. Always somewhere in the deepest hems of her skirts, she carries her Baba Yaga mortar and pestle. Every day she will need them to process new energy. She knows that all the information in her head, all the rationalizations, all the polarities—all will have to be ground through her crucible if they are to be embodied in her sacred body. Her big tears and her big Buddha laugh make her a good companion in life.

She brings strength to face what is to be faced with vulnerability and wide-awake fact. What is happening now is meant to be happening now. If we are walking through the valley of the shadow we know we are present where we are; if we are in waiting, we wait until we begin to see the constellation lining up without our trying to make it so. Eventually, all comes into place and we know it is time to do what is to be done.

Mother Teresa, the founder of the Order of the Missionaries of Charity in Calcutta was a crone. Along with her, we now tend to think of Diana, Princess of Wales. The two were friends. Powerful images of the tall, regal princess bending down to greet the tiny, wizened nun are stamped permanently on our memory. Princess and nun are irrevocably joined in our imagination, because almost immediately after the tidal wave of grief for Diana swept over the Western world in September 1997, an equally powerful wave of grief for Mother Teresa swept over the Eastern world, and the two waves commingled as they washed over the earth. For more than a week, the globe was encircled with love for these two very different women: one glamorous, seductive, rich; the other unadorned, self-effacing, sworn to poverty and committed "unremittingly" to caring for the poor, abandoned, sick and dying. Mother Teresa's experience of the world made her tough, wily, totally realistic in the face of death, and totally cherishing of the human soul. During her later years, her frail body was held together by love, a fierce love that fought all the way for its own values. Her authority was in her presence, not her power.

In our fairy tale, Ivan has progressed to a point where he is able to enter the crone's hut, immediately partake of her food and drink, and enter into dialogue with her. He is strong enough to relate to her because he has created an inner container in which his soul is seen and heard by his inner crone. He tells her he is **"going to the thrice tenth kingdom to find the Maiden Tsar,"** his betrothed. **"Ah,"** says the old woman, **"she no longer loves you; if she gets hold of you, she will tear you to shreds."** Instantly, we hear echoes of the warnings of the second Baba Yaga as Ivan set out on his way to the third: **"If she gets angry at you, and wants to devour you, take three horns from her and ask her permission to blow them."** Psychologically, the masculine is once again in danger of being annihilated by the feminine. This time, however, the danger is coming from the opposite pole. Whereas the Baba Yaga energy can mire the masculine in matter—bills to be paid, taxes for two homes, insurance for two cars, pension, charitable donations, all the snakes on Medusa's head always grasping for more—the energy inherent in the swan maiden can carry him off into the air and dissolve him into spirit.

The Romantic poets were terrified of being seduced into death by this spiritual energy that despised life on this earth while yearning for the release and perfection of death. John Keats, for example, in one of the greatest odes in the English language, is listening to the sweet song of a nightingale in his garden. As he listens, he is gradually seduced out of this world "where men sit and hear each other groan."[3]

> *Now more than ever seems it rich to die,*
> *To cease upon the midnight with no pain,*
> *While thou art pouring forth thy soul abroad*
> *In such an ecstasy!*
> *Still wouldst thou sing, and I have ears in vain—*
> *To thy high requiem become a sod.*[4]

The song, which begins in ecstasy, becomes transformed into a "plaintive anthem,"[5] a "high requiem," which at the end of the poem lies "buried deep/In the next valley-glades."[6] Shaken out of his bewitchment, Keats becomes aware that the transformation of full-throated summer song into high requiem is a product of his own seductive imagination, a "deceiving elf"[7] to whose wiles he very nearly succumbs. Once the magic spell is broken, the song fades, and with it the inspiration. On this earth, that creative fire of inspiration must be embodied in experience; the sheer labor of the Baba Yaga cries out for the inspiration of spirit, even as spirit yearns for its realization in matter, lest its music flee, leaving us with Keats's final question, "Do I wake or sleep?"[8]

Shelley, in "Epipsychidion," describes his fusion with his feminine soul as "one annihilation."[9]

> *Woe is me!*
> *The winged words on which my soul would pierce*
> *Into the height of Love's rare Universe,*
> *Are chains of lead around its flight of fire—*
> *I pant, I sink, I tremble, I expire!*[10]

Like many of the great Romantic poets, musicians, and artists in the early nineteenth century, Keats and Shelley were dead before the age of thirty. Their firebird did not set them down soon enough. The intensity of their creative fire carried them too far into the thrice tenth kingdom before they made friends with their Baba Yaga and their crone. They lacked the balance between spirit and embodied soul. Yet, what outpourings of "full heart/In profuse strains of unpremeditated art"[11] their young spirits bequeathed to us!

Now, why is the feminine so angry that she would tear the masculine "to shreds"? Why did Mary Shelley's Frankenstein create a monster who destroyed him? So long as the patriarchal masculine projects goddess perfection onto the feminine (the feminine as swan maiden), he keeps her imprisoned. Of course, she is furious, unless she is young and gullible and too inflated to want to live her own life. In a relationship, some women easily accept the goddess projection from men because they grew up as "Daddy's little princess." If they remain in that projection, they carry an invisible bell jar around them that can quite easily turn into a glass coffin, as Sylvia Plath knew only too well. Plath, like so many other women, was furious at being rejected in her own humanity.

The feminine of most men experiences a similar kind of fury for the same reason. What that feels like and looks like in the imagery of dreams is a beautiful body being thrown into prison and left there, being brought out occasionally to be penetrated, scorned, or starved. In the movie *Blue Velvet,* the terrified and silenced Isabella Rossellini is eventually dragged out by her persecutors onto a wooden platform on which she cringes naked against a cold skyline, her body taking the form of a cross.

Images of the sacrificed feminine abound in Western culture: Iphigenia, Jephthah's daughter, Joan of Arc, thousands of "witches," Tess of the D'Urbervilles, Marilyn Monroe, fourteen women gunned down in the Montreal Massacre. The imprisonment of the feminine is nightly in the dreams of men and women as they rush and rush faster to escape that inner horror. When they have acceptable reason to weep, because others are weeping, as they were for the dead Diana, their body breaks into sobs of anguish.

As the year 1997 came to an end, the sad patriarchs and matriarchs on television, speaking from their heads, pontificated on what the year was all about. One said, "This was a year of emotion." Another countered, "No, I can't think it was genuine emotion. I would call it sentimentality—a vicarious kind of feeling." A third told us, "Diana's death had nothing to do with our daily lives. If anything of importance had been going on—a major recession, for instance—this upheaval of sentimentality would never have occurred." Another pointed out that our vast electronic culture opens the way for the whole world to become involved in one incident. Another tentatively suggested that people now want to be machines, but this desire creates an undercurrent of melancholy, anxiety, and emptiness that was released in Diana's death. The one who had the last word reminded us that this was the fin de siècle, the passing of an era.

Yes, it was the passing of an era, but let us not cut our arrogant heads off from our anguished bodies and faintly smile and label the weeping millions sentimental, indulging in vicarious feeling. Nothing to do with our daily lives? Nothing to do with our culture's unexpressed shame, guilt, anger, yearning? If we are in touch with our dreams at all, then we will hear our femininity, our matter, our feminine soul screaming out every night for release from her incarceration, whether from a prison, a concentration camp, or a bag tied on the end of an exhaust pipe. She is also calling out to us in our bodily symptoms, especially in illnesses affecting the autoimmune system, where the body is turning against itself. The death wish is stronger than the life force. Yes, we're anxious. We're terrified—blind terrified. Our firebirds, whether masculine or feminine, are carrying us so high into idealization that they are tearing us to shreds. We need ground, the ground of our own bodies, the ground of our own Earth—and the consciousness of the sacredness of that ground.

As the sacredness of matter increasingly permeates the culture's consciousness, the battle will rage more fiercely. What has never before been brought to consciousness does not at first want to be dragged into the light, as anyone following a dream process knows, or as anyone listening to the comments in a modern art gallery overhears. Once that new energy begins to experience itself, however, it will not be stifled. Attempting to re-imprison it is asking for death—the death of individuals, the death of a culture. Life expands. The conscious feminine is now among us, demanding that we honor our bodies, our environment, our Earth. She is determined to find embodiment. Like the crone's daughter in our story, she who lives in the palace, we have to find out in what remote place the Maiden Tsar's love is stored away.

· PART IV ·

The Still Point

When her daughter flew in for a visit, the mother-crone **"turned Ivan into a pin and stuck the pin into the wall."** This action is characteristic of crone energy. Often in dreams she cuts through with laser-beam energy: "I'll show you what your problem is. Come." With no sentimentality and great love, she takes the dreamer into a cave, a tunnel, or a grove and points her finger at a scene that makes the core issue nakedly clear. The dreamer is forced to look at it. Running away is no longer possible. In being turned into a pin, Ivan is reduced to the negative essence that is his sleeping self at the beginning of the fairy tale. Why does the crone do this to him? Before Ivan can find and unite with the Maiden Tsar, he needs to stay still and silent and confront fully his own absence from his true self. He will then be able to assume full responsibility for his growing presence.

This is a pregnant moment. Will Ivan be able to remain still? Will he be able to listen, to sacrifice his illusions so that he will be able to comprehend and follow through to his next task? This is the real growing up—moving beyond narcissistic adolescence and polarization. This is the holding of paradox. This is the move beyond gender wars.

Speaking of this point in *Four Quartets,* T. S. Eliot writes,

> *Except for the point, the still point,*
> *There would be no dance, and there is only the dance.*[1]

This is the still point of soul. The psychic pendulum will continue to swing in its inevitable rhythm, but the "I desire" is now coming from a different place. Soul watches the ego swinging without becoming identified with its yearnings. The first "I desire" is for physical survival; this "I desire" is for soul survival. Here is the holding of the tension of the opposites in the still point.

Anyone who has seen the workshop on "The Maiden Tsar" that we filmed in Belleville, Canada, in 1991 will realize that the group was not able to reach the "still point" at that time. Perhaps Robert and I had not reached it in our own lives; perhaps many of the participants were still caught in the polarization that could not hold the tension of the opposites; perhaps the pressure of clock time made soul time impossible. Perhaps some readers are at this moment finding themselves sleepy or irritated because this part of the book is "not as interesting as what came before." If so, consider the possibility that your journey has not yet brought you to a still point. However, you can still envision, if not yet embody.

That inner place of concentrated listening changes every day, but the first experience of it is pivotal in a life. It dismantles the past. Ego desire is sacrificed to make room for soul. The central axis of life becomes the axis between soul and what Jung calls the Self, what fairy tales call the King and Queen, what some religions call God/Goddess. New sensitivities open our eyes to ways in which we have crushed others with our criticisms and judgments, ways we have crushed ourselves in our complexes, and restricted our lives. If, like Ivan, we have been working to develop both sides of ourselves, we recognize that masculinity without femininity is a killer. Likewise, femininity without masculinity is a devourer. In that first still point, we have an intuitive flash of the journey that lies ahead.

I remember my own dream at this point. I dreamt my analyst was a dentist. He was extracting a rotten tooth (transformer) from the back of my mouth. He had been pulling with all his might until we were both exhausted. Then one more pull and out came my tooth, and hanging from it, my entire spine.

I awakened shaking from head to foot, feeling like a powerless jellyfish. I tottered to my analyst's office and told him I thought perhaps he was not right for me. He smiled, and said, "Your parents probably said you needed lots of backbone. The oak laughed at the bamboo because it couldn't stand up straight. But when the lightning struck, the oak split down the middle and the bamboo continued swaying." I heard him because I loved him, but I still felt like an invisible nobody yearning to *be* somebody.

Presence is not the opposite of absence. It is what remains hidden in absence. Ivan as a pin in the wall hears everything that he needs to know. He hears where the Maiden Tsar is. He hears where he is. Ivan as a pin in the wall is not the sleeping Ivan who missed all three encounters (the thrice tenth kingdom) with the Maiden Tsar. Rather, he is envisioning the living embodiment of love, the masculine in whom the feminine is fully present. Now as a pin in the wall, as his own sleeping essence, he is no longer asleep. He is conscious of the content of his sleep. As pin, he carries the Maiden Tsar's love, which he could not carry before. The negative now contains the positive. Absence contains presence.

Ivan has to learn to inhabit this psychic space. Somewhere in himself, Ivan is still holding the feminine out of life, idealizing it into perfection on the one hand, demonizing it on the other. Either way, it tears him "to shreds." His task is still to let his dead mother go and out of her death give birth to his own Bride. In other words, he needs to cherish the mystery of life as it is.

This is the space of the crone in which apparent contradictions belong together in true friendship as the very condition of consciousness. Until Ivan arrives in that psychic space, he will not be able to receive the love of the Maiden Tsar. "Then how will I get it?" he asks. When he is able to hold himself in that psychic place, remote from what culturally passes for consciousness—a place where contradiction cancels out what must be held together—then he is moving into the inner space of the inner marriage.

The Inner Marriage

When the crone's daughter, one of the foster sisters of the Maiden Tsar, flies in the next day, she has found out from the Maiden herself where she has hidden her love: **"On this side of the ocean there stands an oak: in the oak there is a coffer; in the coffer there is a hare; in the hare there is a duck; in the duck there is an egg; and in the egg lies the Maiden Tsar's love."** Ivan does not have to cross the eternal ocean to find his true essence. He does not have to literally die to find the "happily ever after" of the fairy tale.

Still compelled by his love for the Maiden Tsar, Ivan sets out to find her love hidden in an egg in a duck in a hare in a coffer in an oak tree. Such a journey will surely take him into the mythical world if it is to have any meaning at all. He is now developing metaphorical vision. All these last images suggest the divine within the human, and the eternal feminine pattern that moves from life into death into rebirth. His meetings with the Baba Yagas and the crone have initiated him into the dark side of the feminine; now he will initiate the eternal feminine into life. To do this he needs metaphorical vision. He will find the tree, the coffer, the hare, the duck, the egg, and he will experience them within himself. That is what matters.

As children, we see with metaphorical vision. We see the physical object; we ask the impossible question about its meaning. "Where does the wind come from? Where did the baby go? Why did the baby die? What is death?" As we grow older, we may deny the impossible questions until eternity bisects our temporal path. And we may remember them through music, poetry, prayer, nature. Gradually, we may realize that we are beginning to see from two perspectives at the same time—as we do with a pair of glasses that is correcting our vision in one eye or both eyes so that we may see the world in non-dual focus. We may still ask, "Where does the wind come from? What is death?" While our one eye is seeing temporally and our other eternally, the focus is becoming one. In the glory of the lily we see radiant life, we feel its mystery, we feel the poignancy of life moving into death. We feel ourselves fully present in that non-duality.

The perfection of that moment of seeing abides in its paradox. Such moments do not happen with silk flowers. Nor do they happen with a plastic Christmas tree. It does not hold a mystery. The incarnation of the divine in matter is not present. Physical energy is not being transformed into spiritual energy. As a child, you may have gone with your folks to cut down the tree, brought it home, set it up in your own living room, tied on the silver bells, said your prayers beside it, projected worlds upon it. If so, you understand seeing one object with two eyes—one physical, one mythical—each enhancing the other. In healing an addiction, this might mean the coming together of compulsion and freedom in one Christmas treat if, for one instant, spirit were to release thirst from its compulsion.

The journey Ivan is about to make will open his soul to that non-duality—that most precious of mysteries that is always already there for us to see, hear, smell, touch when we return to the mighty oak that is the axis of our life, our connection between earth and heaven. There we find the treasure that we buried when we left our childhood vision behind. In that place, contradictions are robbed of their power to polarize. Instead, they carry, as a Zen koan carries, the spark of oneness best articulated by silence—the daffodil laughing in the spring sun.

And so Ivan goes to that oak tree, and in the oak he finds the coffer. Now, the coffer can be anything from a treasure box to a coffin. In this place of paradox, it is both. In the tree of life it holds the part of Ivan that was buried alive when his goddess mother wasn't there to love him anymore and his god father left him in the care of a tutor. All his dreams of the perfection of she who could love him are in that coffin, and his memories of the goddess who disappeared on the golden boat. And the man in himself who died with her when she left, and died again when he heard she did not love him anymore. His soul buried in that box is not dead.

And when he opens it, a living hare jumps out. Again we need our double-vision glasses. A hare is a rabbit with extra large ears, so it brings to mind rabbit, bunny, many bunnies, Easter eggs, maybe Easter Sunday dawning—the resurrection from the dead of the new god who was also human. We are working with a Russian story and the archetypal roots that are feeding this imagery are Christian. They are even deeper, going back to the Great Goddess of fertility (life, death, rebirth) throughout Europe, Egypt, China, Africa, North America. The goddess of the spring equinox was Eastre, the hare was her ritual animal and the egg her fertility symbol. The image suggests the lasciviousness of the goddess, the sheer lusciousness of life, sexuality, and birth. And with the goddess, the moon, the luminous white of the moon that carries the imprint of the hare, shines.

Moon Goddess imagery carries the cyclic pattern; it is simply a law of life. The forest knows how to sacrifice the parts of itself that have to give way to new growth. The grief in the dying gives place to the miracle of resurrection. The hare willingly sacrifices itself for the sake of spirit: unconscious matter sacrifices itself to conscious awareness.

Farmers who know hares well think of them as sacrificial animals. When fields and hedges are burned off, they see hares who refuse to run before the fire reaches them, suddenly leap, their fur on fire, to run to their death aflame. The more we meditate on the hare, the more we love this animal that, like the moon, dies to be reborn.

Within the hare, Ivan finds a duck, an amphibious creature with the added advantage of being able to transport itself through the air. In the process of integration, Ivan has to learn to live not only on land (consciousness) but also in the water (the unconscious) and in the air (refined consciousness, where contradiction becomes paradox). At home in all three living environments—land, water, and air—the duck transcends the limitations of other creatures bound to a single habitat. Thus the duck is always an encouraging image in dreams, because it suggests the imminent arrival of something totally new in the dreamer, something that transcends the limitations of the dreamer's conscious life. A person torn on a cross between two loves may have a dream in which a duck appears. The flying duck represents what is called the "transcendent function," which unites the opposites in the psyche in a way that the consciousness of the dreamer could not have imagined. From the air, one can see both land and water. However, the airborne duck does not locate the dreamer up in the air, on a higher plane outside the reality of daily life. In flight, the duck remains as much an inhabitant of the earth as it does when it moves upon the land or in the waters. Its flight suggests a reconciliation of the divine and the instinctual, spirit and matter. Rather than excluding each other, the two embrace each other, enhancing the human being. In relationships, this might mean the coming together, through suffering, of love and lust in one relationship, rather than continuing the splitting of body from soul.

Ivan has carried two images of the feminine: one, an ethereal maiden too high up on a pedestal to be real; the other, the shadow counterpart, the devouring mother. The transcendent function, represented by the duck, would connect heaven and earth—bring both the love of the swan maiden and the lust of the Baba Yaga into human form, creating one integrated human being. So long as the duck is in a dream, the union is still only a whiff of intuitive possibility. The real possibility lies in the egg within the duck. The egg provides the means of bringing the new consciousness into lived reality.

The love of the Maiden Tsar lies hidden in the egg, which Ivan will take back, and which she will eat. There is a sweetness in this coming together of energies, a sweetness we often find in dreams. Here is masculinity concentrated on returning the precious egg to the feminine, and the feminine ingesting, with her own love, the golden orb (yolk) of her masculine spirit. In that union, the masculine is coming to consciousness through the feminine, and the feminine is coming to consciousness through the masculine. In the egg lie all the new possibilities of their new relationship.

The inner marriage cannot take place until the projections are identified as projections and withdrawn. Initially, the projection itself is the unconscious messenger of the inner Beloved, a signal sent to announce its hidden presence. Until the projection is withdrawn so that the love it constellates is drawn back, the inner Beloved remains unknown except as a *desire to be known*. Love as the desire to be known is the state of being in love with love. It is a love that feeds on isolation, darkness, withdrawal. It is narcissistic because it is a state of being in love with one's own projected image, one's own fantasized image of oneself. This state of love is the unconscious form of the inner marriage. While from the outside it is rejected as adolescent and immature, from the inside it is important to recognize what it does contain as distinct from merely criticizing the dangers of becoming blocked at this stage. Because the projection of the inner Beloved onto another person is so often accepted as the ultimate goal of a relationship, the inner marriage remains too often identified with Romantic narcissistic love. The fact that narcissistic love is also suicidal is often overlooked or idealized. The inner marriage should not be identified with Romantic love, which is not a healing of narcissistic love, but perhaps the most deadly form of it.

The withdrawal of the projection that is essential for the achievement of the inner marriage transforms the object of the projection, the Beloved, into a stranger. It is this confrontation with the stranger, with the otherness of the Beloved, that creates an "energy field" of love. When that field of love is established within, the archetypal projections are taken off the outer partner. No need, then, for either partner to attempt to be god or goddess. An immense unnatural weight is removed from both. A freedom enters the relationship, which may be quite alarming at first. Gradually that freedom will be recognized as the freedom to love another human being as a human being without any hidden agenda and false expectations and needs. The inner marriage makes the outer marriage possible.

When Ivan at last becomes the still point and takes time to listen to find out where his soul's love is hidden, surely his question then, as for all of us, is: "What was the journey all about?" The bringing together of his lifetime search for the Maiden Tsar into a final series of interlocking symbols, one embedded in another, like Dante's multifoliate rose at the end of the *Paradiso,* brings the fairy tale together at its point of highest tension. There the arrow is spontaneously released and goes directly to its target: the reader's heart. To hold the image there as the whole soul in activity is to find ourselves impregnated by the still point of the ceaselessly turning world, like the chicken leg on which the hut of the Baba Yaga ceaselessly turns. How many angels can dance on the head of a pin? Or on a grain of Sophia's salt? At the core of this question, absurd to some, costing no less than everything to others, lives the masculine indwelling in the feminine, the feminine indwelling in the masculine, as in the divine embrace of Shiva and Shakti, or the two fish in the symbol of yang and yin. These are images of the androgyne.

It is interesting now to return to Princess Diana as an example of a contemporary androgynous personality. We can see the gradual shaping of the androgyne in her media career, a career governed as much by compulsion as by her own free will. The way in which she attempted to align her will with compulsion can be seen in the way she handled the paparazzi, who ceaselessly pursued her, leaving no part of her life free of their relentless lenses. Simultaneously courting and dismissing them, she knew, consciously or unconsciously, that what in herself she was struggling to achieve had a meaning for the world that extended beyond the range of the British monarchy. At once tentative and tenacious, shy and audacious, her compulsion mysteriously bound to her own will, she was shifting her own relationship to herself and the global attitude of relationship between the sexes. Perhaps nothing better symbolizes her changing relationship to herself than exchanging her Versace gown for the jeans and helmet necessary to go forth to release the earth and its citizens from land mines. Significant in the auctioning of her gowns is the fact that this was an idea put forward by her son, William.

How much was conscious in Diana we do not know, but we do know that she was capable of carrying intense projections from a global public that targeted her as the bearer of their unconscious yearnings. When she died, millions grieved for what they felt they lost in themselves—their own femininity and their burgeoning masculinity. This Maiden Tsar who rebelled against the entrenched British monarchy that was prepared to treat her as little more than a breeder of future kings armed herself for a "masculine" role that the patriarchy that sought to control her knew nothing about. She had to assume in herself a masculine role strong enough to release her from the outworn tyrannical grip. This new masculinity, wedded to her own emancipated femininity, she offered as her service to the healing of the world.

The public Diana was gradually developing androgynous characteristics. The androgyne is not to be confused with the hermaphrodite, an image of unisex in which masculine and feminine are sexually joined in a union of unconscious opposites. Androgynous consciousness demands hard work in bringing to union a well-differentiated femininity and an equally well-differentiated masculinity in an inner marriage in subtle body. Diana was going through the difficulties of that painful inner courtship. Her actual fairy-tale marriage beneath the dome of St. Paul's was not really her marriage at all. Instead, it was a parody of the inner marriage that marked the end of a long patriarchal era rather than its renewal. What replaced it, costing no less than everything (her life), was the emergence of potential androgynous consciousness. The Maiden Tsar as an androgynous figure can be understood as the whole person having within himself/herself the source of his/her own integrity.

What Diana achieved within herself, what would have happened had she lived, will forever remain a mystery. What is clear is what came into consciousness when she no longer carried the mass projections. The bashful maiden whose Prince Charming will arrive to save her is obsolete. The androgyne is still in the unconscious, but it *is* there and ready to be born. Whether the masses will do the work necessary to bring it to birth or whether it will drop again into unconsciousness until someone else comes along to carry the projection is the question.

To embrace the androgyne as a symbol of the inner marriage,

as the God/Goddess within, requires a long, painful process of differentiation, as Ivan found out. The archetypal and the human worlds are not the same. In the perfection of the "once upon a time" world where "they lived happily ever after," the circle is complete. In our clock-and-calendar world the circle is a broken arc. During a painful process of differentiation, Robert wrote:

> *Wrens*
> *make their nests of fancy threads*
> *and string ends, animals*
>
> *abandon all their money each year.*
> *What is that men and women leave?*
> *Harder than wrens' doing, they have*
> *to abandon their longing for the perfect.*
>
> *The inner nest not made by instinct*
> *will never be quite round,*
> *and each has to enter the nest*
> *made by the other imperfect bird.*[1]

As we differentiate between the perfection of the inner and the imperfection of the outer relationship, gradually we find ourselves honoring the soul's beauty shining through human impossibility. Part of the rainbow has the luminosity of the whole arc.

By the end of the story, Ivan has actually brought the treasure home. To glimpse what he has, by compulsion and will, consciously achieved is to see who we, in our becoming, "always already" are. Like so many of us who buried our youthful vision of the divine in a treasure box in our own tree of life, he, step upon step, has reconnected with his own eternal identity, and recognizes his garden for the first time. Part of that recognition is the necessity for the Beloved to eat the egg. To taste it, swallow it, assimilate that divine energy through every cell of our earthly body is to bring the swan maiden into life, to redeem the ethereal bird that would escape into the air. As the feminine connects with her humanity, she unites the idealized goddess and the outlawed sexuality of the Baba Yaga—her love and her lust. That mature femininity awakens mature masculinity in full equal partnership within and without.

The marriage that is finally celebrated in our story is not a postmortal one that transcends matter. Imagine the care with which Ivan carries back the raw egg that contains the buried essence of life itself. The crone bakes that egg in the fire of passion and serves it as the centerpiece of her birthday world which is being celebrated. In eating the egg in which her love for Ivan is hidden, the Maiden Tsar is ingesting all that he is now bringing back to her.

Mythologically, the egg is the eternal germ of life, a symbol of immortality, and a vessel of transmutation. In Egypt, it was related to the red sun of morning (the resurrection), its golden yolk the sun, the wheel of fire, and by extension, the firebird.

As she ate the egg, the Maiden Tsar **"at once conceived a passionate love for Ivan."** The Maiden Tsar eating the egg is an exquisite image of soul opening herself to spirit, light hidden in body released by a shower of gold. This is a moment of reshaping, the resurrected body becoming the body of passionate love. As she ingests the egg, she ingests Ivan's entire initiation into his own inner feminine. She becomes the full consciousness of it— the full Being and Bride of Ivan as her own inner masculine. The eating of the egg is her own inner marriage that fills her with passionate love—the love of Shiva and Shakti in divine embrace.

Ivan, too, is moving toward the inner marriage. Being received by a feminine that can love him *as he is in all his becoming* is Ivan's final, triumphant step. That he dares to make it shows how hard he has worked to redeem his mother—natural and unnatural—integrate his Baba Yagas and relate to the crone. Now he can receive them as the Maiden Tsar—his own Bride. Her love of her masculinity is embodied in Ivan; his love of his inner feminine is embodied in the Maiden Tsar. What he experiences, she digests. Their union is born out of the inner marriage that both have accomplished. Their "happily ever after" will be their inner work together in ceaseless transformation.

When we are young, few of us have established an inner marriage when we commit to an outer partner. We believe the outer partner is the Beloved, while the true Beloved is hidden away in a coffin—maybe a coffin that traps the soul in insatiable desire that freezes it in matter. As life continues, however, we begin to realize we cannot enter an outer relationship unless we are coming from our own inner marriage. The sacramental ground has to be prepared. Until the inner Bride and Bridegroom creatively love each other, the outer relationship is starving, becoming a substitute that may collapse into crippling codependence. In the new paradigm, we are sooner or later pushed toward our own maturity—the androgyne.

And what is the Maiden Tsar thinking as she eats of the egg?

Ivan, I think I still love you. Yes, I have been angry with you. Yes, I did withdraw. I am weary of being imprisoned behind Adam's ribs. Try to understand I had to protect myself from your blunderings and bludgeonings. Know, too, I saw your courage when you met me in the Baba Yagas and the crone. You have endured the dignity of your own pain.

Something in you was determined to fly up and out into eternity; something in me was determined to go down and in to blood and bone. I have done my work too. I have sacrificed some of my wing feathers . . . for now. I know the perfection I sought is not realizable on Earth; it is a tapestry of delusion. I see now the Light at the center of our love and at the center of the Earth as one creation of which we are a part, here and now.

Through each other's suffering we have matured. I know you have looked for me in women, and when you didn't find me you felt betrayed and angry. Hear me, Ivan. Hear me. I am not a woman, though you may fleetingly see me in a woman as you look into her eyes, kiss her, make love to her. Your love of a woman will enhance your love of me.

I am a mystery, not a problem to be solved. You no longer fear me, no longer idealize me. Now we are free to love each other. I am forever fresh, forever alive. And so long as we love each other, you too will be a mystery that we will celebrate together.

Let me flow through you, Ivan. Let us celebrate my flow through your conscious form in writing, painting, singing, dancing, whatever we choose to do right here in life.

I am your soul, Ivan. We are standing together on the top of a hill in the dawn of a New Day. Dark times may lie ahead. Do not sentimentalize me. I am strong; you are strong. You are my spirit that ignites the fire in every cell of my Being. Do not forsake me. Let the Light of our love shine through you. Let it illumine your dark places. Let us create together.

Dearest Ivan, can you love me as I have loved you?

And even as Ivan had brought back the Maiden Tsar's love from its hiding place, the crone brought back Ivan from his hiding place. **"How much joy there was, how much merriment. The Maiden Tsar left with her betrothed, the merchant's son, for her own kingdom; they married and began to live happily and to prosper."**

And maybe the mourning doves chortle to each other in their garden, and the swans swim in their stream, and maybe, just maybe, a firebird bursts over their horizon every morning in the rising sun.

Epilogue

A Brief Conversation Between
Robert Bly and Marion Woodman

R.B.: I think I do look at this male journey to the underworld
a little differently than you do, because I consider this descent into the underworld partly a punishment for insen-
sitivity toward the feminine during a man's whole life.

M.W.: I don't see that sense of punishment at all, Robert. Thinking like that has a big shadow; it could leave a man trying
to please women instead of living his own reality. To me,
the descent is simply the way life is. It's the *felix culpa,* the
fortunate blunder. We make these mistakes; they are the
mistakes that throw us into our own destiny; we go
through our own initiation into our own experience.

    Sometimes when you are talking, I sense you coming
forward with some old assumptions, old patterns toward
women. It's too easy for both sexes to allow the feminine
to slip into service to the masculine, and vice versa. I think
those assumptions are rooted in archaic "judge and
blame" games that end in punishments for both sexes.
Luckily for us, we both have a good sense of humor that
pushes us out of those games. Where else do we disagree
on our interpretations?

R.B.: Let's go back a bit to the section of the book when you
were talking about the Conscious Virgin and Princess Di.

I disagree with you there. There is tremendous evidence that a strong feminine is returning, and it is a good sign. Nora's slamming the door on *The Doll's House* was one of the loudest sounds of the nineteenth century. Women have decided not to live in a doll's house and are taking part in the life of the whole culture.

M.W.: And we are doing it consciously, Robert. This has never happened before. What was going on in ancient times was very unconscious.

R.B.: I'm not sure I agree. I'm not convinced the ancients were unconscious. But I don't find Di to be that clear an example of the Conscious Feminine as you do.

M.W.: I think that she herself was quite a frail vessel. Had she not died exactly when she died, had she actually received that ring from Dodi, and had she chosen to go to France to live in the Duke of Windsor's house, she would have betrayed the intensity of the projection she carried, especially for the English people. I don't think she was a clear example of the Conscious Feminine. However, what is important is that she carried enough projections that her death released the feminine into the consciousness of millions of people. Her efforts to be herself turned many lives around.

R.B.: It's not clear to me how long the power of her example will last. What troubles me is the presence of pop culture around that phenomenon.

M.W.: In what way?

R.B.: I find it hard to believe that the long-expected Conscious Feminine would arrive surrounded by bad songs of Elton John and by the culture of the media and the paparazzi. There's something about pop culture that is inimical to the feminine. Pop culture, I think, is profoundly hostile to the genuine masculine as well. It's noticeable that in those days around the funeral, pop culture could celebrate Princess Di's death but not Mother Teresa's death.

M.W.: So you think more in the sacramental sense, don't you? Elton John singing "Good-bye, England's rose" does not belong in Westminster Abbey?

R.B.: Pop culture is making all life on earth horizontal with the help of global capitalism. It is suceeding all over the world. That makes me suspicious of the association of Princess Di with the Maiden Tsar. You're absolutely right when you say that her death was an amazing mythological event; but it can be looked at in many different ways. I'll look at her death this way: In England, with hard work, she had become the Queen of the May. But in some traditions, whoever moves into that position will die. The woman who represents the spring has to die, one can say, when summer comes, just as the young man representing the old year has to die when the new year comes. These events take place in trance. Forces are moving so far below the surface that no human being can understand them or know when they have taken hold.

M.W.: Diana was walking right into them.

R.B.: She was. I don't think she really knew she was going to die. So I don't think one can call her a conscious person.

M.W.: Robert, I'm not a Dianamaniac. I'm not interested in her as an actual, historical person living a just-sort-of-fumbling-around life and getting herself killed by a drunken driver. I'm not about to romanticize her going to heaven with a dead lover in the back seat of a smashed Mercedes. I'm not interested in the facts as facts. I'm interested in them as metaphor. I'm interested in what the collective unconscious spontaneously did with those facts, with the mythical shape it put on them. Joyce said that history was a nightmare. His writing was his struggle to wake up. I think the fact of Diana's death became a wake-up trumpet call that sounded right across the planet. I believe that long after the actual historical Diana is forgotten, the wake-up call will remain and will go on sounding until what it is sounding is fulfilled. As a starter, I think the funeral in the Abbey helped a lot. It set the resurrection going in the right direction. It certainly helped to keep me going. My image of Diana as she was presented at her funeral was of an extraodinary ordinary woman. That's the way I see all women.

R.B.: I'm half convinced! There's one more disagreement I sense. You have referred to Ivan idealizing the Maiden Tsar. He projects, so to speak, interior energies onto her in a kind of arc going upward. But I see the arc of energy coming down from the Divine toward him. The divine realm is symbolized here as the horizon, and an arc of energy comes down toward him, not the other way around. He is faced with something so much greater in intensity than he is that he cannot take it in.

There's a Sufi poem by Jami dating from the fifteenth century in Iran, called *Yusuf and Zulaikha,* which gives an image much like that in our story. The scene takes place in what the Muslims call "pre-eternity." Jami says:

> That bride whose beauty could touch every heart remained in her bridal chamber. The magnificent mistress lived in her joyful solitude, dealing the cards of love with no one but herself; she had no one with whom to drink the wine of her beauty. At that time no human being had heard of her. Even the mirror was ignorant of her face.
>
> But it is a principle of beauty that beauty can endure hiddenness only so long. Handsomeness will not put up with concealment. If you close the door, she will show her face at the window.
>
> So the bride pitched her tent outside the sacred precincts, showing herself throughout creation, and inside the soul. After that her face, so long hid-

den, looked out from every mirror: wherever there were human beings, storytellers told her story. One spark from it flashed forth and set heaven and earth on fire.

The Sufi story adds clarity, actually, to the image that we have in our story, in which we have these two little mortals floating around on a raft, and then this enormous, brilliant energy comes toward them because it or She wanted to set heaven and earth on fire.

M.W.: I see that as incarnation. That Sufi bride and the Maiden Tsar are goddess figures manifesting Beauty. One spark flashes forth and sets heaven and earth on fire.

R.B.: Our story begins with this incredible beam of light that comes down and hits you when you are twelve or thirteen. A girl can hear it in music, see it in a painting. And we call it feminine beauty. But it's just beauty. To me that's terrifically exciting. I love that image in this story: the idea that the entire religious life of the human race is described here in this energy coming toward the raft with the two little guys on it.

M.W.: What is Baba Yaga in relation to that bride?

R.B.: Perhaps we couldn't have this great transcendent energy all by itself, so to speak, without its dark side. On this planet, lions eat gazelles. Perhaps one can get too far away from reality by talking about the transcendental light coming down. You can cure that by looking at history; then you are looking at Baba Yaga.

M.W.: Yes, you move too close to the transcendent light and the darkness comes crackling at your back door. The danger comes in allowing those two energies to polarize. Either side can be a killer or a healer. I love the idea of the Baba Yaga as death in the service of life.

R.B.: Baba Yaga's humor suggests that she is in the service of life.

M.W.: Oh, yes. Her humor is part of her authentic life, so it holds the paradox. Ivan, in that moment of cutting off the tutor's head, began his journey into his authentic life.

R.B.: The other day I read Tolstoy's *The Death of Ivan Ilyich*, which is a terrific description of an inauthentic life. He marries his wife because the bureaucracy thought she was the right wife for him. Now why is it that Ivan Ilyich could not pull out of his inauthenticity in the way Ivan did? Just before death, Ivan Ilyich was still, so to speak, inauthentic. Why did Ivan in "The Maiden Tsar" pull out of it? He too had inauthenticity pressing in on him.

M.W.: Whatever that bolt was that came from the Maiden Tsar, it woke him up to his own personhood. He could receive, tentatively at first. I do think we should notice that there is an underlying difference in our views of the feminine.

R.B.: We didn't talk about these differences around the feminine before we started. We each just wrote. But now after reading each other's sections, it does seem clear that we are seeing the feminine differently.

M.W.: Well, let's just jump into it. Robert, how would you describe the feminine as you see it now at this time in your life?

R.B.: The Maiden Tsar arriving at the raft is an image of the Feminine Ecstatic. I don't think Ivan is idealizing the Divine Feminine—can you idealize the Divine? I do agree that in some cultures men tend to idealize a woman in such a way that she becomes all angel—indistinguishable from the Virgin Mary—without sex or mud between her toes or vulgarity. Women are justly angry about being idealized in such a way that their genuine human substance is ignored. But we can make a distinction between the vision of the Divine Feminine and a sickly idealizing of a living woman. I think this story is about the Feminine Divine which includes not only the Virgin Mary, so to speak, but this Baba

Yaga who is so much at home in blood and flesh that she can stand for death as well as a very high-spirited life.

M.W.: It is the Feminine—as matter—which makes the bridge between the divine and the human. The new feminine stands for a new kind of consciousness which can hold the divine and the human in one thought. Women feel angry about the distrust and rejection of matter by men in so many traditions and sciences. Women don't want to be idealized when they are not recognized in their humanity. They want to be honored in their own sacred matter.

R.B.: I'm not sure about that. All over the world I see statues of the Virgin Mary appearing prominently in churches, and women are attending those churches. I think they're still responding to the Feminine Divine.

M.W.: That's the point, Robert. Most women that I know are responding to the divinity in matter—soul living in matter. Women are tired of having matter depreciated and themselves depreciated with it. I know that in *News of the Universe,* you fight strongly for nature and matter as having consciousness, so I know we are not at loggerheads on this question. It's a matter of emphasis, and I think it's fine for us to hold this diversity of opinion. After all, it's the main gist of this story that men and women learn not to take adversarial positions on these matters so important and so essential.

R.B.: I know that it's possible that when I admire the vision of the Feminine Divine arriving in thirty boats, I can be accused of having a patriarchal view. It could be called patriarchal to the degree that it keeps the feminine elevated. I do agree that the patriarchal loves to elevate the feminine so far that the only ones left on earth to decide about material matters are men.

But the Feminine Divine that appears on the horizon also includes Baba Yaga. That double vision is not a patriarchal invention. It is the matriarchies themselves and cultures that are called matrilocal in which this vision of the feminine is brought forward: ecstatic on one side and tigerlike on the other. The Marxist position is that there is no divine, only lies about it. I think there is a Feminine Divine and a Masculine Divine.

M.W.: I think so, too. I think Ivan had to let go of his Divine Maiden and learn to love an inner divinity that was not so far removed from reality. That shift would make both his inner and outer marriage possible. This is his story, but I think there is another whole story in the last series of images—the feminine story. What was the Maiden doing all the time Ivan was struggling? How did her love get into the egg, into the duck, into the hare, into the coffer in the Tree of Life? From the opposite direction, she moved toward Ivan with no assurance of his being there for her. Like many fairy-tale heroines, when she loses her way, she goes into Nature, which puts her in touch with the wisdom of her own body.

This Maiden is Ivan's Bride. His inner strength makes it possible for her to reconnect with her own love. He at the same time is embodying the sacredness of his own Being, recognizing her as the connection between human and divine. The egg she eats, he eats. In human experience, eating the egg, digesting it for a lifetime is what it's all about. It's the reward that consciousness brings to the struggle, the labor.

R.B.: You like these lines of Yeats:

> *Labour is blossoming or dancing where*
> *The body is not bruised to pleasure soul!*[1]

M.W.: A fairy tale has a happy ending. It is a divine comedy.

Notes

Introduction

1. Antonio Machado, trans. Robert Bly, *Times Alone: Selected Poems of Antonio Machado* (Middletown, CT: Wesleyan University Press, 1983), p. 113.
2. Ibid., p. 57.
3. Ibid.

The Fishing Trip

1. Lecture by Marie-Louise von Franz, Notre Dame University, 1982.

The Moment When the Worlds Meet

1. Robert Bly, "After Working," in *Silence in the Snowy Fields* (Middletown, CT: Wesleyan University Press, 1962), p. 51.
2. Thomas Traherne, *Centuries, Poems, and Thanksgivings,* Vol. 1 (Oxford: Clarendon Press, 1958).
3. Robert Johnson, *Balancing Heaven and Earth: A Memoir of Visions, Dreams, and Realizations* (New York: HarperSanFrancisco, 1998), p. 7.

The New Life

1. Rumi, trans. Coleman Barks, *The Essential Rumi* (New York: Harper-Collins, 1995), p. 37.
2. Wallace Stevens, ed. Frank Kermode and Joan Richardson, "Sunday Morning," *Collected Poetry and Prose* (New York: Library of America, 1997), p. 55.
3. William Shakespeare, *Romeo and Juliet*, in *The Norton Shakespeare* (New York: W. W. Norton, 1997), p. 890.
4. Rainer Maria Rilke, trans. Robert Bly, *Selected Poems of Rainer Maria Rilke* (New York: Harper, 1981), p. 161.

The Maiden Tsar's Second Visit

1. *The New York Times,* Jan. 11, 1998.

The Great Disappointment

1. Joseph Chilton Pearce, *Evolution's End: Claiming the Potential of Our Intelligence* (New York: HarperCollins, 1992), p. 190; also *Magical Child Matures* (New York: Dutton, 1985).
2. Gerard Manley Hopkins, "The Leaden Echo and the Golden Echo," *Poems and Prose* (New York: Penguin, 1953), p. 53.

The Tutor as Destroyer of Imagination

1. Charles Dickens, *Hard Times* (New York: Heritage Press, 1966), p. 3.
2. William Blake, *The Marriage of Heaven and Hell*, in John Sampson, ed., *The Poetical Works of William Blake* (New York: Oxford, 1913), p. 251.
3. Bill Holm, private conversation.
4. D. H. Lawrence, "Healing," *The Complete Poems, Vol. 3* (London: William Heinemann Ltd., 1957), p. 50.
5. Nicole Gauette, "Are colleges coming to praise Shakespeare, or to bury him?", *Christian Science Monitor,* January 27, 1997, p. 12.
6. Marion Woodman, *The Ravaged Bridegroom* (Toronto: Inner City Books, 1990), p. 17.

A Parallel Mayan Story

1. Martín Prechtel, private conversation.

The Maiden Tsar's Third Visit

1. T. S. Eliot, "The Waste Land," *Collected Poems 1909–1935* (New York: Harcourt, Brace, and Company, 1930), p. 69.

Using the Sword

1. Kabir, version by Robert Bly, *The Kabir Book: Forty-four of the Ecstatic Poems of Kabir* (Boston: Beacon Press, 1977), p. 3.

Baba Yaga's Hut on a Chicken Leg

1. Bob Dylan, "Like a Rolling Stone," *Highway 61 Revisited* (New York: Columbia Records, 1965).
2. Federico García Lorca, trans. Robert Bly, *Lorca and Jiménez: Selected Poems* (Boston: Beacon Press, 1973, 1997), pp. 169–71.
3. Robert Johnson, *Balancing Heaven and Earth*, p. 292.
4. Emily Dickinson, Poem #599, ed. Thomas H. Johnson, *The Complete Poems of Emily Dickinson* (Boston: Little Brown, 1960), p. 295.

Who Is Baba Yaga?

1. Alain Daniélou, trans. K. F. Hurry, *Shiva and Dionysus* (London: East-West Publications, 1982), p. 80.

Baba Yaga's Question to Ivan

1. Tomas Tranströmer, trans. Robert Bly, "At Funchal," in *Truth Barriers* (San Francisco: Sierra Club, 1980), pp. 38–39.

The Baba Yaga Who Eats People

1. Erich Neumann, trans. Ralph Manheim, *The Great Mother: An Analysis of the Archetype* (Princeton: Princeton University, 1955), p. 149.

Why Is Baba Yaga Female?

1. Sherwood Washburn, quoted in Dorothy Dinnerstein, *The Mermaid and the Minotaur: Sexual Arrangements and Human Malaise* (New York: Harper & Row, 1976), p. 19.
2. Melaine Klein, "Some Theoretical Conclusions Regarding the Emotional Life of the Infant," in *Envy and Gratitude and Other Work 1946–1963* (New York: Free Press, 1975).
3. Dorothy Dinnerstein, *The Mermaid and the Minotaur*, pp. 161–66.

The Reply to Baba Yaga's Question

1. Robert Frost, "The Lovely Shall Be Choosers," Edward Connery Lathem and Lawrance Thompson, eds., *Robert Frost, Poetry and Prose* (New York: Holt, Rinehart and Winston, 1972), pp. 102–04.
2. Marie-Louise von Franz, *Shadow and Evil in Fairy Tales* (Zurich: Spring, 1964), p. 168.
3. Sri Ramakrishna, quoted in trans. Swami Nikhilananda, Heinrich Zimmer, *Philosophies of India* (New York: World Publishing Company, 1956), pp. 564–67.

Arriving at the Second Sister's Hut

1. Bernadine Jacot and Liam Hudson, *The Way Men Think: Intellect, Intimacy and the Erotic Imagination* (New Haven: Yale University Press, 1991).
2. Jacot and Hudson, *The Way Men Think*, p. 172.

Who Goes to the Underworld?

1. Terence Real, *I Don't Want to Talk About It* (New York: Scribner, 1997).
2. W. B. Yeats, "The Second Coming," *The Collected Poems of W. B. Yeats* (New York: Macmillan, 1956), pp. 84–85.
3. Federico García Lorca, trans. Robert Bly, *Lorca and Jiménez: Selected Poems*, pp.169–71.

How Kali Belongs in the Malls

1. David Kinsley, *Hindu Goddesses: Visions of the Divine Feminine in the Hindu Religious Tradition* (Berkeley and Los Angeles: University of California, 1986), p. 126.
2. James Mellaart, *Çatal Hüyük, A Neolithic Town in Anatolia* (London: Thames and Hudson, 1967).

Part III

1. William Blake, *The Marriage of Heaven and Hell*, in *The Poetical Works of William Blake*, p. 254
2. Sean Kane, *Wisdom of the Mythtellers* (Orchard Park, NY: Broadview Press, 1994).

The Firebird

1. Joachim Berendt, trans. Tim Nevill, *The Third Ear: On Listening to the World* (New York: Henry Holt, 1992), p. 16.

What Is the Firebird?

1. Robert Bly, "The Adventures of Ganesha: A Hindu Story," *The Sibling Society* (Reading, MA: Addison-Wesley, 1996), pp. 67–88.
2. Juan Ramón Jiménez, trans. Robert Bly, *Lorca and Jiménez: Selected Poems*, p. 65.
3. Federico García Lorca, trans. Christopher Maurer, "Play and Theory of the Duende," in *Deep Song and Other Prose* (New York: New Directions, 1980), pp. 44 and 52.
4. Wallace Stevens, "Of Mere Being," *Collected Poetry and Prose*, p. 477.
5. Rumi, version by Robert Bly, "Praising Manners," in *Night and Sleep* (Somerville, MA: Yellow Moon, 1981), unpaginated.
6. García Lorca, trans. Ben Belitt, "The Function and Theory of the Duende," in *Poet in New York* (New York: Grove Press, 1955).
7. William Shakespeare, *A Midsummer Night's Dream*, in *The Norton Shakespeare*, p. 851.
8. Rumi, trans. by R. A. Nicholson, *Mathnawi* (London), 1925–40, Bk VI, v. 573.
9. William Blake, in *The Poetical Works of William Blake*, p. 254.

The Realm of the Crone

1. Marion Woodman and Elinor Dickson, *Dancing in the Flames: The Dark Goddess in the Transformation of Consciousness* (Boston: Shambhala, 1996), pp. 133–34.

What Can Be Done

1. W. B. Yeats, "Michael Robartes and the Dancer," *The Collected Poems* (New York: Macmillan, 1958), p. 174.
2. Takeo Doi, trans. John Bester, *The Anatomy of Dependence* (Tokyo, New York: Kodansha International, 1973).

The Three Mothers

1. Ted Hughes, *Shakespeare and the Goddess of Complete Being* (New York: Farrar, Straus and Giroux, 1992), p. 107.

Part IV

1. Kabir, version by Robert Bly, *The Kabir Book,* pp. 24–25.
2. Herschel Parker, *Herman Melville, Vol. 1* (Baltimore: Johns Hopkins Press, 1996).
3. James Wood, "The All of the It," *The New Republic,* March 17, 1997, p. 34.

The Metaphor of the Oak

1. Robert Graves, "To Juan at the Winter Solstice," *Collected Poems 1975* (New York: Oxford, 1975).

The Metaphor of the Coffer

1. Jeremiah Curtin, *Myths and Folk-Lore of Ireland* (New York: Weathervane Books, 1974), p. 74.
2. Wallace Stevens, "Poetry Is a Destructive Force," *Collected Poetry and Prose,* p. 178.
3. Lewis Hyde, *Trickster Makes This World: Mischief, Myth and Art* (New York: Farrar, Straus and Giroux, 1998).
4. William James, *The Will to Believe,* in *Writings 1878–1899* (New York: Library of America, 1992).

The Metaphor of the Hare

1. Mrs. Wright, quoted in John Layard, *The Lady and the Hare: A Study in the Healing Power of Dreams* (Boston: Shambhala, 1988), pp. 48–49.
2. Layard, *The Lady and the Hare,* p. 63.

3. Ted Hughes, *Shakespeare and the Goddess of Complete Being*, p. 73.
4. Goethe, translated by Robert Bly, "The Holy Longing," in Robert Bly, ed., *The Soul Is Here for Its Own Joy: Sacred Poems from Many Cultures* (Hopewell, NJ: Ecco Press, 1995), p. 209.

The Metaphor of the Duck

1. Rainer Maria Rilke, "The Swan," translated by Robert Bly, *Selected Poems of Rainer Maria Rilke*, p. 141.
2. William Shakespeare, Sonnet #146, *The Norton Shakespeare*, p. 1973.
3. Kabir, version by Robert Bly, *The Kabir Book*, p. 45.
4. William Blake, *The Marriage of Heaven and Hell*, in *The Poetical Works of William Blake*, p. 252.

The Metaphor of the Egg

1. Gerard Manley Hopkins, "Spring," *Poems and Prose*, p. 28.
2. Francis Ponge, trans. Robert Bly, "The Asiette (The Plate)," *Ten Poems of Francis Ponge Translated by Robert Bly and Ten Poems of Robert Bly Inspired by the Poems of Francis Ponge* (Riverview, New Brunswick: Owl's Head Press, 1990), p. 27.
3. John Layard, *The Lady and the Hare*, pp. 171–72.

Ingesting the Egg

1. Emily Dickinson, Poem #249, *The Complete Poems of Emily Dickinson*, p. 114.
2. Mirabai, version by Robert Bly, "His Hair," in *The Soul Is Here for Its Own Joy*, p. 185.
3. Rumi, version by Coleman Barks and John Moyne, *Open Secret* (Putney, VT: Threshold, 1984), p. 6.
4. Rumi, version by Coleman Barks, *The Essential Rumi*, p. 37.
5. Hafez, version by Robert Bly, "The Lost Daughter," *The Soul Is Here for Its Own Joy*, p. 239.

The Maiden Tsar

1. T. S. Eliot, "Little Gidding," *Four Quartets* (London: Faber and Faber, 1952), p. 43.
2. Letter to Benjamin Bailey, 13 March 1818, in *The Letters of John Keats,* ed. Maurice Buxton Forman (London: Oxford University Press, 1947), p. 112.
3. William Shakespeare, *Macbeth,* 2. 2.37.

Positive Mother vs. Stepmother

1. William Blake, "The Marriage of Heaven and Hell: Proverbs of Hell," l. 10, in *The Complete Poetry and Prose of William Blake,* ed. David V. Erdman (New York: Doubleday, 1988), p. 36.
2. John Milton, *Paradise Lost,* bk. 4, l.299, in *John Milton: Complete Poems and Major Prose,* ed. Mettit Y. Hughes (Indianapolis: Odyssey Books, Bobbs-Merrill, 1976).
3. John Donne, "The Ecstasy," ll.7–8, in *The Norton Anthology of Poetry,* 3d. ed. (New York: W.W. Norton, 1983), p. 213.
4. Emily Dickinson, no. 772, in *The Complete Poems of Emily Dickinson,* ed. Thomas H. Johnson, (Boston: Little, Brown, 1960), p. 377.

Loss of the Positive Father

1. William Shakespeare, *Hamlet,* 4.7.181.
2. Shakespeare, interestingly enough, ended his career by writing plays that were close to fairy tales, as if at the end, choosing to bring his great tragedies into some final realignment with the inner marriage enacted in the fairy tale, a vision of wholeness seems to have been demanded by his psyche.
3. In relationship with her mother, she may find her mother's masculinity sparks her creativity, in which case she might later find a lesbian relationship profoundly creative.
4. Marion Woodman, with Kate Danson, Mary Hamilton, and Rita Greer Allen, *Leaving My Father's House* (Boston: Shambhala Publications, 1992), pp. 355–66.

A Vulnerable Triumvirate: Power Without Presence

1. Carl Gustav Jung, *Collected Works*, trans. R. F. C. Hull (London: Routledge & Kegan Paul, 1960), vol. 17, para. 313.

The Fishing Trip: Deep-Sea Collusion

1. William Shakespeare, *Macbeth*, 4. 1.21–22.
2. Ibid., 1. 5. 55.
3. Ibid., 4. 1. 45.

The Pin

1. William Stafford, "A Ritual to Read to Each Other," ll. 17–20, in *The Rag and Bone Shop of the Heart*, eds. Robert Bly, James Hillman, and Michael Meade (New York: HarperCollins, 1992), p. 233.
2. I Corinthians 13:1.
3. William Shakespeare, *Othello*, 5. 2. 1.
4. Ibid., ll. 3–7.
5. T. S. Eliot, "Journey of the Magi," in *Selected Poems* (London: Faber & Faber, 1970), p. 98.

The Sword

1. Marie-Louise von Franz, in *The Feminine in Fairytales* (New York: Spring Publications, 1972), p. 64.
2. *Selected Poems of Lorca and Jiménez*, chosen and translated by Robert Bly (Boston: Beacon Press, 1997), p. 63.

The Conscious Virgin

1. Emily Dickinson, no. 627, *Complete Poems*, p. 309.
2. Emily Dickinson, no. 506, *Complete Poems*, p. 246.
3. Quoted in Jeremiah Abrams, *The Shadow in America: Reclaiming the Soul of a Nation*, comp. and ed. Jeremiah Abrams (Novato, CA: Nataraj Publishing, 1994), p. 34.

4. Marie-Louise von Franz, *The Feminine in Fairytales,* pp. 121–22.
5. William Shakespeare, *Romeo and Juliet,* Prologue, l. 6.
6. Ibid., l. 8.
7. William Shakespeare, *Othello,* 5. 2. 246.

The Descent: Journey into the Unconscious

1. Emily Dickinson, no. 443. *Complete Poems,* p. 212.
2. This theme is further developed in Woodman's *The Ravaged Bridegroom* (Toronto: Inner City Books, 1990), pp. 131–58.

The Baba Yaga

1. William Shakespeare, *Hamlet,* 5. 2. 10–11.
2. William Shakespeare, Sonnet 146.
3. John 15:27.
4. Philippians 4:7.
5. T. S. Eliot, "Journey of the Magi," ll. 35–36, in *Selected Poems,* p. 98.
6. William Wordsworth, "Ode: Intimations of Immortality," l. 203, in *The Norton Anthology of English Literature,* 5th ed. (New York: W.W. Norton, 1987), p. 1433.
7. William Blake, "The Tyger," ll. 23–24, in *Norton Anthology of English Literature,* 3d ed. (New York: W.W. Norton, 1975), p. 1314.
8. William Shakespeare, *King Lear,* 5. 3. 20–21.

The Crone

1. William Butler Yeats, "Sailing to Byzantium," ll. 9–12, in *Norton Anthology of English Literature,* 3d ed., p. 2364.
2. Matthew 11:30.
3. John Keats, "Ode to a Nightingale," l. 24, in *Norton Anthology of English Literature,* 5th ed., p. 1845.
4. Ibid., ll. 55–60.
5. Ibid., l. 75.
6. Ibid., ll. 77–78.
7. Ibid., l. 74.

8. Ibid., l. 80.
9. Percy Bysshe Shelley, "Epipsychidion," l. 587. in *The Complete Poetical Works of Percy Bysshe Shelley*, ed. Thomas Hutchinson (London: Oxford University Press, 1960), p. 424.
10. Ibid., ll. 587–91.
11. Percy Bysshe Shelley, "To a Sky-Lark," ll. 4–5, in *Norton Anthology of English Literature*, 5th ed., p. 1783.

The Still Point

1. T. S. Eliot, "Burnt Norton," in *Four Quartets* (London: Faber & Faber, 1952), p. 9.

The Inner Marriage

1. Robert Bly, "Listening to the Köln Concert," in *The Rag and Bone Shop of the Heart*, eds. Robert Bly, James Hillman, and Michael Meade (New York: HarperCollins, 1992), p. 352.

Epilogue

1. "Among Schoolchildren," by W. B. Yeats, ll. 57–58, in *Norton Anthology of English Literature*, ed. M. W. Abrams (New York: Norton, 1962).

The Story: The Maiden Tsar

In a certain land, in a certain kingdom, there was a merchant whose wife died, leaving him with an only son, Ivan. He put his son in charge of a tutor, and after some time took another wife; and since Ivan, the merchant's son, was now of age and very handsome, his stepmother fell in love with him. One day Ivan went with his tutor to fish in the sea on a small raft; suddenly they saw thirty ships making toward them. On these ships sailed the Maiden Tsar with thirty other maidens, all her foster sisters. When the ships came close to the raft, all thirty of them dropped anchor. Ivan and his tutor were invited aboard the best ship, where the Maiden Tsar and her thirty foster sisters received them; she told Ivan that she loved him passionately and had come from afar to see him. So they were betrothed.

The Maiden Tsar told the merchant's son to return to the same place the following day, said farewell to him, and sailed away. Ivan returned home and went to sleep. The stepmother led the tutor into her room, made him drunk, and began to question him as to what had happened to him and Ivan at sea. The tutor told her everything. Upon hearing his story, she gave him a pin and said: "Tomorrow, when the ships begin to sail toward you, stick this pin into Ivan's tunic." The tutor promised to carry out her order.

Next morning Ivan arose and went fishing. As soon as his tutor beheld the ships sailing in the distance, he stuck the pin into Ivan's tunic. "Ah, I feel so sleepy," said the merchant's son. "Listen, tutor, I will take a nap now, and when the ships come close, please rouse me." "Very well, of course I will rouse you," said the tutor. The ships sailed close to the raft and cast anchor; the Maiden Tsar sent for Ivan, asking him to hasten to her; but he was sound asleep. The servants began to shake him, pinch him, and nudge him. All in vain—they could not awaken him, so they left him.

The Maiden Tsar told the tutor to bring Ivan to the same place on the following day, then ordered her crews to lift anchor and set sail. As soon as the ships sailed away, the tutor pulled out the pin, and Ivan awoke, jumped up, and began to call to the Maiden Tsar to return. But she was far away then and could not hear him. He went home sad and aggrieved. His stepmother took the tutor into her room, made him drunk, questioned him about everything that had happened, and told him to stick the pin through Ivan's tunic again the next day. The next day Ivan again went fishing, again slept all the time, and did not see the Maiden Tsar; she left word that he should come again.

On the third day he again went fishing with his tutor. They came to the same old place, and beheld the ships sailing at a distance, and the tutor straightaway stuck in his pin, and Ivan fell sound asleep. The ships sailed close and dropped anchor; the Maiden Tsar sent for her betrothed to come aboard her ship. The servants tried in every possible way to rouse him, but no matter what they did, they could not waken him. The Maiden Tsar learned of the stepmother's ruse and the tutor's treason, and wrote to Ivan telling him to cut off the tutor's head, and if he loved his betrothed, to come and find her beyond thrice nine lands in the thrice tenth kingdom.

The ships had no sooner set sail and put out to sea than the tutor pulled the pin from Ivan's garment; he awoke and began to bemoan his loss of the Maiden Tsar; but she was far away and could not hear him. The tutor gave him her letter; Ivan read it, drew out his sharp saber, and cut off the wicked tutor's head. Then he sailed hurriedly to the shore, went home, said farewell to his father, and set out to find the thrice tenth kingdom.

II

He journeyed onward, straight ahead, a long time or a short time—for speedily a tale is spun, but with less speed a deed is done—and finally came to a little hut; it stood in the open field, turning on chicken legs. He entered and found Baba Yaga the Bony-legged. "Fie, fie," she said, "the Russian smell was never heard of nor caught sight of here, but now it has come by itself. Are you here of your own free will or by compulsion, my good youth?" "Largely of my own free will, and twice as much by compulsion! Do you know, Baba Yaga, where lies the thrice tenth kingdom?" "No, I do not," she said, and told him to go to her second sister; she might know.

Ivan thanked her and went on farther; he walked and walked, a long distance or a short distance, a long time or a short time, and finally came to a little hut exactly like the first and there too found a Baba Yaga. "Fie, fie," she said, "the Russian smell was never heard of nor caught sight of here, but now it has come by itself. Are you here of your own free will or by compulsion, my good youth?" "Largely of my own free will, and twice as much by compulsion! Do you know, Baba Yaga, where lies the thrice tenth kingdom?" "No, I do not," she said, and told him to stop at her youngest sister's; she might know. "If she gets angry at you," she added, "and wants to devour you, take three horns from her and ask her permission to blow them; blow the first one softly, the second louder, and the third still louder." Ivan thanked the Baba Yaga and went on farther.

He walked and walked, a long distance or a short distance, a long time or a short time, and finally beheld a little hut standing in the open field and turning upon chicken legs; he entered it and found another Baba Yaga. "Fie, fie, the Russian smell was never heard of nor caught sight of here, and now it has come by itself," she said, and ran to whet her teeth, for she intended to eat her uninvited guest. Ivan begged her to give him three horns: he blew one softly, the second louder, and the third still louder. Suddenly birds of all kinds swarmed about him, among them the firebird. "Sit upon me quickly," said the firebird, "and we shall fly wherever you want; if you don't come with me, the Baba Yaga will devour you."

III

Ivan had no sooner sat himself upon the bird's back than the Baba Yaga rushed in, seized the firebird by the tail, and plucked a large handful of feathers from it.

The firebird flew with Ivan on its back; for a long time it soared in the skies, till finally it came to the broad sea. "Now, Ivan, merchant's son, the thrice tenth land lies beyond this sea. I am not strong enough to carry you to the other shore; get there as best you can." Ivan climbed down from the firebird, thanked it, and walked along the shore.

He walked and walked till he came to a little hut; he entered it, and was met by an old woman who gave him meat and drink and asked him whither he was going and why he was traveling so far. He told her that he was going to the thrice tenth kingdom to find the Maiden Tsar, his betrothed. "Ah," said the old woman, "she no longer loves you; if she gets hold of you, she will tear you to shreds; her love is stored away in a remote place." "Then how can I get it?" "Wait a bit! My daughter lives at the Maiden Tsar's palace and she is coming to visit me today; we may learn something from her." Then the old woman turned Ivan into a pin and stuck the pin into the wall; at night her daughter flew in. Her mother asked her whether she knew where the Maiden Tsar's love was stored away. "I do not know," said the daughter, and promised to find out from the Maiden Tsar herself.

IV

The next day she again visited her mother and told her: "On this side of the ocean there stands an oak; in the oak there is a coffer; in the coffer there is a hare; in the hare there is a duck; in the duck there is an egg; and in the egg lies the Maiden Tsar's love."

Ivan took some bread and set out for the place she had described. He found the oak and removed the coffer from it; then he removed the hare from the coffer; the duck from the hare, and the egg from the duck. He returned with the egg to the old woman. A few days later came the old woman's birthday; she invited the Maiden Tsar with the thirty other maidens, her foster sisters, to her house; she baked the egg, dressed Ivan the merchant's son in splendid raiment, and hid him.

At midday, the Maiden Tsar and the thirty other maidens flew into the house, sat down to table, and began to dine; after dinner the old woman served them each an egg, and to the Maiden Tsar she served the egg that Ivan had found. The Maiden Tsar ate of it and at once conceived a passionate love for Ivan the merchant's son. The old woman brought him out of his hiding place. How much joy there was, how much merriment! The Maiden Tsar left with her betrothed, the merchant's son, for her own kingdom; they married and began to live happily and to prosper.

Index

Copies of the film mentioned by Marion and Robert are still available. *Bly and Woodman on Men and Women* can be ordered by contacting Applewood at http:www.applewood.com, or at the Applewood Centre, Box 148, Belleville, Ontario, Canada K8N5A2 (phone: 1-800-361-0541).